RINGSIDE

ALSO BY BUDD SCHULBERG

FICTION

What Makes Sammy Run?
The Harder They Fall
The Disenchanted
Waterfront
Some Faces in the Crowd
Sanctuary V
Everything That Moves
Love, Action, Laughter, and Other Sad Tales

NONFICTION

From the Ashes: Voices of Watts Writers in America
Loser and Still Champion: Muhammad Ali
The Four Seasons of Success
Swan Watch (with Geraldine Brooks)
Moving Pictures: Memories of a Hollywood Prince
Writers in America
Sparring with Hemingway

PLAYS AND SCREENPLAYS

A Face in the Crowd (screenplay)
Across the Everglades (screenplay)
The Disenchanted (play, with Harvey Breit)
What Makes Sammy Run? (musical libretto, with Stuart Schulberg)
On the Waterfront (screenplay and stage play)

BUDD SCHULBERG

RINGSIDE

A Treasury of Boxing Reportage

With an Introduction by Hugh McIlvanney

Ivan R. Dee

Chicago 2006

www.ivanrdee.com

Library of Congress Cataloging-in-Publication Data:
Schulberg, Budd.
    Ringside : a treasury of boxing reportage / Budd Schulberg ; with an introduction by Hugh McIlvanney.
        p. cm.
    Includes bibliographical references and index.
    ISBN-13: 978-1-56663-707-7 (cloth : alk. paper)
    ISBN-10: 1-56663-707-4 (cloth : alk. paper)
    1. Boxing matches—United States. 2. Boxers (Sports)—United States. 3. Schulberg, Budd. 4. Sportswriters—United States. 5. Sports journalism—United States. I. Title.
GV1125.S34 2006
796.860973—dc22
                                                        2006011639

This book is for those noblemen of the ring I'm proud to call dear friends: the late Fidel La Barba, Billy Soose, and Rocky Marciano; and for Archie McBride, the original Golden Boy Art Aragon, Roger Donoghue, Jose Torres, Muhammad Ali, Gerry Cooney, Diego "Chico" Corrales, trainer Joe Goossen; and for my fellow pigeon fancier, Mike Tyson

Contents

Acknowledgments

M ERE THANKS doesn't begin to describe my appreciation for Professor Nick Beck's expertise and selfless devotion to this work in his role as editorial consultant, reading and rereading a Niagara of words and putting up with the author's defensive vanities. His background as both an amateur boxer and veteran journalist has provided him with the ideal tools to cope with all the copious demands involved.

My thanks also to the indefatigable photo maven and working archivist Betsy Schulberg, who concentrated her boundless energy on tracking down the photographs that illustrate the text. Putting up with the author's sometimes over-the-top enthusiasm for a sport that is not at the top of her list, she undertook the task with a professional attention to detail that helped round out this book effectively.

I am also indebted to Margaret Schwarz's dedication to this collection. She tracked down all those missing pieces and ran them through the computer again and again as I tested her patience by adding "just one more little change" each time she thought the work was done.

If I sported a big fedora like fistic historian and incorrigible jokesmith Bert Randolph Sugar, I would doff it to Nigel Collins, whose knowledgeable column "Ringside" graces the boxing "bible" he edits, *Ring Magazine.*

I am grateful to the following publications where these articles first appeared:

American Rebels edited by Jack Newfield (New York: Nation Books, 2003), for "Joe Louis and Social History."

Boxing Illustrated for "Return to the Mecca": "Genius at Work"; "Bowe-Holyfield: Act III (The Rubber Match)"; "The Softer They Fall"; and "Tyson Redux: Act I."

Collier's Magazine for "Machiavelli on Eighth Avenue."

Esquire for "Boxing Movies 101."

Fight Game for "Confessions of an Ex-Fight Manager"; "The Welters Are Coming! The Welters Are Coming!"; "De La Hoya-Trinidad: A Tale of Two Champions"; "Mosley-De La Hoya: My Home Town"; "The Real Main Event: Arum vs. King"; and "Lennox Lewis: A Want of Passion."

International Boxing Digest for "Good Night, Sweet Princes"; "Arturo Gatti: The Manly Art of No Defense"; "The Guessing Game: De La Hoya-Whitaker"; "The Oscar Express Rolls On"; "Lewis-Golota: The Bigger They Are . . ."; "The Emperor Has No Clothes"; "Jones vs. Griffin: Pretty Boy Loses Ugly"; "The Mouthpiece Hamlet"; "A for Ability, B for Bored"; "Reenter Evander: A Big Night for Him and HIM"; "Evander the Holy: The Once and Future Undisputed King"; "Evander's Homecoming and Going"; "Requiem for a Heavyweight"; and "The Little Prince: Good Hit, No Field."

New York Times Book Review for "King of the World."

Sports Illustrated for "Paynight for Old Archie" and "The Champion of Communications."

Sunday Herald (Glasgow, Scotland) for "My Very Own Ali Movie"; "Mosley-De La Hoya: Act II"; "Move Over, Ruby Bob—Here Comes Roy Jones!"; "Lewis Takes Tyson to Finishing School"; "The Night of the Undisputed"; "The 'Heavyweight Championship of the World'—or, Four for the Price of One"; "Ricky Hatton and Kostya Tszyu: The British Are Coming!"; "Requiem for a Middleweight"; "Trinidad vs. Mayorga: Brain vs. Brawn"; "Winky Wright vs. Felix Trinidad: The King Is Dead! Long Live the King!"; "No. 1 Pound-for-Pound: Pretty Boy Floyd Mayweather, Jr."; "Weightgate, and on to World War III: Diego Corrales vs. Jose Luis Castillo II"; and "Fighters and Writers: At the Boxing Hall of Fame."

True Magazine for "Tom Cribb vs. Tom Molineaux: The First International Championship Fight" and "Charles Freeman: The Primo Carnera of the Nineteenth Century vs. The Tipton Slasher."

When Boxing Was a Jewish Sport by Allen Bodner (Westport, Conn.: Praeger, 1997), for "When Boxing Was a Jewish Sport."

Introduction
by Hugh McIlvanney

BOXING HAS a long tradition of attracting the attention of serious writers but, once in the vicinity of the ring, not all of them
have deserved to be taken seriously. At that early stage of the
Rumble in the Jungle, when Muhammad Ali had decided to adopt
the perilous strategy of planting himself against the ropes in the
hope of letting George Foreman "blast his ass off," a figure prominent in the literary world turned to the famous novelist beside
him in the press seats and shouted: "The fix is in."

To some of us for whom the tension of those minutes is an im-
perishable memory—who can recall as if it happened an hour ago
how the raw immensity of the risk Ali was embracing put a knot in
our stomachs and nearly made us want to shield our eyes from the
drama—the thought that somebody could have associated the violence taking place two or three yards in front of us with a fix has a
hilarious, almost a sweet absurdity. Where had that man of letters
acquired his outlandish perspective on events inside the ropes? If,
as must be suspected, he absorbed it from movies, they certainly
weren't the kind of films identified with Budd Schulberg, who was
another of the writers on hand in Kinshasa when the hours before
an African dawn were filled with perhaps the most extraordinary
experience sport has produced in the past fifty years.

Schulberg's lifelong love affair with boxing has never been
tainted with the romantic naiveté rampant in the mind of that
conspiracy theorist in Zaire. Budd's has always been a clear-eyed

passion. Thanks to a father who took an admirably broad view of what constituted the essentials of a boy's education, he was around fights and fighters from an early age. Both his knowledge (historical and technical) of sport's roughest trade and his warm regard for the men who ply it are deeply rooted. Being in his company anywhere is a rich pleasure, but having him as a companion at ringside is a privilege to be cherished.

Obviously, his longevity alone makes him a living archive of the fight business, and the recollections he can summon up from as far back as the 1920s are informed by such perceptive observation that distant decades come alive as he evokes them. The same is true, naturally enough, when he talks of writers with whom he had close encounters long ago, of Ernest Hemingway or Scott Fitzgerald, William Saroyan or Nathanael West. Of course, Hemingway has always been linked with boxing, unimpressively as a participant ("not particularly evasive" was A. J. Liebling's assessment of the Nobel Prize–winner's technique) but brilliantly in print (his short story "Fifty Grand" is as good as fiction about the ring can be). He once rashly sought to engage Budd in a rapid-fire interrogation about fighters and their deeds that was meant to be a crushing humiliation for the younger man. But it was Papa who retired on his stool after being pummeled by more vivid specifics than he could handle.

But it is not Schulberg on the past but Schulberg on the present that I appreciate most when we are together at the fights. I have come across few men with as profound an understanding of the imperatives that govern the quality of a performance in the ring. I confess to a lack of enthusiasm for sporting chroniclers who are fine with description but feeble in judgment, who give us plenty of color but don't know a hawk from a handsaw. It is a species exemplified by some horse-racing correspondents of my acquaintance, fellows whose words can present a picture of a thoroughbred that Stubbs might envy but whose tips would put you on welfare.

Plainly, that last point is not meant to be anything more than the facetious complaint of a frequently impoverished bettor. Anybody who claimed to be consistently accurate in forecasting the outcome of races or fights would be a bigger fraud than Nostradamus. But I do think we can ask of reporters of both kinds of contest that they should be able to comprehend and interpret the action as it is unfolding and that, once it is over, they should have a clear idea of what they have seen.

At ringside, Budd Schulberg invariably does all of that, and more. The voice that will come through the ensuing pages is not just engaging and eloquent. It is wise.

RINGSIDE

Tom Cribb vs. Tom Molineaux: The First International Championship Fight

PRIZEFIGHTING in the old bare-knuckle days was a basic, brutal business, highly unlike the stuff you see being dispensed on your television sets today. Fighters then didn't rely on the critical judgment of boxing "experts" with intricate scorecards. They fought round after round, sometimes hour after hour, until one or the other was unable to come off his second's knee and stagger back to the line of scratch. It was not twelve three-minute rounds to a decision but as many rounds and as much time as it required for one man to knock another man completely senseless.

And yet even rules as decisive as these could lead to controversy when the stakes were high and feelings even higher. There have been disputed title fights in our own country—was the Johnson-Willard fight on the level and did Dempsey really knock Tunney out in that "long count" affair in Chicago? But a bare-knuckle fight for the heavyweight championship of the world in 1810 is probably the most controversial fight in the history of the division. It was certainly one of the most thrilling.

The rivals were Tom Cribb, the celebrated champion of England, and Tom Molineaux, an underrated ex-slave from Virginia. Molineaux was the first of a gallant line of African-American boxers to win worldwide acclaim. And his fight with Cribb was the first international match for the heavyweight championship. To-day their names come alive only for historians of the old prize ring who treasure the pages of Pierce Egan's eyewitness accounts in that ebullient if sometimes inaccurate masterpiece, *Boxiana*. But in the nineteenth century, when fight fans by the thousands cheerfully waded through muddy lanes and across miles of open fields to wager and cheer on their favorite bruisers, Tom Molineaux's threat to English boxing supremacy provoked a national crisis and an international incident. The first Napoleon might have been more feared throughout England than this American challenger, but to read the sports pages of that day you would not think so. A victory for the ex-slave from Virginia over the mighty Cribb was widely considered a no less tragic prospect than a successful Napoleonic invasion.

In these days when press agents are as essential to prizefighters as to movie stars, Tom Molineaux surely would have been tagged the first "Cinderella man." He came from a fighting family on the Molineaux plantation in Virginia. Boxing was not yet an organized sport in America, but plantation owners used to pit their slaves against each other for side bets, and Tom's father Zachariah was a local champion. Tom grew to bull-like proportions. Although his full height was only five feet eight, he weighed two hundred pounds. He succeeded his father as the plantation's best bare-knuckle man and is said to have won his freedom as a reward for knocking out a rival plantation champion. Tom worked his way to New York, earned a living as a dock-walloper and a reputation for walloping his fellow men as well. These waterfront battles are unrecorded, but he seems to have won enough of them to style himself Champion of America, a title apparently deserved.

American pugilism was a scorned and lowly activity in 1810. But its English counterpart was at the height of its glory and popularity. An English sailor who saw Molineaux fight on the docks thought he should try his luck on the other side of the Atlantic. But not even an overenthusiastic jack-tar could have predicted that this powerful but untrained dockhand would soon be whipping to a standstill one of the great bare-knuckle champions of all time. Or that Molineaux, working his way across the Atlantic on a clipper ship, was to come within a disputed hair of snatching the championship of England from its Anglo-Saxon foundation.

Penniless and unknown, Tom landed in Liverpool and somehow found his way to the only place in London where he had some hope of finding hospitality—to the Horse and Dolphin Tavern operated by a fellow American black already celebrated in England for his fighting ability. Although only a middleweight, Bill Richmond had squared off with Tom Cribb himself, and his public house was a gathering place for the fancy and the sports. Lord Byron was one of Richmond's friends and boxing pupils. Richmond welcomed Molineaux and was soon seconding him against a promising novice from Bristol who was handled by Cribb. The burly youth beat Cribb's man so badly that he was reported as "not having a single distinguishable feature left on his face." Molineaux next was given a more formidable test in the person of Tom Blake, who had earned the fighting *nom de boxe* Tom Tough, as durable a trial horse as England had in those days.

The day he met Molineaux, Tom Tough arrived at the scene of the contest in a baronet's carriage, accompanied by Cribb. A large crowd was on hand, for Pierce Egan tells us, "There was considerable curiosity among the swell division to see the new specimen in ebony, on whose merits Massa Richmond was so eloquent to all visitors to the Horse and Dolphin." Richmond had not oversold his man. Tom Tough hardly lived up to his name and crumbled under Molineaux's vicious pummeling. Not only was Tough unable to come to scratch within the allotted thirty seconds, but he lay unconscious for several minutes. The American was ready for Cribb.

The ease of Molineaux's victory convinced Bill Richmond that he had a coming champion on his hands. Cribb had won the title from the great Jem Belcher a year before but was in virtual retirement because his superiority had been so convincingly established that no one dared challenge him. But now a challenge was made that shook the complacency of a British sporting scene patriotically confident that its fighting men, like its fighting ships, were masters of the world. It was no accident that Molineaux's startling challenge to Cribb drove sportswriters of the day to these lines of Shakespearean defiance:

England that never did nor never shall
Lie at the proud foot of a conqueror.

In the sporting taverns of London this challenge from a lowly American, and one of African ancestry at that, was considered rank impudence, unparalleled effrontery. Gentlemen of rank who never before had concerned themselves with the crude goings-on of the pugilists admitted, in the privacy of their clubs, their anxiety lest Molineaux take the measure of England's pride. National feelings and racial presumptions brought the match to the attention of countless thousands who would have scorned the ordinary prize ring brawl.

Additional excitement came from Molineaux himself, who held forth at the Horse and Dolphin with tall prophecies about the destruction he would vent on the champion. Cribb, on the other hand, though he had seconded the fighters Molineaux had clubbed into submission, could not believe that this swarthy newcomer could stand up to him for more than a few minutes. While the betting was brisker than it had been for many years, the most popular wager was whether or not the American challenger could absorb his punishment for more than fifteen minutes.

Amply fortified with spirits to shorten the arduous journey over rocky road and muddy dale, let us climb into a coach with our loquacious guide Pierce Egan, who has given us the fullest eyewitness account of one of the memorable prize ring battles of all time.

"The day selected for this grand milling exhibition was December 10, at Copthall Common, in the neighborhood of East Grimstead, Sussex, within 30 miles of the Metropolis. . . . The ring was formed at the foot of a hill (24 foot roped) surrounded by the numerous carriages which had conveyed the spectators thither, to ward off the chilling breezes and rain which came keenly from the eastward. Immediately . . . Molineaux came forward, bowed, threw up his hat in defiance, and retired to strip; Cribb immediately followed, and they were soon brought forward by their seconds; Gully (another former champion) and Joe Ward for the Champion, and Richmond and Jones for Molineaux."

The crowd gave a great hand to Cribb and then fell intently silent as these rugged antagonists waited for the referee to cry "Time." Cribb looked solid if slightly fleshy at five feet ten and a half and two hundred pounds. Molineaux's weight equalled Cribb's, though he was two inches shorter. But any height deficiency was more than overcome by his long arms and powerful muscles.

Molineaux lost no time in showing the oddsmakers that they had held him too cheap. Staggered by a hard punch over the right eye and rushed to the ropes by the confident champion in the second round, Molineaux rallied fiercely, and Cribb "received a dreadful blow on the mouth that made his teeth chatter, and exhibited the first sign of claret." "First blood" was hotly wagered in those days, and the longshot bettors had won on Molineaux.

Round after round the men fought toe to toe, Cribb with some show of science and planning, Molineaux with terrible strength, ferocity, and "gluttony," as the ability to take a punch was described by fight reporters, vintage 1810. In the eighth, according to the round-by-round account:

> Cribb found out that his notion of beating Molineaux off-hand was truly fallacious, as he really was an ugly customer, and he also became sensible that if Molineaux could so reduce him as to make his sledge hammer hits tell, he should not willingly lay his head for the anvil. He therefore now brought forward his science, and began to adopt his usual famous retreating system. The men rallied desperately; success was alternate. At length Molineaux fell; but Cribb from his violent exertion appeared weaker than his opponent.

Somehow this scene never loses its intensity for me: the white champion and the black champion fighting each other to exhaustion while the incessant rain washed the blood from their wounded eyes and mouths and cheeks. On the soggy hillside some five thousand panicky spectators, the highborn in the outer ring, the rabble sprawled out behind them, ignored the downpour as they began to realize with mounting amazement and anxiety that their "unbeatable" Cribb was losing ground to the "American man of color."

After thirty minutes of furious brawling Molineaux was not only on his feet but carrying the fight to the weary champion. The fight had gone into the nineteenth round when the first of two "rhubarbs" running counter to the Anglo-Saxon tradition of fair play checked Molineaux's effort to become the first non-British champion.

At this stage the faces of both fighters were so dreadfully battered that it was impossible to distinguish them by their features. Onlookers reported that only their difference in color made identification possible. Cribb was on the defensive and retreating now. Molineaux pinned him against the ropes and held him so tightly that he could neither throw a punch nor go down. This provoked the first important hassle. The seconds said the men should be separated. The umpires ruled, according to eighteenth-century rules of Broughton, that the contestants could not be parted until one went down. The tension in the audience was unbearable. Finally two hundred persons rushed to the ring and attempted to loosen Molineaux's hold on the ropes. One of his fingers was broken or seriously injured in the melee. When order was restored, the enraged Molineaux chased the champion to one corner of the ring, caught Cribb's head under his left arm and clobbered him unmercifully, Cribb finally falling from the severe punishment.

Despite the injury to his hand, Molineaux pressed his advantage. His left eye was closed and he was arm-weary and close to exhaustion. But Cribb was even more battered, and it was with greater and greater difficulty that he came off his second's knee at the end of each thirty-second rest period. Odds rose as high as 4 to 1 on Molineaux. The twenty-eighth round ended with Cribb "receiving a leveler." At the end of the rest period he lay back in his second's arms, unable to rise. According to Fred Henning's *Fight for the Championship*:

**Cribb and Molineaux battled into the thirty-ninth round until the
ex-slave from Virginia at last had to acknowledge, "I can fight no more."
(© Stapleton Collection/Corbis)**

. . . Tom Cribb could not come to time, and Sir Thomas Apreeee
[an umpire] allowed the half-minute to elapse and summoned the
men three times. Still Cribb could not come and the Black
awaited the award of victory, his just due, in the centre of the
ring. But during the excitement Joe Ward pushed across the ring
to Bill Richmond, and accused him of having placed two bullets
in the Black's fists. This was, of course, indignantly denied, and
Molineaux was requested to open his hands, proving that nothing
was there.

This has been a favorite ruse of cagey managers from Cribb's
day to our own. While Molineaux was on his feet, involved in the
dispute, the fallen champion was gaining an invaluable three- or
four-minute rest. When "Time!" was called again, Cribb was able
to come up to the mark.

Molineaux rushed in to stop his man in the twenty-ninth but
the undeserved rest seemed to have restored Cribb's spirit and
confidence. A desperate blow on Molineaux's right eye closed that

"peeper"—as these early-day boxing writers put it—and brought the gallant Negro down. He was up again for the thirtieth, nearly sightless.

But the desperate trick in the twenty-eighth and the closing of Molineaux's one good eye in the twenty-ninth were the turning points. In the thirty-first he was leveled again by a hard blow in the throat. In the thirty-second "they were staggering against each other like inebriated men." Somehow they went on this way until the thirty-ninth round when Molineaux at last had to acknowledge, "I can fight no more." Cribb himself was near collapse, and Richmond persuaded his deadbeat protégé to try one more round in the hope that Cribb could not come to scratch. But Cribb made it, if barely, and poor Molineaux fell in a heap. After fifty-five minutes of vicious, bloody, and somewhat senseless battling, the "most ferocious and sanguinary" battle in the history of the English prize ring came to an end. Tom Cribb was acclaimed the victor. He had "protected the honor of his country and the reputation of English Boxing," Pierce Egan assures us. But even Egan, an Irish Anglophile, putting the best possible face on it, had to admit that in the disputed and crucial twenty-eighth round, "[Cribb's] seconds, by a little maneuvering, occupied the attention of the Black's seconds, and so managed to prolong the period sufficiently to enable the champion to recover a little, and thus assist him to pull through."

Molineaux's questionable loss brought him overnight fame. And his threat to British boxing supremacy was reemphasized just three days later when the following notice in the London papers rocked the English sporting world anew:

To Mr. Thomas Cribb, St. Martin's Street,
Leicester Square:

Sir, — My friends think that had the weather on last Tuesday, the day on which I contended with you, not been so unfavorable, I should have won the battle; I therefore challenge you to a second meeting, at any time within two months, for such sum as those gentlemen who place confidence in me may be pleased to arrange.

As it is possible this letter may meet the public eye, I cannot omit the opportunity of expressing a confident hope, that the circumstance of my being of a different color to that of a people amongst whom I have sought protection, will not in any way operate to my prejudice.

I am, sir,
Your most obedient humble servant,

T. MOLINEAUX

Cribb promptly accepted the challenge, for his sense of honor had been offended. Molineaux had alluded to the "unfavorable weather," but the champion and his friends, their consciences not entirely clear, knew the dangerous foreigner was not referring to the elements alone. Molineaux had to wait longer than two months for his rematch with Cribb, for a young heavyweight named Rimmer decided to make it a three-way rivalry by challenging the challenger. Rimmer was a protégé of an ex-fighter, Bob Gregson, boniface of Castle Tavern, the pugilistic headquarters of the day. He was close to Cribb, and Richmond saw the challenge as a means of giving the champion more time to prepare for his rematch with this overpowering challenger. Rimmer's friends had been calling him a second Jem Belcher, but he proved no match for Molineaux, who beat him into insensibility in fifteen rounds. Oddly enough, the Rimmer fight was the only Molineaux bout ever to be reported in an American paper. The *Savannah Republican* of July 23, 1811, had this to say:

Civilization!—A boxing match took place at Mously Hart, in the neighborhood of London, on the 21st of May, for one hundred guineas. The champions were Molineaux (the famous black man from New York) and a young Englishman named Rimmer. In the course of fifteen rounds, the black pounded his antagonist most tremendously; when lords, nobles, sweeps, ploughmen, fighting men and assistants, from pique or sympathy, crowded into the ring and fought promiscuously about twenty minutes. There were at this brutal exhibition about fifteen thousand spectators of all ranks.

Englishmen, it would seem, despite their traditions, had difficulty accepting the sight of one of their countrymen stretched out at the feet of this dark intruder. The dreadful possibility that this might happen to their idol, Tom Cribb, made the second Cribb-Molineaux battle the most widely discussed in British ring history, even more eagerly awaited than the bitter Richard Humphries-Mendoza "The Jew" title bouts a generation earlier. The issue was nothing less than "Whether Old England should still retain her proud characteristic of conquering; or that an American, and, a man of colour, should win the honor, wear it, and carry it away from the shores of Britain."

Conscious of his patriotic responsibilities, Cribb went into training three months before the fight. He seems to have been the first pugilist to attempt anything like a modern training program. His training camp was on the estate of Captain Barclay, an aristocratic health enthusiast and champion walker who had astonished his countrymen with a series of hundred-mile strolls. Cribb came to Barclay badly out of shape. A life of ease in London had blown him up to 16 stone (224 pounds). In Barclay's own words, "He had become corpulent, big-bellied, full of gross humors and short breathed; it was with difficulty he could walk 10 miles." Barclay soon had him doing 20 miles a day, and then 30, including a half-mile run each day at top speed. His diet was rigorous, he sparred with amateurs to improve his timing, was put through a severe course of calisthenics, and in 11 weeks he weighed in at 192, which Barclay had established as his ideal fighting weight.

Molineaux, on the other hand, lacking a patron, had to pick up his eating money where he could find it. There was plenty to be found, for his near-victory over Cribb made him an object of great curiosity wherever he went. But the money he earned from exhibitions around the country was squandered in self-indulgence. Richmond and Tom Belcher were accused of using Molineaux as a meal ticket instead of seriously preparing him for this crucial fight, and of keeping him "pliable to their wishes by allowing him to drink stout and ale by gallons." Molineaux was openhanded and easygoing. Self-control was not one of his virtues. His contemporaries describe him as "amorous in the extreme." If he was not already sufficiently intoxicated, this sudden fame for an illiterate ex-slave was heady brew. In addition he seems to have had a childish faith in his physical prowess. Tom Molineaux would not believe that any excess could tap his native strength. On the morning of the fight his breakfast consisted of a whole boiled fowl, an apple pie, and a tankard of ale.

There were no million-dollar gates in those days, but all the other familiar trappings of a "Battle of the Century" make that September 28, 1811, sound like a big-time TV pay-for-view at one of the Vegas casino palaces. On the eve of the fight there wasn't a bed to be found for twenty miles in all directions. Twenty thousand fans were on hand at Wymondham, an incredible number considering the total population and the means of transportation of those days. Although the fight was scheduled for noon, hundreds of spectators were on the grounds as early as six in the morning, hoping to get a better view of the battle. Peers were there in their four-in-hands, and watermen, butchers, cobblers, "rustics in their clouted shoes." Among the "Corinthian of the highest rank" were lords, knights, and generals, including the Marquis of Queensberry. Had there been a Don King in those days, the fight would have grossed a hundred million dollars and made wealthy men of both contestants. As it was, both were to die in poverty, the traditional fate of great fighters over the centuries. Not only was there no Don King to maximize the price of the seats, there were no seats. The innovation of seats for spectators at prizefights was nearly a century away. Instead the first row stretched out on the turf, the second row kneeled, and the rest stood behind them. And behind *them* were the horsemen, "some seated, while others more eager stood, circus-like, upon their saddle: these were intermixed with every description of carriage, gig, barouche, buggy, cart and waggon."

For the first five rounds Cribb took another painful drubbing. He was bleeding profusely from the mouth, his right eye was an ugly slit, and his left eye was closing rapidly. But Molineaux could not draw on the superhuman endurance that had carried him so far nine months earlier. Too much ale and too much chicken, winged and otherwise, had him "heaving fearfully" as early as the fourth round.

The sixth round was the convincer. Here it is, blow by blow, as recorded in *Pugilistica*:

> Molineaux, distressed for wind and exhausted, lunged right and left. Cribb avoided his blows, and then put in a good hit with his right which Molineaux stopped exceedingly well. Cribb now got in a destructive blow at his "mark," which doubled up Molineaux. He appeared almost frantic, and no dancing master could have performed a pirouette more gratifying to Cribb's friends. Molineaux hit short and capered about. Cribb followed him round the ring, and after some astonishing execution, floored him by a tremendous hit at full arm's length.

Molineaux was out of gas. But for a few more rounds he kept charging in, borne on a momentum of terrible courage and futile rage. In the ninth round his jaw was broken, and he fell like a slaughtered steer. While the fallen challenger lay senseless, the crowd screamed its pleasure and Cribb danced a crazy hornpipe around the ring. At the end of the allotted half-minute, Molineaux was still out, but Cribb was not satisfied. He waived the time limit so that Molineaux could come again. In a brutal tableau of superiority, a kind of human bullfight with the total destruction of Molineaux the only possible finale, Cribb knocked Molineaux down again, and then again. In a gallant, foolhardy stupor, Molineaux managed to get off his second's knee once more, and again he was leveled. Still not satisfied, Cribb waived the time limit so as to have one more crack at the tottering Molineaux. Molineaux pitched to the stage floor and lay still. Cribb and former champion Gully danced a Scottish reel around the ring. And twenty thousand triumphant sons of Britain went wild with joy.

The fight had lasted only twenty minutes, just a third as long as the first great contest. When Molineaux was carried unconscious from the ring it was learned that not only his jaw but two of his ribs had been broken. Cribb's earnings (on a winner-take-all basis) were four hundred pounds. As a tribute to his gameness, a collection of fifty pounds was raised for Molineaux. Impressive sums had changed hands on the outcome. Captain Barclay was said to have won a fortune of ten thousand pounds. A baker who had gambled his house, his shop, and all his personal property was seventeen hundred pounds ahead. For several days following the fight there were public demonstrations celebrating the British victory. When the champion called on Molineaux to inquire as to his condition, he sported a barouche and four, the horses decorated with blue ribbons signifiying Cribb's colors. When he reached London the public ovation was so great that the streets he approached were impassable. Crowds gathered to applaud him wherever he appeared.

In the tradition of fistic heroes over the centuries, Cribb settled down as a host to the sporting fraternity, and for many years his tavern prospered and legends of generosity and gallantry gathered around him. But true to the same tradition, his luck finally ran out: a few years before he died he was hauled into the courts on a charge of bad debts. In his hometown of Woolwich a monument was erected in his honor shortly after his death in 1848.

After the second meeting with Cribb, Tom Molineaux toured and fought on for five more years with declining success. In the extravagant language of his day we learn that he worshiped more ardently in the temples of Bacchus and Venus than in that of Mars. In 1818 we find him in Northern Ireland, teaching the stick-fighting natives how to fight with their fists, a course of instruction that appears to have left its mark. Fast living had made a gaunt ruin of his powerful physique. His fortunes had sunk so low that he was living on the handouts of two fellow blacks serving in an Irish regiment. Unable to afford the cheapest lodging, and rapidly wasting away from disease and neglect, he muttered his final "I can fight no more" in the regimental bandroom at Galway on August 4, 1818, at the age of thirty-three.

He had come a long way up and a long way down, and a long, long way from the slave quarters of Virginia. But for one glorious hour he had given blow for blow with a great champion of England, he had proved that manly skills and fighting hearts were not exclusive qualities of the English, nor of any race, and for sixty trembling seconds while English sportsmanship wavered and bowed to national expediency, he was indeed champion of England, supreme among men as tough and prideful and resolute as ever assembled, the bare-knuckle fighters-to-a-finish of centuries past.

[1953]

Charles Freeman:
The Primo Carnera of the
Nineteenth Century vs.
The Tipton Slasher

THERE SEEMS TO BE in all of us the urge to create and glorify giants, heroically enlarged extensions of ourselves, who can go forth singlehanded to perform the deeds of strength and annihilation of which we ourselves, mere normals, are incapable.

Greek heroes invariably ran to size. The ancient Jews, when they sought a champion to settle affairs with the rival Philistines, pinned their hopes on Samson. From that day to this, the over-sized, jumbo heavyweight has never failed to excite our curiosity, admiration, and awe, even though this excitement may be a two-sided sensation that anticipates the giant's invincibility and at the same time prepares to enjoy his defeat by a smaller adversary.

Giants getting their lumps from little guys have come to be a common occurrence. But, despite the proof presented by a sad string of fallen giants, the crowds seem to be drawn irresistibly toward any new superman who tosses his hat in the ring.

Of course, the classic example of the last century was the hapless Primo Carnera, all 6 feet 6, 256 pounds of him, who couldn't beat a third-rater without considerable help from his owners. With fights "arranged" all the way to the title, he was finally led to slaughter by Joe Louis and Max Baer.

It may be that every century must have its Carnera. For in the previous century an American giant who outweighed Carnera by fifty pounds and topped him by a half-foot was causing the same kind of furor, some of it just as manufactured, as Carnera did on his introduction to the American sports world in the early 1930s.

His name was Charles Freeman. Performing as a strong man in a circus, like Carnera, he caught the eye of the champion of England, Ben Caunt, who was making an American tour, appearing in *Life in London* at the Bowery Theater, and giving exhibitions of his stiff-stance, slow-moving, bear-hugging style.

In a letter to the leading London sports journal of the day, Caunt wrote: ". . . an unexpected circumstance has brought me back to New York . . . a challenge in the papers from the Michigan Giant. I am quite prepared to fight him. This giant is seven feet three inches high, proportionately stout, and very active; he can turn twenty-five somersets in succession, can hold a large man out at arm's length, weighs 333 pounds and has nothing but muscle on his bones. . . ."

By the time Freeman came to the attention of the New York journals, he had shrunk a trifle and either cast off his Midwestern background or been appropriated by Manhattan. He is described by a reporter as "standing seven feet in his stocking feet and weighing three hundred and fifteen pounds, the tallest specimen of our city that ever came under the notice of Tall Son of York. He has arms and legs strong enough for the working beam or piston rod of a Mississippi steamboat. At Halifax recently, someone sent him a challenge, which was accepted. But upon seeing the New York Baby, the challenger waived the honor of meeting him, except with the muffles on."

The champion, Caunt, apparently saw more advantage in adding Freeman to his road company than in squaring off with him in earnest, for the article concludes with the intelligence that "our specimen youth shall accompany the English champion back to the Old World, where, we'll lay a pile, they'll be graveled to match him."

Billed as the American Atlas and appearing in sparring exhibitions with Caunt, Freeman drew sellout crowds at his first appearance in the Queen's Theater, Liverpool, and continued to turn them away everywhere he went. While the editor of *Sportsman's Magazine* dismissed him with "Freeman has as little pretensions or inclinations to boxing as any noncombative member of the Peace Society," Caunt's press agents were flooding the papers with eloquent accounts of Freeman's prowess, even asserting that no British boxer had courage enough to meet him.

Before he had engaged in a single contest, the New World Goliath, as he was sometimes billed, had become the nemesis of every British heavyweight. Numerous challenges were passed back and forth, all of which Caunt, on Freeman's behalf, chose to ignore. It was not until Freeman's publicity boys began referring to their client as "the champion of the world" (with an impressive list of American triumphs scored exclusively over nonexistent opponents) that the British boxing circle decided it was time to call this colossal bluff.

A council of war was held in what can probably be best described as the Gallagher's of the day, ex-fighter Johnny Broome's Rising Sun. After egging themselves to fighting pitch by reading aloud some of the more extravagant publicity, the fight crowd agreed that a hundred pounds should be posted as a challenge to the American giant to meet any suitable opponent Broome should select.

Much to the surprise of the doubting Toms, the challenge was accepted, with no less a personage than Tom Spring, England's beloved, undefeated ex-champion appearing at the Rising Sun in behalf of Caunt and Freeman. For Freeman's opponent, Broome nominated the Tipton Slasher, an up-and-coming pugilist later to lay a disputed claim to the championship, though never considered much more than a willing second-rater.

As was the custom of the day, the articles of agreement for their match were drawn up at Spring's Castle Tavern, another famous sports hangout, on the understanding that ten pounds would be deposited each week, alternately at the tavern of Spring and Broome, until the full side bet had been posted.

The fame of the untried Freeman and the international aspect of the match, the first since the memorable battles between Tom Cribb and Tom Molineaux half a century earlier, caught the public's imagination. Enthusiastic Americans were going around town offering 2 to 1 on their countryman, though the odds eventually leveled off at 6 to 4. After a final round of exhibitions, benefits, and personal appearances, Freeman finally went into serious training near a country village whose local reporter has left us this happy account of his activities:

"Freeman has been assiduously attended by his friend, Ben Caunt, and has been ranging up hill and down dale like the celebrated giant Gog in his 'seven-league boots' with staff in hand and followed by 'a tail,' which, from the length of his fork, generally manages to keep a respectful distance in the rear.

"Although his nob has been roofed with a shallow tile to diminish the appearance of his steeplelike proportions, he still has the appearance of a walking monument, to the no-small alarm of the squirrels in Squire Byng's Park, into whose dormitories he occasionally casts a squint of recognition.

"By his good humour and playfulness of disposition he has won all hearts and has been a welcome guest on whatever premises he has cast anchor in his walks, which have seldom been less than twenty or thirty miles a day.

"He has been extremely attentive to his training, and has been much reduced in flesh, while his muscular developments stand forth with additional symmetry. On his arrival, he carried some twenty-three stone [322 pounds] 'good meat' but we doubt whether on Tuesday he will much exceed eighteen stone [252 pounds]."

The Slasher was also described as in the pink, down to his fighting weight of 189, "six feet high, a well proportioned, muscular fellow (always deducting the 'baker-knee' which destroys the perpendicular of his pedestal)."

In our own days of televisionary sloth, when fight fans have been heard to complain that it is too much trouble flying all the way out to Las Vegas, one can only wonder at the sacrifices of personal comfort and even safety these early devotees of the ring were willing to make. Despite the widespread publicity the Free-man-Slasher bout had received and the enthusiastic backing of the Prince of Wales and many other of The Fancy, prizefighting was still on the books as a crime. So the site of the bout, in open country some twenty miles outside of London, was to be kept a secret from all except the initiated. But with the entire London sporting world in on the plans, it hardly took Scotland Yard to pick up the scent.

With carriages already on the road toward the appointed site the night before, the law had only to tail them to be on hand for the arrival of the contestants at the rural station the following morning. So the party had to move four miles on into the next county, along muddy backroads which a majority of the would-be spectators had to travel on foot.

Most of these were London dandies, unprepared for such coarse pedestrianism, but even when these stubborn ancestors of present-day ringsiders saw their route lead them directly into a swamp, they pushed on in determination to get their guinea's worth.

These weary, mud-bespattered diehards finally arrived at the ring site with barely time to catch their breath when, as a witness reported, "the Sawbridgeworth police superintendent and Mr. Phillips, the magistrate, once more presented their ill-omened countenances and plainly declared their determination to prevent the fight taking place either in Essex or Hertfordshire. This was a poser."

So back everyone tramped to the station again, ready to re-treat to London for much needed refreshment at the Rising Sun and Castle Tavern. As the disappointed assembly neared the sta-tion, however, it was suddenly noticed that "the conservators of propriety had at last favored us with their absence." So, although already four o'clock and winter evening fast approaching, a ring was hastily formed and the contestants, we are told, "lost no time in removing their superfluous feathers. Both appeared in high spirits and eager for business.

"Umpires and a referee having been chosen, the ring was cleared out, and the privileged dropped contentedly on the damp earth, with such preservatives to their sitting placed as circumstances would permit. It must be acknowledged that these were far from satisfactory, owing to the difficulties to which the commissary had been exposed in the various transfers of his material."

Like many an overpublicized "battle of giants" in our own day, the fight itself hardly justified the ordeal its spectators had endured in order to be on hand. The Tipton Slasher failed to demonstrate how he came by so aggressive a monicker. More wily than scientific, he would beat the ponderous Freeman to the punch and then go down to end the round before "the American Atlas" could even the score. Like Carnera, Freeman's size obviously impeded rather than aided his punching power, and the only damage he seemed able to inflict on the Slasher was by lifting him off the ground and squeezing him, boa-constrictor style, then throwing him bodily.

After thirty-five rounds of this, a round-by-round report tells us "it became so dark that it was difficult to see what was doing in the ring, and the spectators came close to the ropes. The partisans of The Slasher were extremely uproarious, and one of them especially was constantly interfering with the umpires, called 'time' when it was not time and was guilty of other most offensive and unfair conduct."

In darkness and fog so thick the contestants were barely visible from ringside, the fight dragged on into its second hour. In the last few rounds "there was an evident attempt to draw Freeman into The Slasher's corner, where a desperate set of ruffians had collected, who, by the most offensive vociferations, endeavoured to intimidate and alarm him."

Finally, in the seventieth round, with neither opponent showing any real sign of distress, the referee announced that he himself could no longer see the contestants and called the bout on account of darkness.

As if the fans, some of whom had been on the road for twenty-four hours, hadn't already suffered enough, the night was now so black that hundreds were unable to find their way back to the station. They floundered into swamps or pitched headlong into water-filled ditches. The night was filled with anguished cries for help and the choicer cuss words of the day. But at last a large part of the assembly somehow managed to drag itself back to the Rising Sun and the Castle Tavern, where hot rums somewhat restored general morale.

The Slasher and Freeman, at their respective headquarters, were greeted like victors by crowds that lingered into the early morning, fortifying themselves with rum and other manly beverages to compensate for the difficulties of the day.

The story about Freeman the following day might easily have been taken from a more recent description of Carnera in one of his disappointing exhibitions: "It struck us that, with immense power, he wanted judgement in its application . . . many of his hits were rather shoves or pokes instead of coming well from the shoulder."

Despite the inconclusive nature of their first bout, feeling ran high about a rematch, perhaps because the bubble of Freeman's formidability had been pricked and the Slasher's backers were more confident.

Once more the participants and their indomitable followers had to play hide-and-seek with the law. Once more, after being driven back and forth across an entire county, a ring was finally established and the fighters stripped for action, only to be intercepted by a police captain who had been chasing them on horseback. Old Tom Spring helped set up another ring several miles from the last one, but a third time their nemesis, the police captain, tracked them down.

To cut down on the roadwork, for which many of the followers did their training in the back room of Castle Tavern, and to make sure that the score between Freeman and the Slasher would be settled once and for all, a steamer was hired to take the party so far up the Thames as to be beyond the conscientious reach of the "beaks" and "trays," the nineteenth-century equivalent of "fuzz" and "pigs."

The atmosphere on board was not very different from that of a special flight for a big fight, only instead of movie stars, politicos, and socialites, these were scions of the peerage, including a marquis, a number of high-ranking military men, university men, doctors, barristers, and sportsmen, along with the famous boxers and prominent proprietors of chophouses and taverns.

The custom of enjoying refreshments en route apparently has changed little from that day to this, except perhaps in the quality of the commissary. The facetiously named Bishop of Bond Street, who catered to the party, offered a magnificent hamper with everything from ham to pigeon pie, "various comestibiles for which Fortnum and Mason are renowned," and an abundance of precious amber-colored bottles, plus a generous supply of cognac, sherry, and champagne.

Except for a sportsman or two who overestimated his capacity and fell into a champagne slumber from which not even the impending battle could rouse him, the voyage passed without incident. Unless you consider the prank of the practical joker who spread the word "that the swells down below had arranged with the captain for a trip to France, to make sure of no more stoppages from beaks or blues." At this point an unidentified passenger, insisting that his wife would be done with him for good if she should hear of his unannounced trip to the continent, leaped overboard. "Great was the laughter at the victim of this sell," a reporter for *Bell's Life* in London recorded, "for moments later the paddles were backed, the chain cable run out and our good ship anchored for the day."

This time the ring was formed in an ideal spot on the bank, just across a single-lane footbridge guarded by ring constables. The privileged ticket holders, newspapermen, and officials were issued stools. Forming in rows behind them were the second-class spectators, who carried folding seats from the ship, trestles, bundles of straw, and cushions. Soft-seat concessions had not yet been introduced, though a couple of enterprising vendors were offering beer from enormous barrels they had managed to lug across the flimsy bridge. Spreading out behind the second-class spectators sprawled a great crowd of East Enders, who, the *Bell's Life* reporter tells us with obvious distaste, were conveyed for a very low tariff by tugs which had formed a flotilla behind the main steamer.

Although this second battle was fought only two weeks after the first one, the New World Goliath seemed to have expanded considerably, weighing in at 265. The Slasher, thinner and paler, was spotting his elephantine rival some 80 pounds.

The cautious, shifty, evasive style of the inaptly named Slasher and the ponderous, badly timed attack of Freeman once more produced the kind of fight today's fight crowds would taunt with unison applause and Bronx cheers. For the bloodthirsty, however, there were rounds like this, quoted from the round-by-round account:

"Round 10: The Slasher dropped a heavy smack on the Giant's ivories with his left, which, coming in contact with his teeth, inflicted a wound on his own finger that bled profusely. He tried it again but was short, as was the Giant in his attempt to return, and The Slasher fell on his knees.

"Round 15: The Slasher led off and popped his left on the Giant's mouth. The Giant's lips were swollen and a tinge of blood was perceptible. The Giant caught The Slasher heavily on the ear, which became seriously swollen. A rally, in which there were some heavy hits exchanged, and in the close The Slasher got down."

In the seventeenth round, Freeman "popped a heavy smack on The Slasher's neck" for one of the few clean knockdowns of the fight. In the thirty seconds allowed before having to come up to scratch, "The Slasher's seconds were observed rubbing his neck, and there was a little of the doldrum appearance in his phiz."

But this kind of punishment on Freeman's part seemed largely accidental, and in the inimitable words of the round-by-round reporter, "there was a want of precision in Freeman's deliveries which forbade the hope of execution."

A typical round was the twenty-seventh: "a wild, blundering round, in which there was no precision on either side. The Slasher slipped down but was up again and renewed the round, planting a right-hand chopper on the Giant's pimple. After a scrambling rally, The Slasher again got down and slipped completely under the Giant's fork, at whom he looked up and grinned."

Then, somewhat as in the Carnera-Sharkey fight, the match suddenly ended controversially in Freeman's favor. In the thirty-seventh round, after only (for those days) forty minutes of fighting, the Slasher rushed in, struck Freeman on the shoulder, and before the Giant could return the blow, fell without being hit. Freeman's seconds promptly claimed foul. When the umpires disagreed, the referee ruled the Slasher disqualified and Freeman the winner.

The Slasher protested that he had merely fallen from the recoil after hitting the Giant's shoulder, but the ruling was final and so, after fighting a total of 107 rounds, inciting London sports fans to a pitch where they would wade through swamps and engage in cross-country tag with the constabulary of five counties, this latter-day David-and-Goliath affair ended in fiasco.

As in the cases of Jess Willard, Carnera, Buddy Baer, Big Ben Moross, and other mammoths of the ring, Freeman's failure to live up to his overwhelming appearance proved once more the inability of giants to cope with smaller, better-coordinated men.

"That Freeman is a game man we have no doubt," ran a newspaper account of the thirty-seven inconclusive rounds, "but he is unwieldly, and possesses too much of 'the milk of human kindness' ever to become a 'star' in the ring. We recommend him to choose some more suitable occupation, although as a sparrer, from his great size, he will always be an object of curiosity."

Apparently the harmless Giant took this reporter's unsolicited advice, for the next year found him back in the circus, once more exhibiting himself to packed audiences. But even his feats of strength were illusory and tinged with irony, for suddenly, in his twenty-fifth year, he was struck by an attack of tuberculosis which doctors discovered he had carried since childhood.

One account of the period attributes his early death to "the dreadful injuries received in his terrible combat with the formidable bruiser known as the Tipton Slasher—injuries which, from the tremendous stature of the combatants, must have been beyond ordinary calculation."

But an ardent advocate of the British prize ring lost no time in labeling this as an uncalled-for attack on Britain's glorious sport by a "mere penny-a-liner." It was sheer nonsense to blame the Giant's untimely passing on his unsatisfactory showing in the ring, this enthusiast maintained, for it was quite clear that "the Giant's end was of necessity accelerated by repeated colds, caught in the light attire of fleshings and spangles in which he exhibited in draughty canvas erections and crowded theaters and booths."

Whether Charles Freeman, the biggest American who ever fought, died from exposure to the fists of the Tipton Slasher or to the drafts of chilly circus tents is a question that can no longer cause us concern.

But should you ever be accosted by an adversary who towers over you from six inches to a foot, you may take heart from the gigantic ineptitude of this American man-monster whose heroic proportions made it seem improbable that any man in the world could stand up to him but who was unable to overcome a second-rate English trial horse weighing less than 190 pounds.

[1948]

▪ 3 ▪

When Boxing Was a Jewish Sport

ALTHOUGH I WAS RAISED in the film business—where my father B.P. for many years ran the Paramount Studio—my idols weren't the movie stars who worked for him: Maurice Chevalier, Fredric March, Cary Grant, Gary Cooper. . . . I knew them well but they didn't get to me as the boxers did. The moviemaking that went on all around me, at the studio and on location, was fascinating. But my most vivid, early memories involved going to the fights with my old man.

He was a passionate boxing fan who went to the fights twice a week. In my mind's eye I am with him in the first row at the Hollywood Legion every Friday night. Great fighters came to the Legion—the young Archie Moore, Tony Canzoneri, Bud Taylor, Fidel La Barba, and Henry Armstrong. Boxing has always been an intensely ethnic sport, and so I must confess we had a special *qvell* for the exploits of our Jewish heroes. The 1920s and '30s into the '40s were a Golden Age for Jewish boxers, and in Hollywood, my hometown, we couldn't help feeling a surge of pride when the fighters with the six-pointed star on their trunks proved their mettle against the toughest and most skillful of the Italians, Irish, and blacks, of whom there were so many stars in those star-studded times.

If not only my father but all of the Paramount "family" were fight fans, they came by their passion honestly, with a sense of Jewish tradition and history. The sturdy and inspired little founder of Paramount (originally Famous Players), Adolph Zukor, had been part of the stream of penniless Jewish immigrants who came to America in the late nineteenth century with their pockets empty and their heads full of dreams. Before he was a low-paid, piecework furrier, young Adolph was hustling to make a dollar here, a dollar there. One of the ways he stumbled into making a buck was to fight for a dollar a round in a neighborhood boxing club.

By the time my father was working for Zukor as a twenty-year-old wunderkind writer and press agent for Famous Players, he was drawn to the pioneer company's enthusiasm for boxing. There seemed to be a natural connection between the movie game and the fight game: both offering a way out of the stifling ghetto on the lower East Side, where nearly all first-generation Jews were desperately poor.

If Adolph Zukor enjoyed overnight success making hit movies with magical discoveries of movie stars like Mary Pickford (whom B.P. dubbed "America's Sweetheart"), the Jewish community had a fistic star in the ghetto wonder Benjamin Leiner, who fought under the *nom de boxe* Benny Leonard.

I still think of Benny Leonard as an early-century counterpart to the latter-day boxing saint Muhammad Ali. In the early decades of the twentieth century, ambitious young Jews were struggling to break out of the cycle of poverty in which so many saw their parents hopelessly trapped. They became songwriters like Irving Berlin and Billy Rose, budding movie moguls like Zukor and Sam Goldfish (later Goldwyn), furriers and jewelers, and, most notably for me, stellar champions of the prize ring like Joe Choyinski, Abe Attell, and my father's favorite, "The Great Benny Leonard."

That was the only way I ever heard Leonard described in my household. I wish I still had the scrapbook I compiled as a seven-year-old on "The Great Benny Leonard." I remember the picture I had pasted on the cover, with the trim, athletic body, the look of intelligence, and the slicked-down hair that—so the boast went—never got messed despite fighting in a division, the lightweight, that offered more than half a dozen gifted contenders. As talented young Jews like my father were moving into mainstream America

"The Great Benny Leonard," flag bearer of Jews who were moving into mainstream America. (© Bettmann/Corbis)

at the time of my birth, "The Great Benny Leonard" became their flag bearer, a symbol of their newly found strength and success. The excitement around those early Benny Leonard fights against champion Freddy Welsh, tough Irish Richie Mitchell, and Philadelphia Jewish rival Lew Tendler inspired his Jewish fans in the same way Ali reached out to the black ghettos from Harlem to Watts in the 1960s and '70s. Like Ali with young blacks, Benny Leonard, with the six-pointed star he wore so proudly on his trunks, sent a message to Jewish ghettos across America: "You may think of us as pushcart peddlers and money grubbers. But we can climb into the ring with you, the best you have to offer, and maybe you can knock us down (as Richie Mitchell floored the Great Benny), but you can't keep us down. We've got the skills and the courage to beat you at your own game. Ready or not, we're moving up." Not just in the prize ring with Leonard and Tendler, Jackie "Kid" Berg, "Battling" Levinsky, Maxie Rosenbloom, Ben Jeby, and our host of champions. Their victories in fierce and memorable battles reinforced my father's generation's belief in themselves in their battle in what I've always thought of as the ring outside the ring.

In Hollywood from the twenties to the forties we responded with unabashed ethnic pride to the exploits of our local Jewish champions. Mushy Callahan (Morris Scheer), Jackie Fields, Newsboy Brown, and Maxie Rosenbloom were not only sports heroes but personal friends. When Callahan took the junior welterweight belt from Richie Mitchell's brother "Pinky," I proudly hung the winning gloves on the wall behind my bed. And even though Jews had come a long way up in the world from the 1910s when Leonard was in his ascendancy to Mushy's wins over Mitchell and his formidable local rival Ace Hudkins in the 1930s, even though Jews were now leaders in the film industry, the music business, dominant in the arts and even challenging the WASP movers and shakers in banking and Wall Street, there was still a healthy reassurance that "some of our boys" could fight their way to the very top of the hardest and most demanding of all professional sports.

I've always thought of boxing not as a mirror but as a magnifying glass of our society. It is hardly accidental that out of the poor Irish immigration of a people being brutalized by their British overlords, we had a wave of great Irish fighters—from John L. Sullivan and Gentleman Jim Corbett to the "Toy Bull Dog" Mickey Walker and the brash, nimble, and brave Billy Conn. As the Irish moved up into the mainstream, there was less economic need to use the prize ring as their way out and up. The wave of Jewish boxers followed exactly the same pattern, as did the Italians. The almost total domination of the ring today by African Americans

and Hispanics speaks directly to the continued economic depriva-
tion and discrimination of large sections of our inner-city commu-
nities.

But the first half of the twentieth century was a Golden Age of
Jewish Boxing, with score on score of Jewish champions of the
world, not to mention all those fierce and gifted contenders like
Allie Stolz, Artie Levine, Maxie Shapiro, Georgie Abrams, Leach
Cross . . . the brave boys who made their statement for all of us
when boxing was a Jewish sport.

[1997]

▪ 4 ▪

Good Night, Sweet Princes

WATCHING AGED, grizzled, overmatched legend Roberto Duran take an unmerciful beating from young, scrappy, up-and-coming William Joppy a few weeks ago, I felt a little ashamed of myself for wanting to see what we all knew in advance had to be the humiliation, at age forty-seven, of the greatest lightweight champion of the modern era. Unranked by the WBC, the IBF, the WBO, and Father Time, in his thirty-first year in what my knowledgeable colleague Hugh McIlvanney of the *Sunday Times* calls "the hardest game," the ancient Roberto was in there one more time to challenge Joppy for his WBA middleweight belt.

Alas, we doubt that even the hoary veteran from the mean streets of Panama City climbed into that Vegas ring believing he could win a sixth world title, thereby becoming the oldest man ever to gain such honors. Showtime's own commentator, "Fight Doctor" Ferdie Pacheco, set the tone in his preamble to the mismatch: "Hopefully, we won't see a tragedy. But the very fact Duran's still in there is a tragedy. . . . This could be a very sad night for boxing."

And so it was, with the quick-fisted, fast moving Joppy hitting his aged opponent with all the punches in the repertoire—jabs, uppercuts, left hooks, and a hard right hand to Duran's battered head to end round one; the punishment continuing in round two with Duran wobbled by a series of left hooks; and finally, in what would be the ultimate round three, trapped in senile immobility, eating punches, unable to escape the flurries he used to slip,

33

block, duck, and neutralize. Never the conventional boxing master, in his good years he had developed his own street-fighter defensive style built into his *"Manos de Piedra"* relentless aggression. "It's heartbreaking to see a great fighter just stand there unable to get away from the punches," the Fight Doctor gave it to us straight, honorably foreswearing the conventional commentator hype. And when referee Joe Cortez finally moved in belatedly to save the *Viejo* any more unanswered blows from what had become an exercise in brutalized futility at the end of round three, Pacheco summed up the floundering mess that had once been the indomitable Roberto Duran: "Unfortunately, he'll pay the price later on, as they all do."

As he delivered this requiem for the forty-seven-year-old wreck of what had been the pocket-sized terror of the late 1970s, I was reminded of McIlvanney's tough-love farewell on watching a used-up forty-year-old Ali laboring through ten lackluster rounds with an out-of-shape journeyman, Trevor Berbick. "A king rode into permanent retirement on the back of a garbage truck."

As I sorrowed for the retrogressed Roberto, I remembered glory nights, when he savaged the nifty Scot, Ken Buchanan, to become the twenty-one-year-old lightweight champion of the world; how he took the welterweight crown from Sugar Ray Leonard in a trademark Duran performance eight years later; and, in his early thirties, when he knocked out that very tough Mexican Pipino Cuevas and beat Davey Moore into insensibility for the WBA junior middleweight crown.

But there's always that night, if you must fight on into your late thirties and forties, when suddenly the magic's gone and all that pretty fistic music becomes a terrible silence. Great fighters are able to fight from memory for a few years past what their bodies are trying to tell them is their natural retirement. As I watched our once matchless Roberto succumb to fistic Alzheimer's, I found myself drawing up a misery list of all-time champions I have had the upsetting experience of seeing on the dark night that prompts this observation: Old fighters don't fade away, they just slowly die in front of our eyes.

My first geriatric champ was Benny Leonard. The Great Benny Leonard. The boxer my fight-fan father loved to boast about as the best he ever saw. I had seen all those Leonardian triumphs through the eyes of my doting old man. And when Benny retired as undefeated lightweight champion when I was ten years old, I despaired that I would never see him. But came the depression, the loss of Benny's savings, and he was back at his old trade again. When they matched him with the young boxer-puncher I had followed as a kid in Hollywood, Jimmy McLarnin, I remember the excitement as I drove down from Dartmouth College to see father's idol in action at last. Alas, my Benny Leonard was a faint carbon of my old man's hero. No magic, no music: begloved Alzheimer's. The thirty-six-year-old ghost of Great Benny was knocked down and out in the sixth, the first time he had suffered that humiliation since he was a teenage novice two hundred fights ago.

The tragedy becomes the ritual sacrifice of the king. I saw the greatest before the Greatest, Joe Louis, run through his money, including a fixed fight with the IRS, a tired fighter when he took a pasting from Ezzard Charles in what should have been an unnecessary comeback, and then back again, fat, old, and damaged, against the hungry and ferocious Rocky Marciano. If you were not there to see old Joe on his back with his leg trembling over the lowest strand of the ropes, you were spared another of those royal rides on the back of the garbage truck.

Take our twentieth-century nonpareil who for his weight could punch like Louis while moving like Ali, Sugar Ray Robinson. How I wondered at his genius, able to lick great fighters—Fritzie Zivic, Sammy Angott, Henry Armstrong, Jake LaMotta—while still in his early twenties, able to come out of retirement in his mid-thirties and win middleweight titles from Bobo Olson, Gene Fullmer, and Carmen Basilio. Did I have to see him follow the downward path of great champions out of money and fighting for chump change in his forties? Did I have to see him lose a dreary ten-rounder to journeyman Phil Moyer (at least Moyer didn't have the power to chop him up, as Joppy chopped Duran)? And was it masochism or boxing history that led me to what some people called "the outhouse for San Diego," Tijuana, to see a forty-four-year-old impersonator of the greatest fighter I ever saw get cuffed around in losing to a Mexican middleweight who might once have qualified as a willing sparring partner, Memo Ayon?

Yes, Ray spent money as if he had his own private press for grinding out the green. Yes, if you traveled to Europe with your own private barber, your private court jester, musicians, and enough friends to fill the entire floor of a world-class hotel, one of those days you were going to run out of time and money.

One of the most remarkable figures of all time is boxing's Old Man River Archie Moore, who kept rolling along for 27 years and 229 fights with 131 KOs, who didn't even get a shot at the light heavyweight title until he was past the age when most fighters have retired, 39, who knocked down and almost stopped the un-stoppable heavyweight champ, Rocky Marciano, when he was 42, and then went on to defend his light heavyweight championship nine times in the next nine years, his final successful defense at the unbelievable age of 48—and if this is a long sentence, so was Archie's career. Did we really have to see the weary ghost of this venerable champion, almost 50 years old, humiliated and knocked out by the 20-year-old new kid on the block, Cassius Clay, on his way to becoming the iconic Muhammad Ali? No, and remember-ing fights I wish I had never had to see, flash forward 18 years to see the proud but fistically senile Ali take an unmerciful beating from Ali's able successor and former sparring partner, Larry Holmes. Holmes didn't want to hit him anymore, and Ali had nothing left except pride. When trainer Angelo Dundee tried to stop it, the dead-tired, dead-game Ali refused to quit. What moti-vated this ill-advised comeback? Well, in that whirlpool of a mind, he was still The Greatest. And let's face it, no matter how many big paynights he shared with his manager, Herbert Muhammad, his three wives, promoter Don King, and all those hangers-on his loyal and savvy business and camp manager Gene Kilroy tried to jettison, he needed the money.

That's the epitaph to almost every great fighter's career. "He was a true champion, but at the end he needed the money."

And thinking of all those humbled champions, I keep harking back to pensions. Boxers are the only professional athletes without a pension fund. A point or two off the top, honestly administered, would have afforded those great if prodigal athletes the dignity they deserved in retirement. As the original and irrepressible Golden Boy, Art Aragon, once said to me, "When you quit the ring, if you're a big success you're only a few thousand dollars in debt and only a little bit brain-damaged. Now, how can you knock a sport like that?" I wasn't knocking the sport, but I couldn't help thinking of its hero-victims as I watched poor old, great old Roberto Duran take his lumps and, with what's left of his $300,000 purse after IRS and child-support attachments, shamble out of the ring for what we hope for his and boxing's sake is the last time. From Tom Cribb and Tom Molineaux two hundred years ago to more recent champions like Ike Williams and Riddick Bowe, it's the same old downward path.

Old fighters never fade away. They simply die slowly in front of our eyes. Sophocles had his tragic heroes. We have Sam Langford and Joe Louis and Roberto Duran and Beau Jack, and now, pathetically dreaming of still another comeback, talking of his vainglorious hope of winning a fourth heavyweight championship when he is getting beaten up by second-raters, the man who once lived up to his fistic hype as the Real Deal and has now played out all his cards but refuses to leave the table will finally go back to that beautiful estate outside Atlanta with chronic bells beating in what's left of that warrior's brain. Evander, Evander Holyfield for God's sake, for your sake, for all our sakes, go home. Once a role model for boxing integrity, you're going out as a role model for boxing senility. We remember you *when*. Please, please stop asking your old admirers to remember you now.

[1998]

▪ 5 ▪

Confessions of an
Ex-Fight Manager

IT'S HALF A CENTURY AGO and I'm living on a farm in New Hope, Pennsylvania, minding my own business, which is writing novels. After an unexpected success with the first one, *What Makes Sammy Run?*, I've had good reviews and a movie sale on the second, *The Harder They Fall*, and wondering what to do for an encore.

I've got a big barn, and no cows in it, so I figure I'll set up a boxing ring. Going to fights with my old man as a Hollywood kid, I had always liked to box. I had only one serious weakness. I didn't like being hit on the nose. Make that two weaknesses: I never devised a strategy to avoid being hit on the nose.

At the New Hope post office I always lingered to talk fights with a fellow fan who worked there, Bob McNamara. An ex-amateur boxer, he was ready to train our local Golden Gloves prospects. How about using my ring? Writers are always looking for distractions to help them procrastinate. I couldn't think of a happier one than having the young boxers training in my barn.

Into our amateur mix came a rugged-looking young black man from Trenton, just under 6 feet tall and weighing an already well-conditioned 190 pounds. Archie McBride pounded hell out of the heavy bag and moved sturdily around the ring. McNamara thought we had a good Golden Glove novice class candidate.

38

But this serious eighteen-year-old didn't want to waste his time fighting for free. He wanted to help his family. So I phoned the little operator who ran the fights in Trenton, Willie Gilzenberg, and told him I had a big, strong kid in the barn and could I get him a four-rounder? Willie asked me how many tickets I'd buy. Buy enough and we'd open the show. I was learning on the job.

Willie was a slippery little guy who ran a low-level, one-man show. He was right there at the ancient ticket window taking the money. The money wasn't exactly flooding into that hoary Trenton arena, and Willie made sure every nickel of it went into his pocket.

With no experience and the most primitive kind of preparation in the New Hope barn, Archie went in there against a kid who had a few fights and who looked formidably muscular, with a formidable *nom de boxe*, Babe O'Blinnis. Archie took him out almost as fast as Joe Louis took care of Max Schmeling in their historic second fight. So we got invited back again and knocked out another young Trenton heavyweight. Soon Archie McBride was building a local reputation, with a string of early-round KOs.

I was working hard on a book drawing on my ill-fated journey to the Dartmouth Winter Carnival with Scott Fitzgerald, but with Archie training in the barn and all the fights taking place in Trenton or Asbury Park, I was having a lot of fun and excitement without a sense of guilt at taking too much time away from what was still my main line of work.

By this time Archie was fighting local main events, and it got a little more serious when "my Archie"—as I called him to separate him from the venerable Archie Moore—was matched with the much bigger, far more experienced Cuban heavyweight Nino Valdes. Valdes had a reputation as a big puncher, with a dozen knockouts in nineteen fights. He had boxed a number of ten-rounders while Archie had never gone beyond six.

I remember the Valdes fight in Reading as a turning point in my managerial career. I was into my novel now, *The Disenchanted*, but I found myself looking up from that yellow legal pad to worry about Archie. I had always complained about managers bringing their boys along too fast and putting them in over their head, and now I wondered if we shouldn't have picked up some more six-rounders in Trenton before taking on Valdes in Reading.

But Archie took Valdes that night. It was hard fought, but the pride of New Hope was bobbing and weaving, getting under the long jabs and scoring with body punches in close. That was Archie's style. Nothing flashy, a very solid performer, especially when he was able to move under punches and stay close without clinching. Every time he got hit, I hurt. Every time the bell rang ending a round and he came back to our corner unscathed, I wished it could end right there. Feeling close to and responsible for a fighter is an indescribable feeling. I had watched good friends, including some champions, in action and always felt nerved up for them. But this was different. If anything happened to Archie, it was my fault. I could have said no. But it might have been the end of Archie's career, for we were still in the hands of Willie Gilzenberg. In Jersey, wily Willie was the only game in town.

In the dressing room after the fight, along with a deep swallow of relief, I remember the touching gesture of the defeated Cuban's coming into Archie's dressing room to check a small cut over Archie's left eye. Like an unbelievable scene in a sentimental movie, Valdes actually took the scissors and cut the tape that was to go over Archie's eye.

I remember driving back from Reading to my farm with Archie and Bob McNamara that night, realizing that we had a pretty good country heavyweight on our hands and wondering how far we could take him. I was also wondering how I was going to get a tough book done if I spent too much time worrying about the future of Archie McBride.

But this managing stuff gets in the blood. When I came out of my little stone writing house for a breather, I could hear the pounding music of the heavy bag, and I couldn't resist going to the barn to talk things over with Archie and Bob. A good win in Philly finally brought us to New York, not all the way to Madison Square yet, but to Sunny Side Gardens where Archie lost a close one to a more experienced fighter and then came back in the rematch and knocked him out.

Next came a fight with Mickey Carter, who didn't worry me too much when I checked his record. I didn't start worrying until I got a call from a stranger in Queens wanting to bet me two thousand dollars on his boy Carter. That was out of my league, and his confidence worried me. From my friend Jimmy Cannon, the then famous sports columnist, a drinking buddy in those days, I found out that Carter's guy ran numbers in Queens. He called me again and made me feel like a piker. We settled for five hundred. He said he'd see me at ringside.

That was the first money I made on Archie. He blew Carter out of there in two. I thought we were ready for the Garden. But the Garden wasn't ready for us. Archie looked so strong that none of the boys on the way up wanted to take a chance. And none of the names on top wanted to come down to a no-name who might lick them.

My Archie was in a twilight zone that would shadow him through his long and checkered but memorable career. While he kept on training, I was also getting a lesson in practical fight-game politics. Teddy Brenner didn't come right out and say so, but I got the message. If I wanted to bring Archie into the Garden, I'd need a Managers Guild co-pilot. It was a cozy little closed shop, and most if not all the members would have had to take the Fifth if questioned under oath on their relations to Frankie Carbo, Boxing Commissioner Without Portfolio.

To move to the Garden we took on board one of the in-boys, Sammy Richman, who promised us a fight in the Garden. Writing books seemed unimportant. We were on our way to the Mecca. Our opponent was Floyd Gibson, whose main claim to fame was winning on a foul from the more famous Archie, the ageless Mr. Moore.

Sammy lived at the Great Northern Hotel. It seemed as if all the managers on Mike Jacobs's Beach lived at the Great Northern. The lobby was filled with little Jewish guys with big cigars right out of *Guys and Dolls*. Some of them had name fighters and some of them wannabes. When they fell behind on their rent, they'd promise the desk to pay it off out of their kid's next purse. They hung out at Lindy's, and their other homes were the Garden and St. Nick's. None of them seemed to have wives or even steady girlfriends. It was all broads and "hoors" and one-night stands. The dialogue was almost exclusively fight talk, and when they talked about fighters it was all about money.

I loved the Great Northern and the Edison where Jimmy Cannon and a lot of fight mavens lived, but my home away from home was the Algonquin where the shades of Dorothy Parker, George S. Kaufman, and Alexander Woollcott wandered the lobby and where you were apt to bump into Bill Faulkner and Aldous Huxley in the corridors. We checked in the day before the fight, and my bellboy chums, Michael, Earl, and Phillip, asked if they could come in and meet Archie. Pulitzer Prize winners were a dime a dozen in the Algonquin, but a real live prizefighter on his way to the Garden brought a new excitement to the old hotel. Next day in the *New York Herald-Tribune* Red Smith described Archie as "the only fighter who ever fought out of the Algonquin. . . ."

My entourage was much more Algonquin than Great Northern: my venerable editor Saxe Commins, who brought Eugene O'Neill to Random House and had never seen a prizefight; Harvey Breit from the *New York Times Book Review*, and Irwin Shaw.

I introduced sensitive, intellectual Saxe Commins to cynical, cigar-smoking fight writer Al Buck and felt as if my two worlds were smashing together. Saxe had already lectured me about neglecting my work for what should be a hobby on the side. I tried to explain that what he was to me, a guide and nourisher, I had become to Archie. Others could teach him in the gym, but I could give him emotional support in the hotel room.

We won the Garden fight big, with a sixth-round knockout, and I was more relieved than when I got thumbs-up reviews on that nervous-making second novel. And let me explain that "we." In my pre-managing days, I had laughed at the managers with their "we're fighting the semi at the Garden Saturday night";

"We're fighting a tough son-of-a-bitch from Youngstown." What's with the "we" shit? I used to think. They're not doing the bleeding. They're not taking the shots to the head. But in my managerial mode I actually heard myself saying, "We're going back to Trenton. Willie is paying us more money now that we've got a name." And, "We're fighting Red Applegate for the Jersey State Heavyweight Championship." And, oh what a fight "we" had. They didn't come tougher than Applegate. He was the only one to go the distance with Rocky Marciano that year. Red may have been nicknamed for the color of the liquid that oozed from cuts all over his face. But he kept coming. It could have been the fight of the year.

It was heady stuff. We—well Archie helped—were the heavyweight champions of all New Jersey! Until a few months later, when we ran into a nobody from Newark, with a famous name, Jimmy Walker. Archie came out and got stopped by a very hard and very straight right hand. Twenty fights and he had never even been down before. He had chin. But Jimmy Walker had punch. My wife Vicki, in the second row, broke down and sobbed theatrically. The referee came down from the ring and tried to console her. "I got knocked out a coupla times," he said soothingly. "It isn't that bad."

He was right. Archie recovered. I asked Willie for a rematch, we lost a close one, but in the third one Archie solved the Jimmy Walker problem. We were champion of the great state of New Jersey again, and ready for prime time.

We were back in the Apple again, back in venerable St. Nick's, which looked exactly like Thomas Eakins's painting of it because it was a throwback to the nineteenth century and hadn't changed. There was a low-slung balcony and an intimacy; the cigar smoke from ringsiders in the '20s and '30s still floated through the lovely old place. Damon Runyon's guys and dolls were all around ringside, and the balcony was full of blue-collar holler guys ready to fight themselves.

I had dearly loved St. Nick's as a spectator, but now I was a participant. The opponent was a comer from Far Rockaway, the original Hurricane, Tommy Jackson. It was the Tortoise and the Hare, Jackson flashing and showboating and Archie landing the solid punches. Jimmy Cannon and Al Buck, the cognoscenti, thought we won. But they gave it to Jackson. I was in the middle of a rewrite on our movie about the waterfront and being pushed by Elia Kazan to get on with it—he even wanted me to move into his home on Seventy-second Street, but I had Archie working in the barn for an even bigger fight than Hurricane, a rematch with Nino Valdes who had gone up in this world with a win over Ezzard Charles. A top contender for Marciano now. I talked to Sammy Richman about putting it in the Garden, but the money said Havana. Kazan wanted to talk post-production *On The Waterfront* and Saxe Commins was scolding me for deserting my *Waterfront* novel. I had a tiger by the tail, and his name was Archie McBride. I wasn't sure enough to put him in with Rocky Marciano, but even cynical Sammy Richman said McBride could hold his own with the best heavyweights in the world. So I said goodbye to Kazan and Saxe Commins, and on we went to Havana. We had a big welcome, Famous Gringo Writer with his formidable American fighter whose win over Valdes the Cuban heavyweight champion was determined to avenge.

It was in the sold-out Havana sports arena, and the voices of the patriotic rooters sounded like bongo drums. Archie and I had talked about the crowd scene, the deafening "Ni-no, Ni-no" that could get to a fighter before the opening bell. Archie said he wasn't worried about the crowd, and he thought he could lick Valdes again. He was always very quiet, very self-contained, a lovely man who's now in his mid-70s. We still stay in touch with each other.

The fight was a rouser, with both men down once, and of course every time Nino landed the crowd went wild, and every time Archie scored, punching Nino to the body, there was dead silence. So the atmosphere said Valdes was winning. But as in the Jackson fight, Archie's were the more telling punches. The close decision went to Valdes, to the banging of the bongos and impromptu dancing in the aisles. But the truth is, we wuz robbed. Fifty years later I'm telling you, we beat the No. 1 contender that night. I tried to make my case in a radio interview at ringside, throwing in a little fractured Spanish along with a lot of outraged English. I called the judges *ladrones*, and you don't do that in Havana. *Dios Mio*, I needed the head *policia* to protect me. It was only a month to the Oscars, our movie was in the running, and Kazan and our producer wanted me to go out there and ask Marlon to stop knocking the Academy or we wouldn't have a chance. But all that was happening to somebody else on some other planet. That was Tinseltown. This was real, the only reality I knew that bitter night in Havana.

It was a natural rematch, only natural rematches don't happen too often in boxing when there's more money with somebody else. In this case the somebody elses were Hurricane Jackson and Archie Moore. Sammy Richman worked all his Garden connections to get Valdes back for us again. But Nino was hoping for a title shot. Archie was dangerous and didn't sell that many tickets. My entourage was growing, but how many poets and novelists and book editors could I bring? But then we were back in the Algonquin for another rematch we wanted—Hurricane Jackson. Bob McNamara and I both urged Archie to move in on Jackson. It was the Tortoise and the Hare all over again, Hurricane flailing and flashing but inflicting no punishment, Archie taking his time with his solid but not eye-catching style. In the hotel room that afternoon I had been a pale carbon copy Angelo Dundee, urging Archie to match Jackson's flurry at the end of rounds and to go back to the corner with the body English of winning the round— little tricks I had seen boxers do all my life.

Archie was an honest and solid performer, but that sort of theatrics was not his bag. This was another spirited contest, almost a repeat of the first, with Archie doing by far the heavier punching and even having Jackson in trouble a couple of times. I felt sure we had won it this time, but the decision went to Hurricane again. The crowd booed, the working press saw it almost unanimously our way. The AP had it 5-3-2 for McBride. Robbed again. In a way it was an easy fight for Archie. In the dressing room he was uncharacteristically upset. "They didn't count punches," he said.

"They counted slaps. Just little pitty-patty slaps. I know I won this fight."

On his deathbed years later, one of the judges confessed he had had his hand out to slip the fight to Jackson for a miserable five hundred bucks. And of course everybody in the game knew the hopped-up Hurricane had the right connections.

As the unofficial winner of the Jackson fight, Archie drew a dangerous assignment, meeting Bob Satterfield on that awesome puncher's home turf, Chicago. This time I was on a collision course with my writing career. I was locking up my *Waterfront* novel; I followed a no-nonsense pub-date deadline, and I had to tell Archie I wasn't going to be able to make the journey to Satterfieldland. I was a nervous wreck for Archie, but I was in the Random House ring now, with demanding editor Saxe Commins as my corner man.

We told Archie to circle clockwise away from that explosive right hand of Satterfield's for ten rounds nonstop. He followed instructions to a T and came home with an upset decision.

I was back on the farm being pushed by Kazan to get on with our follow-up to the waterfront movie, *A Face in the Crowd*, when I got a call from matchmaker Teddy Brenner. Off the Satterfield win, Archie was getting a shot in the Garden again. I mentioned Bob Baker, a big guy with a name I figured Archie could take. Archie looked good with big strong guys a little slower than him. No, Teddy said, it'll be Floyd Patterson.

The name stuck in my throat. Patterson was the current sensation. He had knocked out everybody he faced that year, including the tough Canadian Yvon Durelle. The maestro Cus D'Amato was crafting his masterpiece. When Archie came in from his workout in the barn, I told him who he'd be meeting. He said quietly, "Do I have to fight Floyd?" This wasn't fear. Archie had pride and heart. Just realism setting in.

It wasn't easy for me to concentrate on my work after that. I kept fighting the Patterson fight in my sleep. Archie wasn't just my fighter, he was family. It was like putting my two little boys Steve and Davey in there with D'Amato's tiger. On the Sunday

"My Archie"—Archie McBride—sparring with the author before his fight with Floyd Patterson.

morning before the fight, a light heavyweight from Trenton with nice moves was due to work out with Archie, to simulate those fast hands of Patterson, Roosevelt LaBord. I'll never forget his name. He never showed up. Even after thirty pro fights, we were still something of an amateur operation. In my anxiety and guilt, I said I'd get into the ring with him and try to move around with him a little. "But, Archie, please don't hurt me." Archie was positively insulted. Me, his mentor? "Mr. Schulberg," he said, "Would I hurt you?"

Thirty seconds later Archie held his left hand out to jab me and my old weakness exposed itself. I had never faced a left hand that didn't find its way to my nose, and Archie's, not even thrown in earnest, smashed against that prominent part of my physiognomy. I saw a wave of blood in which I felt I was drowning. The next day I was due to speak at a book-and-author luncheon in Philadelphia. I had a bandage across my resculptured beak, from cheek to cheek. I was embarrassed to tell the book people what happened. Too much like Papa Hemingway. So I said car accident and picked up sympathy points.

The butterflies felt more like seagulls beating in my belly the night of the Patterson fight. In there with a prodigy. The fastest hands in the history of the heavyweight division. And Archie held his own for the first five rounds. Holding his own was the stamp of McBride. But in the sixth round the fast hands caught up with him, and Archie was down twice. All over in the seventh. That was the year before Floyd stopped Archie Moore to become champion of the world.

I was rushing back to the dressing room with a fluttering heart when Jimmy Cannon stopped me. "Schulberg the great fight reformer! That was a fixed fight if I ever saw one." Until that moment I thought Cannon knew more about fights and fighters than anybody in town. "Jimmy, I always thought you were a little crazy. I underestimated you. You're certifiable."

It got worse. He repeated this hallucination in his column next morning. We had been such good friends, talking about everything from Joe Louis and Sugar Ray to Hemingway and Fitzgerald. But we never talked again.

Old Man River McBride rolled on. Alex Miteff . . . Willie Besmanoff . . . good names in the '50s. Then came Ingemar Johansson. In Goteborg, Sweden, Ingemar's hometown, Archie wants me to go. Not so much for the boxing expertise. Just used to having me with him in the room the day of the fight. But I was lost in the Florida Everglades that month, producing with my brother Stuart a film I had written about saving the plume birds from the feather hunters. We're up to our ears in Cypress swamp, with a temperamental Burl Ives, the young and gifted Christopher Plummer in his very first film, and director Nick Ray, of *Rebel Without a Cause* fame but now ruinously junked out on the hard stuff.

But Whitey Bimstein will be with him, I console myself. Best in the business. And a very nice man. When Whitey came back, he was with Ingemar now. That's the gritty logic of the fight game. "Very close fight," he says. "Archie really won it. He'd have to knock Ingemar out to win it in Goteborg." Three fights later, Johansson takes Floyd out in three and he's champion of the world. Whitey loved Archie, but boxing is a money business and a white heavyweight who could fight a little bit was still gold in America.

When I asked Archie, "How good is Johansson?" he gave me a funny answer. "Remember Jimmy Walker, back in Newark? That's Johansson. All he's got is that big right hand." And, he might have added, the right epidermis.

I thought back to Willy Gilzenberg in Trenton, in what felt like our fistic infancy, when I thought Archie would pick up a few dollars in four-rounders and I'd have a little diversion from sitting at that desk writing words all day.

Thank God Archie came out of it with his mind and dignity intact, a home he bought with his ring earnings, a devoted husband and father who put his sons through college. And as for me, I just write about fighters now, my fight manager days well behind me.

Of course I do talk fights with another fellow fan in the Westhampton Beach Post Office. But if Ted O'Kula, Jr., wants to bring me a likely local prospect, I'll tell him I've been there, done that, and gone the distance with Archie McBride. *Ring Magazine* described him as "one of the most dangerous heavyweights in the business." A long, long way from my barn in New Hope, Pennsylvania, sometimes I rub the bridge of my broken nose and long for the good old days.

[2003]

■ 6 ■

Joe Louis and Social History

RALPH ELLISON'S *Invisible Man* was an apt title for the entire black race in America in the 1930s. In the eyes of white people, it simply did not exist. The *New York Times*'s boast that it printed "all the news that's fit to print," should have added "for white people." When young Joe Louis was winning amateur boxing titles in the early '30s, the outstanding black men in our country, like W. E. B. DuBois and A. Phillip Randolph, were nonpersons to every white newspaper. Even famous entertainers like Louis Armstrong, Paul Robeson, and Bojangles Robinson were ignored. For a black baseball player to play in the big leagues was unthinkable. The National Football League was no better, and as for the colleges, when a Southern college objected to playing Columbia with its one black player, New York's great liberal arts college obligingly dropped him from the lineup.

It's only against that backdrop of know-nothing, racial prejudice that the impact of Joe Louis can be understood. The heart of the Joe Louis Story is his historic break through the race barrier. Earlier in the century there had been another great black champion, Jack Johnson, but there was no way he could challenge for the heavyweight title in America. He had to chase the champion all over the world before finally catching up with him in Australia. There he beat on the hapless white Tommy Burns so fiercely that the police finally intervened at the end of the fourteenth round.

The myopic racism of the day was nakedly expressed by Jack London, at ringside to cover the fight for the *New York Herald*. "He is a white man and so am I," wrote this avowed socialist who preached international understanding (apparently for whites only). "Naturally I want the white man to win." And when Johnson's hand was raised, London called on the undefeated ex-champion, Jim Jeffries, to come out of retirement to put this overweening black boy in his place. "But one thing remains," London begged in his postmortem for the *Herald*, "Jeffries must emerge from his alfalfa farms and remove that smile from Johnson's face. Jeff, it's up to you."

"The Fight Between the White Champion and the Black Champion," as it was billed in Reno in 1910, was less a boxing match than a primitive tableau in bitter race relations. In Jeffries's corner were all the previous champions, the impassioned Caucasians John L. Sullivan, Bob Fitzsimmons, and "Gentleman" Jim Corbett, who mouthed racist epithets at Johnson through the fight. When the hopelessly overmatched old champion finally went down for the count, a deathly silence fell over the crowd. As our bereft Jack London typed out his lead, "Once again has Johnson sent down to defeat the chosen representative of the white race. . . ," race riots were breaking out all over the country.

As a resented black champion in a rabid white world, Johnson did nothing to endear himself. In a time of uptight segregation, Johnson not only consorted with white women but flaunted them, lording it around Chicago in a chauffeur-driven open phaeton with two white women all over him. The entrance to his notorious nightclub Café de Champion displayed a blowup photo of him lip-locking with his white wife. Her suicide, partly due to his having so many other white lovers, including a scandalous affair with his white eighteen-year-old secretary, provoked a lynch atmosphere with Johnson being railroaded to jail and jumping bond to escape to Europe, leaving behind the unwritten law of boxing: never again a black heavyweight champion.

It may have been unwritten in the 1910s and '20s but it was adhered to as faithfully as if it had been engraved in stone. After the gifted troublemaker Johnson held up his black middle finger to white America, there would be eight successive flour-faced champions through the 1920s to the late '30s. The most frustrating example of a top heavyweight contender being denied his deserved title shot because of the wrong pigmentation was Harry Wills. When Wills knocked out a brace of white contenders and clearly outclassed the "Wild Bull of the Pampas," Luis Firpo, famous for knocking Jack Dempsey out of the ring in the first round of their celebrated fight, the New York State Athletic Commission finally made Wills its No. 1 contender, ruling that Dempsey could not defend his title until he met Wills. Dempsey's promoter, the same old foxy Tex Rickard from Johnson-Jeffries days, finessed that one by taking his champion to Philadelphia to face Gene Tunney. The white race was saved again.

As a young fight fan growing up in Los Angeles, I knew an impressive heavyweight by the name of George Godfrey. When I asked him about fighting in Madison Square Garden, in those days the pot of gold at the end of every boxer's rainbow, he shook his head. "Only if I lost, son. My color can't win in the Garden." That was the hard truth when teenaged Joe Louis was coming out of the Bottoms, a ghetto within the ghetto in hard-times Detroit. When Joe's discoverer, John Roxborough, the soft-spoken, community-minded numbers man from Detroit, and the hard-nosed numbers boss Julian Black in Chicago, brought their young amateur champ to the veteran trainer Jack Blackburn, Blackburn turned them down. A bitter ex-fighter still smoldering at the way the race barrier had prevented him from earning a decent living at his trade, Blackburn told them, "I don't care how good he is. He's the wrong color. Bring me a white boy so I c'n make some money." It was only when Black promised the mean-spirited trainer thirty-five dollars a week and expenses, sweet money in '34, that Blackburn lucked into the job that would become his legacy.

He was a master teacher, and the twenty-year old prodigy was a master pupil. From mid-'34 to mid-'35 the Louis-Blackburn team had twenty-two straight victories, in the Midwest almost all knockouts, including two over the highly rated Lee Ramage. Roxborough and Black felt their boy was ready for New York. "Yes, but is New York ready for Joe?" asked the old cynic Blackburn. Roxborough put in a call to Jimmy Johnston, the "Boy Bandit," who ran boxing for the Garden. Roxborough told Johnston he had a fighter so good he should be fighting in the Garden.

"Yeah, I hear he's pretty good, but if he comes in here he's got to lose a few."

"He's undefeated, and we want him to stay that way."

"Look, I don't care if he knocks out Ramage. He's still colored. Don't you have any white boys out there?"

Roxborough hung up. Johnston had made a ten-million-dollar mistake. Nobody had told him Roxborough was black. Blackburn said, "I told you so." But he hadn't figured on a most unlikely do-gooder, "Uncle" Mike Jacobs, "Machiavelli on Eighth Avenue." A ticket scalper from the age of twelve, Jacobs had a genius for squeezing that extra dollar from the box office. He didn't care whom he was touting—Enrico Caruso, the Barrymores, the suffragette Emmeline Pankhurst, World War I. He made a million dollars from his concessions at military posts. He had no pretensions as a social thinker, but Jacobs's sixth sense of what the public would and would not buy gave him an insight into society that was color-blind. He knew his New York, he knew fight fans were tired of the mediocre white heavyweights after Tunney with their fixed fights and foul tactics. And maybe the times had something to do with it. Roosevelt and his New Deal promised social change if not revolution. Jacobs might still call African Americans *schwarzes*, but his favorite color was green, and he smelled money in bringing to New York the devastating puncher who had captured the imagination of the Midwest.

This was a social experiment, and Louis's managers were taking no chances. Determined to make Joe the un-Johnson, Roxborough let the press know his seven commandments: (1) He would never have his picture taken with a white woman; (2) He would never go into a nightclub alone; (3) There would be no soft fights; (4) And no fixed fights; (5) He would never gloat over a fallen opponent; (6) He would keep a "deadpan" in front of the cameras; (7) He would live and fight clean.

Condescending rules, perhaps, but after the Johnson debacle the twenty-year-old was clearly on trial in the court of white public opinion.

One gets the feeling in history that the right man has a way of coming along at the right moment. George Washington in 1775. Abe Lincoln in the Civil War. FDR in the depression. Aside from his blistering talent in the ring, the man-child Joe Louis had exactly the right personality for the role he was thrust into—as an ambassador from the Negro race (as it was called then) to the white ruling class. Joe didn't have to feign modesty or behave himself in public. He was naturally shy, especially as an uneducated youth from the Bottoms suddenly thrust into the limelight in Eastern society. It wasn't his nature to lord himself over inferior opponents; his mother had raised him well. He was a mother's boy. The first thing he did with that big advance from Jacobs was buy her a nice house and drive her there to show it off to her completely furnished.

At the same time he was never the Uncle Tom the white press was hoping for. He didn't have to be programmed to act with dignity. It came as naturally to him as his punching power. Hyping his New York debut against the Italian giant Primo Carnera, a tabloid photographer brought him a watermelon as a prop and asked him to pose with it. "Sorry, I don't like watermelon," Joe said. Polite but firm. His handlers smiled. They knew Joe loved watermelon. They also knew he could spot a black stereotype as quickly as a telegraphed right hand.

Overnight this totally unprepared twenty-year-old was thrust into a tense international conflict he knew nothing about. The fascist dictator Mussolini was ready to invade the North African black nation of Ethiopia. There were fascist sympathizers and "Save Ethiopia" placards at the press conferences. It wasn't the first time a prizefight had been identified with nationalistic fervor, all the way back to the early nineteenth century when the former slave from Virginia, Tom Molineaux, challenged the bare-knuckle champion Tom Cribb, even the august London *Times* had sounded the alarm: "The honor of the English nation is at stake."

Young Joe had to deal with a hostile American press, with two of the most famous columnists, Arthur Brisbane and Westbrook Pegler, both devoted racists, warning of the riots that would erupt if "an American colored man" is allowed to face "the Italian military reservist." The canny Mike Jacobs actually played up the racial tension to fill Yankee Stadium that long ago summer evening. The announcer, Harry Balough, felt obliged to beg the overwrought audience not to satisfy the doomsday warning of Brisbane and Pegler: "Ladies and gentlemen, before proceeding with this most important heavyweight contest I wish to take the liberty of calling upon you in the name of American sportsmanship, a spirit so fine it has made you, the American sporting public, world famous. I therefore ask that the thought in your mind and the feeling in your heart be that, regardless of race, creed, or color, let us all say, may the better man emerge victorious. Thank you."

When Louis destroyed his Goliath in less than six rounds, the multitude of Italian Americans and an official cheering section from Benito himself quietly folded their Il Duce banners and stole away. Next morning newspapers across the country signaled the breakthrough: the first time the name of a black man appeared on their front pages. Years later Joe would remember that night as the best he ever had. "If you was ever a raggedy kid and you came to something like that night . . ."

Louis's sudden fame may have been a milestone on the road to racial equality, but the press still was not ready to accept him for what he was, an exceptional young athlete, not yet articulate but basically intelligent and increasingly aware of the awesome responsibilities being thrust upon him. Sportswriters still saw him as a Caliban, a savage, a subhuman force. In describing Joe's victory, a writer for International News Service set the tone: "Something sly and sinister and perhaps not quite human came out of the African jungle last night . . ." The celebrated sportswriter Grantland Rice seconded the motion, describing Joe as a "jungle killer," and the eminent sports columnist Paul Gallico weighed in with, "He lives like an animal, fights like an animal, has all the cruelty and ferocity of a wild thing."

Against this wall of prejudice, the real Joe Louis kept breaking through. There was a quiet decency about the young man that belied all the heavy-breathing "ferocious black panther" metaphors.

He was a world-beater, but he wasn't a man-eater. If black pastors were building their sermons around their new messiah, they weren't alone. A *Time* magazine cover hailed him as the Black Moses. And in the most publicized fight since Dempsey-Tunney, against the quixotic ex-champion Max Baer, even when announcer Harry Balough introduced Joe with his backhanded "Although colored, he stands out in the same class with Jack Johnson and Sam Langford . . .," the fans in Yankee Stadium gave Louis a welcome at least the equal of Baer's. That had never happened in America before. And when Louis hit Baer so hard in the fourth round that the fallen fighter decided to hoist the white (some said yellow) flag, he surrendered with a characteristic quip: ". . . When I get executed, people are going to have to pay more than twenty-five dollars to watch it."

The political symbolism of the great heavyweight championship was never more applicable than in the Louis-Schmeling series. Another ex-champion, Max Schmeling was considered over the hill when Mike Jacobs dug him up to meet Louis, already hailed as "the uncrowned" heavyweight champion. Adolf Hitler and Joseph Goebbels were so upset at the prospect of a member of the Master Race being humiliated by an American "of the mongrel race" that they tried to short circuit Schmeling's challenge. They also urged him to give up his Jewish New York manager, Joe Jacobs (no relation to Mike). But Schmeling stood up to his Führer. He was a professional, and Jacobs had made a lot of money for him in America. When he landed in New York on the *Bremen* there were Jewish pickets to greet him, and when Louis went into training there were German-American Bundists with swastikas. There was also a country-club atmosphere at his training headquarters. The hard-nosed Jack Blackburn was disgusted. Celebrities from both coasts overran the place. And beautiful women. The columnist and later TV host Ed Sullivan introduced Joe to golf, and Louis spent hours chasing little white balls. He had his white fans with him that night back in Yankee Stadium, but for the first time he was less than perfect. After jabbing, he kept dropping his left hand, exposing his chin to Schmeling's

Joe Louis with his wife Marva in Chicago in 1938, just before his second fight with Schmeling. (© Bettmann/Corbis)

straight rights. Fighting with courage but in a losing cause, young Joe was down and out for the first time in his life.

In seclusion with the shades drawn in his apartment in Chicago a few days later, he had lost everything except his sense of humor. Without saying much, he always had a way with one-liners. Asked if he'd like to see movies of the match, he said, "No, I saw the fight."

Hitler and Goebbels were singing "Deutschland Uber Alles." They sent the *Hindenburg* for Schmeling, and he flew home to a hero's welcome. Goebbels greeted him at the airport with a *wehrmacht* band, a troup of SS honor guards, and a chorus of "Heil Hitlers!" The Führer gave a gala reception for him where they watched film of the fight titled "Schmeling's Victory—A German Victory." Hitler ordered Goebbels to dress it up as a feature documentary, and it played to enthusiastic audiences all over

Nazi Germany. It was the best PR for Der Führer since Leni Riefenstahl's *Triumph of the Will*.

How Louis, rather than Schmeling, got the title shot against the aging and vulnerable champion, Jim Braddock, is a story of wheels within wheels, most of them spun by that master spinner, Mike Jacobs. Goebbels and Hitler worked like big-time fight promoters to bring the Braddock-Schmeling fight to Berlin. Braddock's manager, Joe Gould, told me of a phone call he had from Schmeling, who put Goebbels himself on the phone. The Reichmeister for Propaganda told Gould he was prepared to give him whatever he asked to deliver Braddock in Berlin. Joe said he wanted $500,000 in cash in a New York bank. "No problem," said Goebbels. And eight first-class tickets to Germany, suites in the Hotel Adlon, and training expenses. No problem. And one American referee and one British referee. No problem. Anything else? "Yes," Gould told me he told Goebbels, "and I want you to let all the Jews out of the concentration camps." "Goebbels hung up," Gould said. Like all those Jacobs Beach managers, Gould knew the hustle. He knew he had Jacobs and Louis over a barrel. All he wanted, to pass up the Schmeling fight already signed and announced in New York, was 10 percent of Louis for the next ten years. Done deal. Just one of those nasty little things that would contribute to Joe's woes in the postwar years.

When Joe knocked out Braddock, the old champion who had nothing left but pride, the ghost of Jack Johnson was finally laid to rest. While there were cheers for Braddock's courage, the twenty thousand blacks in the nosebleed seats and the even larger white audience spreading from ringside, gave Louis a color-blind ovation for the greatest heavyweight fighter they had ever seen. New champions usually like to rest on their laurels for a while, but the first time someone called Joe "Champ" that night, he said, "I don't want nobody to call me champ till I beat that Schmelin'." So the stage was set for the most politically charged heavyweight championship fight in the history of the ring.

Between Louis-Schmeling I in 1936 and the rematch two years later, the skies had darkened. Germany had swallowed Austria, there was a Berlin-Rome-Tokyo Axis, little Czechoslovakia was threatened, the vilification of Jews intensified. The democratic world had come to realize that Hitler meant every apocalyptic word he had written in *Mein Kampf*. So Louis-Schmeling II was seen as nothing less than the war to come. Democracy vs. Fascism. Good vs. Evil. If Schmeling won, Hitler's fervid theories of a Master Race would be reaffirmed. A victory for Louis would recharge the hopes of everyone who yearned for an order of decency and an end to man's inhumanity to man.

That may sound like hyperbole, but in those almost hysterical prewar days, both sides of the Atlantic looked on Louis and Schmeling as the flag bearers for their respective countries and political systems. It was the first (and surely the last) time in history that the heads of both nations would personally impress upon their fighters the magnitude of the coming conflict. Hitler placed his hand on Max's shoulder and reminded him of his responsibility to prove the superiority of the Master Race by knocking out the black savage again. FDR took time from his pressing day to invite Louis to the Oval Office, feel his muscles, and say, "Joe, these are the muscles we need to beat Germany."

The kid from the Bottoms who had earned just fifty-nine dollars in his first fight only four years before, literally had the world on his shoulders. As if he needed further motivation, in his training camp his backers would read quotes allegedly from Schmeling expressing his confidence that a white man could always beat the inferior "nigger." Actually these were Goebbels-inspired; later the basically decent Schmeling would deny to Joe that he had ever made such statements. But at the time Joe admitted that while he had never felt any animosity for any of his previous opponents, this time he not only had revenge in his heart but a fire in him to defeat a mortal enemy.

When Louis destroyed Schmeling in the first two minutes of the first round, his biggest victory may have been the cheers that rose from everybody when he entered the ring. And seventy million fans glued to their radios across the country were rooting for him too. Never again would the color line be drawn on the most celebrated of boxing titles. Joe Louis had opened the door through which would pour the thousands of world-class athletes who have become household names, from Jackie Robinson and Willie Mays to Jim Brown and Emmett Smith. As he did so often, Heywood Broun in the *New York-World Telegram* summed it up best: "One hundred years from now some historian may theorize, in a foot-note at least, that the decline of Nazi prestige began with a left hook delivered by a former unskilled automotive worker who had never studied the policies of Neville Chamberlain and had no opinion whatever in regard to the situation in Czechoslovakia . . . but . . . exploded the Nordic myth with a bombing glove."

Already an icon in our contemporary culture, Joe actually polished his image when his reaction to Pearl Harbor was to enlist in the army. Sportswriters no longer described him as black or subhuman. Now he was a great American patriot and, with the possible exception of FDR, the most famous man in the country, if not the world. He donated his entire purses for two title defenses, against tough opponents Buddy Baer and Abe Simon, to benefit Army and Navy Relief, giving them over $110,000, for which the government expressed its gratitude by taxing him on the income as if he had put it in his own pocket. That twisted judgment, with compound interest over the years, would contribute to his postwar calamities. But in the immediate aftermath of Pearl Harbor, Joe's stature continued to grow. At the Boxing Writers Association dinner, the charismatic former Mayor Jimmy Walker praised Joe for risking his title for service charities: ". . . you laid a rose on the grave of Abraham Lincoln." At a Navy Relief Dinner in Madison Square Garden, when the presidential candidate Wendell Willkie said we would win because God is on our side, Private Joe Louis went him one better: "I've only done what any red-blooded American would do . . . we will win because we are on God's side."

President Roosevelt sent him a telegram to congratulate him on his choice of words, the slogan over Joe's picture became a favorite recruiting poster, and "Joe Louis Named the War" became a popular poem featured on the front page of the multi-million circulation *Saturday Evening Post*. In later years he would be put down by Ali and others more militant of being an Uncle Tom, but in his own quiet way, Louis stood up to racism in the army. He refused to give boxing exhibitions for his fellow GIs unless the audience was desegregated. When he heard from Jackie Robinson that he and other college graduates had been denied access to Officers Training School, Joe went over the head of his commanding officer to get them admitted. Never part of the civil rights movement, he might be considered its one-man forerunner.

When Branch Rickey, emulating Mike Jacobs, finally gave Jackie Robinson a chance to play with the Brooklyn Dodgers, almost the first thing Jackie said was that he wouldn't have been there without Joe Louis. "He's been an inspiration to all of us. He made it easy for me and all the other fellows in baseball." He went on to say that Rickey must have been thinking of Joe Louis when he decided to let him play big league baseball.

Jackie Robinson was on his way up to the Hall of Fame. But for his mentor, Joe Louis, after that resounding crescendo at the end of World War II, it was all downhill.

After having earned millions in the ring, over $600,000 for the second Billy Conn fight alone, Louis came out of the war not only dead broke but with that IRS monkey on his back. With the clock running on the interest, it built to a million dollars, and counting. It wasn't all the IRS's fault. There were costly divorces, easy-come-easy-go generosities, self-indulgence, 50 percent to his managers, Mike Jacobs's share, and that under-the-table 10 percent to Jim Braddock. You could make a case that every time he fought he was giving away 110 percent of himself. Even so, for America's favorite son in the war years, it was a bitter pill. When he had to wrestle for a living, an IRS agent grabbed his $500 check at the box ofice. When his mother died and left him $600, the IRS took that too. F. Scott Fitzgerald could have had Joe in mind when he wrote, "Show me a hero and I'll write you a tragedy."

Addicted to drugs, reduced to shilling for Caesars Palace, and hounded by the merciless IRS almost to the end of his life, Joe

Louis became practically a forgotten man to the civil rights generation and the throng of cocky young baseball, football, basketball, and boxing millionaires today. But for all their exploits, Emmett Smith, Tiger Woods, and Barry Bonds aren't going to be
buried at Arlington. And there's a very good reason why Joe Louis
is there. He taught white America a lesson it would never forget.
He taught black America, so long denied, its sense of dignity, that
hope was on its way.

The night Joe Louis knocked out Max Schmeling on the eve of
World War II, spontaneous parades erupted all over America. A
democratic carnival. Placards held high proclaimed, "Joe knocks
out Hitler!" An interracial celebration. The old radical slogan:
"Black and white / unite and fight" had suddenly become social
reality. "He was a credit to his race," wrote the epigrammatic
sports columnist Jimmy Cannon, "the human race." The Reverend
Jesse Jackson paraphrased that at Joe's funeral: "Joe Louis came
from the black race to represent the human race."

So on his birthday, April 20, let us all make the pilgrimage to
Joe's resting place at Arlington, at least in spirit, place a rose on
his grave, and pledge ourselves to the complete achievement of
social democracy in America, still a work in progress.

[2003]

7

Archie Moore:
All-Time Senior Citizen Champ

I. Paynight for Old Archie

ONE EVENING last week 8,327 live fight fans and some 20 million TV viewers around the country watched the Madison Square Garden debut of old Archie Moore, the goateed tumbleweed from San Diego, St. Louis, Toledo, Baltimore, or wherever the pickings look good. As debuts go, it was eminently successful, for the oldest headliner in the business caught up with his number one challenger, 26-year-old Harold Johnson, in the fourteenth round with a series of beautifully timed and perfectly thrown right hands that reminded one of well-told stories, short and to the point.

The only trouble with this debut is that Moore was closing in on that age at which Dr. Pitkin argued, questionably, that Life Begins. Archie Moore had to wait until he was 37 years old to see his name go up on a Garden marqee. It had taken him almost 18 years of barnstorm campaigning, from North Adams, Massachusetts, to Panama, from Newark to Tasmania. The boxing story today is often told through likely looking preliminary kids a year or two out of the amateurs who are hustled into Garden main events to keep those razor blades moving. But there was nothing hurried about this maiden appearance of our light heavyweight champion. Behind him were 141 battles with the toughest middleweights, light heavies, and heavyweights of the '30s, '40s, and '50s.

Putting Archie Moore into his first Garden main event at the age of thirty-seven is something like signing Caruso for the Metropolitan Opera in 1920 instead of 1903 when he actually scored the first of his New York triumphs. If Caruso had had to tour the tank towns in moth-eaten opry houses for petty cash while third-raters unfit to carry his music case were pulling down the big notices and the heavy sugar at the Met, he would have become as cynical and money-hungry and unthrilled as Archie Moore seemed to feel in the Garden last week.

When Moore first climbed through the ropes as a pro back in the middle '30s, a twenty-one-year-old Joe Louis was waiting for his chance to come to New York. FDR was still promising to pull us out of the depression. Carole Lombard was a national idol. Adolf Hitler was training his Arbeitssolldaten with shovels. Mussolini was kicking up a rumpus in Ethiopia. People were singing "Goody, Goody." The Oakies were pushing their rattletraps along Highway 66. Mickey Mouse and Joe DiMaggio were hitting their strides. And when you said McCarthy, it meant little Charlie the puppet.

Nearly all the people who were making history when Archie was fighting up and down the West Coast in the late '30s and early '40s have gone back into the ground and the history books. The men who were in there with Moore in the years before Pearl Harbor are old men with stomachs hanging over their belts, and balding heads, living off their scrapbooks and their memories of trial and glory.

Watching old Archie coming on in the later rounds against Harold Johnson, a quality opponent who had taken Ezzard Charles and Nino Valdes and who was nine years old when the champion was belting out tough boys for peanuts in San Diego, you had to admire the old-time moves, the way he got up from an off-balance knockdown and took the fight to the younger man, careful to offer only the smallest pieces of himself and watchful for mistakes on which he could capitalize.

Years ago he had crowded Ezzard Charles, knocked out Jimmy Bivins and worked with the tough ones nobody wanted—

Charley Burley, Lloyd Marshall, Holman Williams, Curtis Sheppard, Billy Smith. He was good enough in those days to be the
light heavyweight champion of the world, but everybody was
looking the other way.

If it had been tennis, his ranking would have top-seeded him
into a shot at the champions. But this was boxing, a bitter and slippery business, where the challenger your manager picked for you
was the one who guaranteed the high money—and who didn't figure to be as tough as Archie Moore. An aging Gus Lesnevich
would rather have the mob-hyped Billy Fox, or the run-down limey
Freddie Mills. And when Mills got his hands on the title, would he
rather fight Archie, still the number one at age thirty-three, or Joey
Maxim, the Kearns concoction, who never resembles a fighter so
much as when he's sitting down between rounds?

It was 1952 and Joey Maxim was in the book as the light
heavyweight champion of the world. At an age (thirty-six) when
the best fighters in the world can't find their legs or their reflexes,
Moore finally got Maxim into the ring with him. The expected
happened. It was one of those nights when Moore was in there for
the glory alone, and Maxim and Kearns got all the money. There
wasn't another light heavyweight around who could bring in a
dollar, so the Moore-Maxim thing became a traveling circus—in
Ogden, in Miami. And now they're talking Omaha. And six figures
for Archie.

At the end of his long and rocky road, Archie is finding the
golden vein that eluded him through the best of his fighting days.
Last week he and manager Charley Johnston were calling the turn
and taking home all the money—around $40,000, including, ru-
mor had it, a fistful out of Johnson's purse.

Moore didn't bother to pick up his check. He's off in his Cadil-
lac and big black cowboy outfit, a dark-skinned, pugnacious Burl
Ives, gypsying around the country talking about fighting Rocky
Marciano. Or the top heavyweight contenders Valdes and Cockell.

What he's really saying is that after all those years in the financial desert he'd like to linger around the International Boxing
Club's oasis. More paynights like that debut in the Garden. There

were times last week when he walked back to his corner like an old man waddling home from a tour of the gin mills. But he's the last of the great journeymen, and it's still a pleasure to watch someone who knows his business in a day when underdeveloped and over-sold kids bob up and down the ladder like the popular songs you can never remember once they've slipped off the hit parade.

[1954]

II. The Champion of Communications

IF ARCHIE MOORE does what he keeps saying he'll do—relieve Rocky Marciano of his heavyweight title—he'll be the first man to write as well as fight his way to the championship. When he climbs into the ring, sporting his resplendent robe and Mephistophelian mustache on the night of the 20th, it will not only climax a notable twenty-year career but a personal publicity campaign that has poured across the desk of American sportswriters literally bushels of telegrams, letters, posters, circulars—some $50,000 worth of words calling all sports editors to come to the aid of Archie Moore in his quest to tangle with Rocky for the championship of the world.

The stuff that cascaded from Archie's headquarters was, by turn, witty, indignant, insulting, bombastic, factual, imaginative—the super press agent from Steve Hannagan to Russell Birdwell could hardly have done it better. If Archie wins this fight it would seem only simple gratitude that the Post Office issue an Archie Moore commemorative stamp, for in a nine-month campaign Archie has written hundreds of sportswriters and sportscasters two or three times a week and has single-handedly swelled the coffers (I've always wanted to set eyes on a coffer, by the way) of the U.S. mails. And Western Union could afford to declare a spe-cial dividend for Archie, who fires telegrams with the speed and cuteness he employs in throwing left and right hooks. The Bell Telephone Company hasn't done too badly either, for Archie is an articulate refutation of the stereotype pug who grunts "Hokay"

Archie Moore during an induction weekend at the International Boxing Hall of Fame in Canastota, New York. He handled the fighting, the training, the promoting, and the talking. (Pat Orr)

when the manager gives him the old line, "You do the fightin' and I'll do the managin." Archie, who was fighting for money when Marciano was twelve years old, handles the fighting, the training, the promoting, and the talking.

Six months ago, when Al Weill was giving Archie Moore the usual brush and trying to decide which bum—Nino Valdes or Don Cockell—was the best meat for Rocky, Moore started talking up his rights again. He ridiculed Weill's handpicked opponents by offering to fight Valdes and Cockell the same night. Archie is a throwback to the good old days when boxers really challenged each other and matches weren't booked mechanically in offices as vaudeville acts are. Archie phoned Pat Harmon, sports editor of the *Cincinnati Post*, saying he would be flying into Cincinnati to launch a petition of one hundred sports editors willing to plump for Marciano to meet Mr. Outside-Looking-In instead of trumped-up importations like Valdes and Cockell.

Harmon enlisted in the Archie Moore Association for the Advancement of Archie Moore and blasted Weilly Al for ignoring the only man in the heavyweight ranks who seemed to have a reasonable chance of standing up to the bruiser from Brockton. But despite the verbal fireworks, Archie was seemingly getting no closer to the pot of gold at the end of the heavyweight rainbow. The AMA for the AAM faced a sturdy roadblock in the chesty-close-to-the-vesty Mr. Weill. In the dressing room after the depressing Cockell affair, Al looked his interviewers in the eye and allowed as how the next logical opponent for Rocky might be Bob Baker. But Archie Moore had knocked Baker out and had beaten Valdes twice? Weill switched off the question as if he were wearing an invisible hearing aid.

But Archie Moore is a stubborn, patient man. A formidable middleweight whose only shot at the middleweight championship was canceled by ulcers, the No. 1 light heavyweight contender carefully bypassed by the light heavyweight champions a decade or so ago, Archie had learned the hard way that the better you were, the less chance you had to get in there for the big one. It had happened to Harry Wills and George Godfrey. The fight game always has had a tough club of guys-ya-want-no-part-of— Charlie Burley, Curtis (Hatchet Man) Sheppard, Holman Williams, Lloyd Marshall. In California we had Jack Chase who met Archie Moore half a dozen times between '42 and '47—sixty-nine rounds of the toughest fighting you'll ever see. Year after year, fighting into his deep thirties, Archie handled the ones nobody wanted no part of—guys you never heard of who would chase Bobo Olson out of the ring. Fought 'em with everything he had for no money until one day he got to Toledo to fight somebody they billed as the Alabama Kid. It had taken Archie twelve years and nearly one hundred fights to get to Toledo. The purse for the Alabama Kid thing was a lousy three hundred dollars.

"Let's face it, I was never going to get a shot at the title," Archie has written of those hungry days. "I was never going to be a champion, except in my heart."

What Archie didn't know, the night he bowled over the Alabama Kid for nickels, was that Toledo housed a fellow by the name of Bob Reese, a prosperous Ford dealer who was waiting to play Fairy Godmother to Archie's Cinderella. Archie had seven fights in Toledo in twelve months, batting 1.000 with five knockouts, including such eminent victims as Bob Satterfield and Jimmy Bivins. But he won more. He won the support of this Bob Reese, whose motor company eventually became the headquarters for his publicity campaign. Reese bankrolled the Archie Moore Story. He wrote a lot of the copy, set up a staff of secretaries to keep the letters and wires flowing, issued catchy posters such as "Wanted—Wanted—Wanted—REWARD for Capture and Delivery of Rocky Marciano to Any Ring in the World for the Purpose of Defending His Heavyweight Championship against the *Logical* contender, *Archie Moore*. *Reward*: the Boxing Public Will See a Great Fight and Witness the Crowning of a New Champion. Advise (Sheriff) ARCHIE MOORE."

Archie's career has been a study in irony, and never more so than two months ago when his fortunes took a sudden upward turn. He had been knocking out overrated heavyweights and light heavyweights for years, but his unprecedented fifty-thousand-dollar publicity campaign might have gone down the drain if he had not disposed of Bobo Olson, a run-of-the-mill middleweight champion who borrows the mantle of greatness in a day when TV and uninspiring promoting has brought us down to what might be called the Chuck Davey-Tommy Collins Era. Archie had knocked out scores of fighters better than Bobo, but at the propitious moment Olson provided the ideal sacrifice to the gods of public opinion.

All his fighting life Archie was kept out of the big arenas on the spurious argument that he was long on ability but short on box office appeal. Now, largely through his efforts, he and Marciano figure to draw the biggest gate since the golden days of Louis. He may not win when he finally gets in there with Rocky, two weeks from next Tuesday night. But win or lose, Archie Moore is the all-time communications champion of the world of sport.

[1955]

P.S. Half a century later how vividly I remember the dramatic ending of Archie's quest. The astonishing old light heavy knocked the champion down with his classic one-two and had the Brockton bruiser in serious trouble in the second round. But as they fought on, age and Marciano caught up with the gallant old man, who took a painful beating until he finally succumbed in the ninth. But the Great Communicator wasn't finished. With his face battered but his pride undaunted, our prize-ring Othello stood on his rubbing table in his gold silk robe, a true King of Fistiana, greeting his subjects, the working press. "Gentlemen, it was a very entertaining evening. I hope you enjoyed it. I know Rocky Marciano enjoyed it. I enjoyed it too. And now, are there any questions . . . ?" The challenger may have gone down. But the Master of Communications was still standing tall.

[2006]

8

Muhammad Ali

I. King of the World

IN THIS REVIEWER'S LIBRARY are no fewer than sixteen books on the singular life, boxing career, and now spiritual journey of the once-brash Louisville amateur whose motormouth equaled the speed of his gloved hands and booted feet, and whose mind— before he was even in his teens—was aflame with his dreams of glory. How does one respond to a twelve-year-old who wins a split decision in a dinky hometown ring and already pronounces himself The Greatest?

Muhammad Ali is our black Paul Bunyan, except that Bunyan's superhuman exploits were fables and Ali's are real. He is not merely our most famous heavyweight champion; indeed, with all respect to Joe Louis, Michael Jordan, Babe Ruth, and Jackie Robinson, the most venerated of our celebrated athletes, he managed to reach a level of global idolization in a manner than can only be described as transcendental. Who could have predicted in the late 1960s, when Muhammad Ali was reviled by the sporting press and most of white America as a black racist, a mouthy troublemaker, that he would be the obvious choice to light the torch at the 1996 Olympic Games in Atlanta, as a symbol of international understanding, peace, and love? What would all the name-callers be thinking now, we wondered, as the puffy-faced, middle-aged icon stood there with torch held high (if tremblingly) in that famous right hand that delivered some of the most punishing right crosses of the twentieth century?

Following his auspicious debut as author of the Pulitzer Prize–winning *Lenin's Tomb*, in *King of the World* David Remnick brings to his reading of the Ali scriptures a helpful sense of recent boxing history, inseparable from political history; since all champions after the early sixties on were black, their lives reflected the social forces at work on them. By choosing to focus on Ali's two predecessors as champions, first Floyd Patterson, then Sonny Liston, the author nicely sets the scene for the impact The Greatest would make when he was ready to shove them aside to take center stage.

In a discerning and sensitive portrait, Floyd Patterson—surely the most unlikely man ever to wear the crown—is the good Negro, an approachable and strangely fearful man, a deferential champion of civil rights, integration, and Christian decency. So anxious about losing was Patterson in his first fight with the stone-faced Sonny Liston that he brought a disguise to the dressing room to escape incognito from his anticipated humiliation. "He was champion in the sense that Chester A. Arthur had been President," Remnick sums up in a particularly felicitous phrase. Some other beauts: Patterson's haunted mentor, Cus D'Amato, is "a cross between the Emperor Hadrian and Jimmy Cagney" ("a 10!" this reader scribbled in the margin) and, a few pages later, "the only modern psychoanalyst who carried a spit bucket in his hand and a Q-Tip in his teeth."

If Patterson was, in Norman Mailer's words, "a liberal's liberal," the tamed Negro literally reformed in reform school, passive, polite, and nice, Sonny Liston was the perfect counterweight, the big, bad, black stereotype in every fearful white man's nightmare. One of at least a dozen children, Liston progressed from overgrown ten-year-old petty thief to knee-breaker for the St. Louis Teamsters and the mob that owned him as naturally as a white middle-class child moves up from elementary school to junior high. It was the only possible career move for this precociously physical muscle boy who couldn't read or write but could knock opponents down with a left jab and cripple them with jaw-breaking rights. By the end of the 1950s Liston was ready for the big time, which meant he was afforded the opportunity to turn over virtually 100 percent of his future earnings to Mr. Gray, otherwise known as Frankie Carbo, acknowledged commissioner of boxing without portfolio. But who needs a portfolio if you run the fight game for the Luchese family?

With racy scholarship, Remnick traces what would seem an unlikely liaison between Mr. Gray (or Mr. Fury, as he was sometimes called) and James Norris, head of the International Boxing Club and heir to a grain and real estate fortune worth hundreds of millions. Madison Square Garden and the top fighters in every division were in their pocket, and this odd couple controlled the fight game until the Feds finally caught up with Mr. Gray (while Mr. Norris, as befitted a scion of Chicago society, was exonerated). But, as Remnick concludes, "through one false front or another, with a succession of ostensible managers, Liston never moved far from the shade of Frankie Carbo." How could he? He knew no other world. In a defining moment that Remnick makes poignant, Liston flies back to Philadelphia after he takes the championship away from Patterson, expecting a triumphant welcome—and nobody shows up. The story of his life. Deep into this carefully written book, Remnick quotes the cynically literate fight promoter Hal Conrad, who knew Lucky Luciano as well as he did Floyd, Cassius, and Sonny. His chilling epitaph for Liston: He died the day he was born.

Like a good playwright setting up the entrance of his hero in Act 2, Remnick gives us Floyd the Good (Victim No. 1) and Sonny the Bad (Victim No. 2) to prepare us for Cassius the Baaad, the upstart to whom champion young blacks and their white hippie allies could relate. Born in still segregated Louisville, "wounded by the accumulated slights of mid-century American apartheid," lying in his bed at night crying "as he wondered why his race had to suffer so," young Cassius was on his way to becoming the symbol of a different kind of black man, whose role model was neither Booker T. Washington nor Martin Luther King. Malcolm X was more like it.

Just as Ali created a new style of heavyweight boxing, "on the principle that a big man could borrow the tactics of a smaller man," a man like Sugar Ray Robinson, he created a new style of black man who went on to shock the world with a challenge both divisive and unifying. With Hegelian logic, in time there would be a synthesis, but when in the mid-sixties Cassius Clay embraced Elijah Muhammad's black separatist Nation of Islam, his "don't have to be what you want me to be" spoke to the white power structure in a way it had never been spoken to before. While Ali's conversion came as a surprise to fight fans and to the public at large, one of the most effective chapters in this book, "Secrets," traces the teenage Clay's attraction to the Black Muslims well before he won the gold medal in the 1960 Olympics. It was the increasingly bitter confrontation between pro- and anti–Vietnam War factions that moved the young black champion from the sports pages to the front pages. Teenagers in Watts wore his famous face on their buttons, and the "Don't tread on me" of black rebellion became "The Cong don't call me nigger."

If Remnick has not come up with new material for *King of the World*—no small task after a score of books on the subject—he's drawn wisely from that body of work to define the arc of Ali's ascendance from superconfident adolescent to Islam-inspired but ecumenical spiritual ambassador (only Ali was multi-dimensional: he could reach out to the world like Mother Teresa, but, as they say in Gleason's Gym, she couldn't lick Sonny Liston, Joe Frazier, and George Foreman).

Remnick—who broke in as a sportswriter at the *Washington Post* and is now editor of the *New Yorker*—explores the difference between the civil rights movement, founded on democratic principles, and the self-sufficient, fiercely independent Black Is Beautiful movement that caught fire with Ali, captured the imagination of his generation, and gave him the courage to refuse the draft, thereby sacrificing his precious championship, facing the prospect of five years in prison, and, while appealing his case on the grounds of conscientious objection, being deprived of the license

**Muhammad Ali: he didn't have to be what we
wanted him to be. (Pat Orr)**

without which he could not ply his trade. The cost to Ali in dollars
was in the millions. But there were rewards. From Bertrand Russell came this message of encouragement: "In the coming months
there is no doubt that the men who rule Washington will try to
damage you in every way open to them, but I am sure you know
that you spoke for your people and for the oppressed everywhere
in the courageous defiance of American power. . . . You have my
wholehearted support. Call me when you get to England." As Remnick quotes the poet Sonia Sanchez: "It's hard now to relay the
emotion of that time . . . when hardly any well-known people were
resisting the draft. It was a war that was disproportionately killing
young black brothers, and here was this beautiful, funny, poetical
young man standing up and saying no!"

How Ali won vindication in the Supreme Court of the United States, 8-zip, how he came back to the ring slower and inevitably more hitable but winning his title back again, and how after the tide turned against our Vietnam misadventure the unpatriotic sinner of the sixties each year grew in stature as a man of honor and respect—maybe only a prophet could have foreseen these events. As Remnick ties it all together in *King of the World*, building on all those books and articles and transcripts along with personal interviews, it doesn't read like the case history of a man (though the man is here in living colors, sometimes funny as hell) but of a comic and cosmic superman who accepts the mission of standing up for Mohammed, Allah, and the human race.

While Remnick's firsthand description of Ali's current physical condition is disturbing—not least, as he notes, "because it is an accelerated form of what we all fear, the progression of aging, the unpredictability and danger of life"—his (our) Ali is "an American myth who has come to mean many things to many people: a symbol of faith, a symbol of conviction and defiance, a symbol of beauty and skill and courage, a symbol of racial pride, of wit and love." That's a lot of symbols for one man. But if ever there was a mighty army of men fused into one, it's the young brash Cassius Clay self-created as Muhammad Ali. If Sonny Liston died the day he was born, here's a fine book to remind us again that Ali was born with a gift for living (and believing) in a world without end.

[1998]

II. My Very Own Ali Movie

SEEING *Ali* the other night, another Ali movie was playing in my head. A strange feeling of double vision as the reel life of the legendary heavyweight champion played out on the screen with the charismatic Will Smith doing his best to impersonate the even more charismatic Muhammad Ali, while the real life as I lived it almost from the beginning kept getting in the way. It was difficult for me to judge the stylish director Michael Mann's film because my personal Ali movie keeps on playing in my mind.

The first time I ever saw Ali he was the twenty-one-year-old *wunderkind* Cassius Clay, the irrepressible "Louisville Lip" given to predicting his opponent's destruction in rhyme—"Archie Moore will fall in four." The unlikely venue was the Bottom Line, an artsy hangout in Greenwich Village, the last place you'd expect to see an undefeated young heavyweight fighter who had starched all but three of his first sixteen opponents and was in New York to face the formidable Doug Jones. But there he was, sporting a little bow tie and standing toe to toe with the long hairs. The hippies had never met a prizefighter before, and no one had ever met one like this charming egomaniac who could give Narcissus lessons on narcissism.

In Madison Square Garden he exhibited that balletic movement and those rapier jabs that would be his trademark and won a controversial decision over the more traditional Jones. He was a curiosity, but I wasn't at all sure I shared his conviction that we were seeing the next heavyweight champion of the world.

My next Cassius sighting came a few months later, at Caesars Palace in Las Vegas where he had come for the second Sonny Liston-Floyd Patterson fight to hype his unlikely challenge to the brutish and seemingly invincible champion. My brother Stuart was producing an NBC documentary on boxing with star newscaster David Brinkley, and I tagged along with them when they called on young Mr. Clay. He was outrageously funny, a bigger, more formidable, and more beguiling version of Norman Mailer's *Advertisements for Myself*.

Stretched out on one oversized bed, his brother Rudolph Valentino Clay, a mediocre boxer, in the other, he was ordering room service. "Hello, room service, this is Cassius, we'd like to order breakfast, eggs, make that a dozen and a half, and bacon, about a pound, and bread—send up a loaf. . . ."

That's what I heard. The most famous news show that year was the Huntley-Brinkley Report, which would end with their signature sign-off, "Good night, Chet"—"Good night, David." So now

Cassius begged him, "David, will you do the 'Good night, David' with me?" and when David responded to Clay's "Good night, David" with "Good night, Cassius," the man-child fell off the bed laughing. "David, let's do it again!" A lovable kid, we thought. What a shame he had set himself on a suicide mission of baiting the dangerous monster who had destroyed the previous champion, Patterson, in a single round and was about to do it again.

Clay's showmanship succeeded in goading Liston into the match, but it was almost canceled when the Black Muslim leader Malcolm X was discovered in Clay's camp, and news spread that Clay was taking instruction in that controversial variation on the religion of Islam. Facing a possible white boycott, my friend the promoter Hal Conrad begged Malcolm to "disappear" and hid the challenger in a Jewish old people's home where the supposedly anti-Semitic Cassius endeared himself to the clientele. "Such a nice boy," an old lady told me. "I can't picture him hurting anyone. We all hope he wins."

The fight was almost called off again after a weigh-in even more hysterical than the one in the movie. Cassius and his alter ego Bundini Brown came thundering in, banging canes on the floor and screaming, "Float like a butterfly. Sting like a bee!" When Cassius saw Liston he flung himself at him, screaming, "Ugly bear! Big ugly bear!" Security guards had to restrain him. Liston gave him the "look" that terrified most opponents into submission. Seasoned fight reporters like Jesse Abramson of the *New York Herald-Tribune* and Jimmy Cannon of the *Post* were convinced the fight should be called off because Clay was so obviously suffering from psychological hysteria. His blood pressure was 200 and going through the roof.

But half an hour later "Fight Doctor" Ferdie Pacheco called me to describe a medical miracle. "As soon as he got back I took his blood pressure and it's perfect. I really believe it was self-induced hysteria as a ploy to penetrate that stolid armor of Liston's. I know nobody gives Cassius a chance of surviving more than a round or two, but Angelo [Dundee, his trainer] says we may be in for a surprise tonight."

The fight I watched from Clay's corner was as controversial as the buildup. The speed of hand and foot tormented the dour bully who was used to fighting men who stood in front of him until they got themselves knocked senseless. Cassius opened an ugly gash in the stone-faced champion's cheek, and blood was oozing from the stone. In the fourth, Cassius was blinded by something—we'll never know what—and came back to his corner screaming, "Cut the gloves off! I can't see."

As Angelo began washing out Ali's eyes with water, a pair of suspicious Fruit of Islam enforcers moved in on the little trainer, accusing him of selling out Ali by wiping some alien susbstance into their hero's eyes. The quick-thinking Angelo slapped the sponge against his own eyes to prove his innocence, and as the two bodyguards retreated, Angelo managed to wash the offending liquid out of his fighter's eyes. Crouched just below the apron of the ring, I was taking all this in as the bell rang for round five and Angelo slapped him on the butt and said, "Big Daddy, get in there. This is your night!"

Cassius, as he was still called, managed to run and recover through that curious round, and then was ready to resume his flashy punishment of Liston in the sixth.

When the old champ refused to come out for round seven, claiming shoulder trouble, the 10 to 1 underdog was the youngest champion in the history of the division, on his way to his legendary place in ring history.

At the press conference the morning after, the new champion scorned the press that almost unanimously had given him no chance to survive. But gone was the loudmouth braggadocio now. In a master stroke of public relations, he made us lean forward to hear his pious whispers. "My name is Cassius X now." No more "slave name." Then he issued his signature declaration of independence: "I don't have to be what you want me to be."

After the conference I managed a few minutes alone with him. Now that he was the champion, I asked, what did he plan to do next? He thought a moment, made a serious face, and said, "Now that I'm champion of the world, I plan to travel all over the world and meet with the great leaders of the world." It was hard to take seriously. He actually saw the championship belt as the emblem of an international ambassadorship. He would be the people's roving ambassador to the world. With due respect for the relative abilities of Lennox Lewis, Evander Holyfield, and Mike Tyson, can you imagine any of them saying with a straight face that he now planned to meet with all the leaders of the world? But the then Cassius X (on his way to becoming Muhammad Ali) not only said it, he did it. A few days after the triumph in Miami, he was off to Egypt, then China, and he's been at it ever since.

With Angelo and Dr. Ferdie, Bundini Brown, and camp manager Gene Kilroy, I traveled to Houston to see him destroy the puncher Cleveland Williams. I saw him beg the referee to stop him from beating any longer on poor Buster Mathis. After the fight, I'll never forget seeing Mathis in his dressing room, sobbing like an overgrown baby. As humane as Ali was with Mathis, a streak of cruelty showed in his punishment of Ernie Terrell and Floyd Patterson, who paid the price for insisting on calling him by that now despised "slave name," Cassius Marcellus Clay.

When he refused the Vietnam draft and had his title and his boxing license promptly revoked by the patriotic boxing commissions, I was one of the Ali loyalists—a motley crew that included James Earl Jones, light heavyweight champion Jose Torres, fellow writers Truman Capote and George Plimpton, film director Sidney Lumet—who posed in a New York ring for the cover of *Esquire* declaring that Ali should be deprived of his title only by losing it in the ring. In vain, Ali's promoter, Hal Conrad, tried to arrange matches for him in Canada and Mexico, offering to bring a U.S. marshal along and to return to the States with him immediately after the fight. I attended several gigs with him at college campuses where he was hailed as a hero of resistance to the war. I remember an improbable night at Harvard where he played to an overflow crowd and where he verbally took on the hawkish Dr. Kissinger in an unforgettable performance.

When the Supreme Court, in an unprecedented unanimous decision, decided Ali's appeal in his favor, qualifying him as a legitimate conscientious objector and restoring his license after a three-and-a-half year exile, I was in Atlanta for his comeback fight with the tough, white Jerry Quarry from my hometown, Los Angeles. At a lakeside cottage twenty-five miles outside Atlanta, Ali held court. Sidney Poitier came from Hollywood, Jesse Jackson from Chicago. It looked like a convention of black celebrities. Ali's no-nonsense trainer Angelo Dundee was having a fit. He liked peace and quiet on the day of a fight. Ali was hosting a coming-out party.

In the dressing room before the fight, the unbelievable happened. Bundini Brown, Ali's incorrigible "assistant trainer" and phrasemaker—"Float like a butterfly, sting like a bee"—had forgotten Ali's protector, the essential leather guard worn under the trunks to protect a man's vitals. A substitute was produced and Ali tried it on, standing on a chair and looking at himself in the mirror. "No," he decided. "It don't make me look pretty." While Ali's army, including the convention of Rolls Royce pimps and their foxes in his-and-hers floor-length minks, patiently waited, the abashed Bundini raced back for the "pretty" protector.

The bloody demolishment of the sacrificial lamb Jerry Quarry was almost an anti-climax to the mad cosmetics in that dressing room.

As a member of the wedding at the historic Ali-Frazier I in Madison Square Garden in '71, I have three seems-like-yesterday memories you won't find in the movie.

(1) I'm driving to the Garden from the New York Hilton with Ali and Angelo. In a little boy voice Ali asks, "Angelo, I'm not only bigger than Jimmy Ellis, [his ex–sparring partner and interim champ during Ali's exile], I'm faster, right?" Angelo: "Sure, champ, Jimmy's fast but you're even faster." Ali: "And I punch harder?" Angelo: "Absolutely, much harder." Ali: "So, if Jimmy held his own pretty good with Frazier until he got tagged, I should be able to do better than Jimmy, right?" Angelo: "No doubt about it, champ. You're gonna win it." Ali leaned his head back and didn't say another word until we reached the Garden. My God, I wondered, was the lionhearted Ali questioning his ability to stand up to the undefeated, heavy-fisted Frazier? When we reached the fabled arena, I had my answer.

As the limo door opened and the waiting fans swarmed in, Ali went through a night-and-day personality change. "I am the greatest!" he shouted. "The Greatest!" Whatever back-seat doubts he had had in the limo were gone now as he went on shouting, strutting in for his "High Noon" shootout with his most dangerous opponent.

The next morning, after being ignominiously floored in the fifteenth round and on his way to losing that bitter encounter, I went to see him in the hotel. A hideous hematoma had rearranged that pretty face into a grotesque gargoyle. It was the first loss of his career, and the talk in Toots Shor's had been that Ali's grandiose ego would be so bruised as to take him to the brink of suicide. "They better have a net outside the hotel," the anti-Alis were predicting.

Instead I found still another Ali, a philosophical Ali focused on his role as a leader of his people: "In every fight someone has to win and someone has to lose. Now I have to show my people we have our victories and we have our disappointments, and when we lose, how to fight back again."

That resilience inspired my writing the book *Loser and Still Champion* from which, somewhat to my embarrassment, he asked me to read aloud in the dressing room before he evened the score with Joe Frazier in Ali-Frazier II.

(2) In Zaire, where I shared a villa with Angelo at President (dictator) Mobutu's estate, N'Sele, Ali presided like an African king. Always the master of pre-fight psychology, he had managed to cast big George Foreman as the personification of white colonialism. Of course, dumb George (a distant cousin to the smart George of today) played into Ali's hands by unknowingly arriving with a menancing German police dog, which happened to be the symbol of Belgian colonial oppression of the native Zairians.

At night, along with all the Westerns he loved, he studied Foreman fight films, particularly Foreman's two ten-round bouts with the Argentine light heavyweight Gregorio Peralta. "Now look at that!" he'd cry out. "There's that little old man, and he's layin' back on the ropes and big George thinks he's killin' 'im an' allatime that little ol' man is givin' 'im nothin' but shoulders 'n el-

Ali at his camp in Zaire, closing in on the author. Camp manager Gene Kilroy laughs in the background.

bows an' big George is gettin' *so* tired!" Ali's fertile mind was spawning the strategy of the rope-a-dope that would sucker Foreman into thinking he was winning when all he was doing was wearing himself out and setting himself up for the knockout that would put Ali back on top of the world again.

Back at N'Sele at dawn, after the tropical downpour that melodramatically lashed the ring moments after the fight was over, Ali came at me outside his villa: "All right. I took care of big George an' now it's your turn!" The once-again king of the ring and the sixty-year-old fight writer engaged in an improbable few minutes of spurious fisticuffs. I wouldn't believe it myself if I didn't have the series of photos in my office to prove it.

(3) Then there was the scene at the Hotel Concord in the Adirondacks where Ali was training for his third Norton fight I was covering for *Newsday*, with my late wife, actress Geraldine Brooks, along as official photographer. Having seen a lot of Gerry's television work, Ali asked for an impromptu acting lesson. She obliged and improvised a scene in which he'd be provoked into anger. His performance fell far short of Gerry's professional standards, and after another unconvincing effort she decided on a strategem worthy

of Elia Kazan. She whispered in his ear with utter conviction, "I hate to tell you this but everybody here except you seems to know that your wife is having an affair with one of your sparring partners." I watched Ali's eyes. Rage. The jockey-sized Geraldine was outweighed by a hundred pounds, but she had a ton of heart. "Let's do the scene again," she ordered, and the Method worked. Ali played angry and won Gerry's hard-earned praise.

Then the mischievous Ali had another idea. "Let's go to the middle of the lobby and you turn on me and in a loud voice call me nigger." Again Geraldine obliged. As they were walking along, Gerry the consummate actress suddenly stopped. "Damn you, Ali, I came up here to do a photo shoot on you and you backed out on me! You promised!" Ali improvised, "Don't bother me, lady. I never promised you nothin', now leave me alone." Then Gerry dropped it on him. "You know what you are, you're just a goddamn lying nigger!"

Ali's bodyguards, his sparring partners, his entourage, the whole bristling Ali brigade started moving in with bad intentions, and I was thinking that this time Ali the mischief maker had gone too far. But at the last moment Ali announced that this whole mad scene was his idea—they were just practicing acting together—and the tension dissolved in nervous laughter.

Whenever I followed Ali there was merriment, along with all the serious stuff. In Dublin, where we went for the Hal Conrad-promoted Blue Lewis fight, Ali was as much of a Pied Piper as he had been in Zaire. Wherever he went, thousands of delighted Dubliners materialized, and the once-reviled black separatist who loved to be loved and loved back so convincingly always took time off for them. He'd do his magic tricks. He'd spar with a half-scared, half-thrilled twelve-year-old. He was the toast of Dublin, and oh do they know how to toast in those delicious Dublin pubs!

There was that sad last hurrah in Vegas when the thirty-eight-year-old Ali came back to face his worthy successor Larry Holmes, who had been one of his $100-a-day sparring partners back in Zaire. In his hotel suite that day the aging comeback kid was admiring himself in the mirror again. "Look at me! Look at me! Same waistline! Same weight! Same pretty face! I'm goin' to surprise the world!" And of course the loyal entourage, who had lived high on the hog all the way and couldn't bear to see their meal ticket falling from under them, obediently fed back to the ex-champ what he wanted to hear. "You look beautiful, champ! You gonna eat 'em up, champ! You look baaad, Ali!"

But alas, we saw the ghost of Ali that night, if you can picture a battered ghost, and this time it was Larry Holmes's turn to beg the referee to spare the defenseless Ali any more punishment.

As time went on, Ali lost another battle, to Parkinson's (though "Fight Doctor" Ferdie diagnosed it as dementia pugilistica). The rapid-fire delivery slowed to a halting whisper. The Nureyev of Fistiana whose winged feet bedazzled all the heavy hitters of the sixties was reduced to a sleepwalker shuffle. Whether this was the Fighter's Disease or its copycat Parkinson's, the motor was gone. But not the mind. The hand that lit the torch for the '96 Olympics in Atlanta might have trembled, but the mind behind that flame knew where he was and who he was. The prickly Black Muslim of 1965, rejected by most of white America as the threatening symbol of Black Power, had somehow morphed into the black Mother Teresa, the heavyweight saint of international peace and interracial, interreligious understanding. Adored from Jackson, Mississippi, to Beijing, China, Ali celebrates his sixtieth birthday with a hundred-million-dollar Hollywood movie, with all those great leaders of the world he once aspired to meet now envious of his popularity, as revered as the pope and an even more ecumenical icon.

From irrepressible teenage Olympic gold medalist to provocative Black Muslim champion to world-acclaimed three-time heavyweight champion to his current elevation to third-millennium sainthood—what a journey of lightning bolts and rainbows!

With all due respect to Michael Mann's *Ali*, I saw something that could never be condensed into even a long Hollywood movie. I saw the life.

[2002]

▪ 9 ▪

Arturo Gatti:
The Manly Art of No Defense

WATCHING GATTI-ROBINSON II in Atlantic City last December, I realized I was watching the Manly Art of No Defense. Once again, young (but aging fast, pugilistically) Arturo Gatti fought like Braveheart, going forward like a battle-crazed soldier charging a machine gun nest. The machine gunner was Ivan Robinson, who withstood charge after charge and fired back without mercy. This was a take-no-prisoners battle, virtually a rerun of Gatti-Robinson I some three months earlier, hailed as the "Fight of the Year." Robinson eked out a split decision in that one, and in a second display of hand speed and fistic character, eked it out once again.

But Robinson prevailed with defensive skills almost as nonexistent as Gatti's. Round after round we counted bursts of five-six-seven-eight power punches thrown by a snarling Gatti. Instead of ducking, slipping, going side to side, or strategically retreating, Robinson patiently endured the punishment, as if to say, "O.K., Arturo, fire away; when you stop, it's my turn." And then, Robinson would fire back with his own barrage, landing a little more accurately than Gatti, making the kind of fight that brings a crowd to its feet while never bringing either of the embattled warriors to his knees.

Round three was pure Gatti at its bloodiest. Robinson was finding the range, and the brave little bull from Montreal was giving still another of his Superman-as-victim performances. The left eye was busted up again, as I had seen it in the Patterson fights, and with Wilson Rodriguez and Angel Manfredy. Through the bloody mask, his eyes were on fire with the glint of combat. It almost seemed as if Gatti thrived on this physical abuse. At times he actually dropped his hands—as I remembered Jake LaMotta doing with the original Robinson in the last of their historic battles—and defied his tormentor to hit him. Our latter-day Robinson obliged, until watching it became either exhilarating or sickening to see, depending on the strength of your stomach.

You kept watching it because you knew, with Gatti, it wasn't over until not only the fat lady sang but a full chorus of heifer-sized divas hit high C together. You remembered Gatti's eyes already swollen and bloodied in the opening round of the Rodriguez ordeal. Knocked down and battered some more in round two, he somehow pressed on through that hailstorm of blood to impose his will on Rodriguez and take him out in the sixth. And who can forget the awful punishment Gabriel Ruelas inflicted on him in their fourth round, which ended with a crimson-faced Gatti barely able to stagger back to his corner? When the referee went over to survey the damage, there were cries of, "Stop it! Stop it!" from the humanitarians sprinkled among the bloodthirsty. But the referee was brave enough to let Gatti come out for round five. Wallowing in a sea of punches, he refused to go under. The humanitarians were taking over now: "Stop it! Stop it!" And, suddenly, the fight was stopped—by a desperate left hook on target to Ruelas's chin. The loser came to the post-fight party, where he was still shaking his head at the explosive, last-second turnaround. And Arturo? He went where he invariably goes after a fight, win or lose. To the hospital.

After his most recent loss, Gatti was in no danger of being abandoned by HBO. "He'll be back as long as he keeps on making great fights," a cable sportsman was saying as the doctor was stitching up the brave Arturo. But how many more times can this glutton for punishment go to the well?

The purses have ranged to $400,000, which means if he's lucky—after the IRS and management get through with him—

he'll be taking home maybe $135,000. Hang on to your money, Arturo. As the once and future champion of the Manly Art of No Defense, you're going to need every dollar of it. Plastic surgery comes high. And, as we approach the twenty-first century, you're still deprived of the pension system for deserving fighters we've been pushing for since the first half of the old century. After going undefeated for six years, Gatti was 0 for 3 in '98. He's in danger of becoming a crowd-pleasing "name" opponent.

Two back-to-back "Fights of the Year" had fans of this bloodfest clamoring, "Rematch!" But Ivan Robinson was looking to move on: challenging the reigning Sugar, Shane Mosley, for his lightweight belt. "If he [Gatti] wants to fight again, he's such an exciting fighter, he can," the winner summed up the rival he had nipped on two of the three scorecards by a single point. "But in all honesty, I don't think Arturo can last another year taking shots like that."

I remember the bravehearts who fought their guts out and kept coming. Ace Hudkins, way back when, whose brothers later had to lead him around like a blind child. And the late Jerry Quarry, who fought 'em all . . . Frazier, Ali, Patterson . . . and wound up groping his way through dark shadows. As we cheer him on and marvel at his truly extraordinary grit, are we writing for young Arturo Gatti a "Requiem for a Lightweight"?

[1999]

P.S. That was seven years ago, and the Gatti Freight Train (never an Express like De La Hoya's) chugs on. Three brutal caveman battles with Mickey Ward. Serving as a human punching bag for Floyd Mayweather, Jr. But coming back to fill the great hall in Atlantic City once again to take out a tough, previously undefeated but unknown Thomas Damgaard in the eleventh round of another of those fights in which he takes too many punches for his future mental health but to the delight of "Gatti's army," fifteen thousand and counting, who love his reckless style and indomitable spirit. We saw him as a junior lightweight champion walking through a storm of punches from good fighters who finally got tired of hitting him and surrendered. He's been doing that for fifteen years, since he was in his late teens, and he's still swinging and catching in his middle thirties. The fine old welterweight, now a top trainer, Buddy McGirt, has been giving him some boxing lessons, and he's an apt student—until he gets hit. Then it's back to the basic Arturo Gatti the fans come to see. But they won't be walking around talking to themelves ten years from now. They'll have a new gladiator to cheer. My "Requiem for a Lightweight" may have been premature. But when it comes to this noble practitioner of the Manly Art of No Defense, as he fights on, he may be able to hum the music of the requiem but, alas, he may have trouble remembering the words.

[2006]

10

Oscar De La Hoya: The Two-Hundred-Million-Dollar Man

I. Return to the Mecca

"RETURN TO THE MECCA," the drum beaters hailed the return of big-time boxing to Madison Square Garden. The main attraction was promoted less like a contest between well-matched combatants, more like "An Evening with Oscar De La Hoya," the good-looking kid from Little Mexico's East L.A., with the fast hands and the fast patter. He could be the best thing to come out of my hometown since our little buzzsaw Henry Armstrong came to the Garden (the third one, on Eighth Avenue and Fiftieth) and shook up first the featherweight, then the welterweight, finally the lightweight division in an incredible triple against Petey Sarron, Barney Ross, and Lou Ambers.

The mood of the healthy turnout for De La Hoya's debut at the Garden—like a hot young tenor's appearing at the Met—was festive, happy, and hopeful. There was electricity in the air when you took your seat for the prelims, a feeling that name fighters were back in the Garden where they belonged. In Vegas there's always the feeling that the high rollers in the casinos are saying, "O.K., let's leave the tables f' an hour an' go out an' see the fight," a momentary distraction but not exactly their main activity. And in Vegas, Michael Buffer intones a seemingly endless litany of film and TV celebrities, a Demi Moore, a Whoopi Goldberg, a John Travolta. . . . Whoever's hot in Hollywood or on the tube gets the roar of the crowd rather than the current fighters and old-time greats who were traditionally intro'd on the Garden nights.

It was good to hear fighters' names on the announcer's lips in the Garden ring—Jose Torres, Emile Griffith, Floyd Patterson . . . though the volume rose to a roar for Roy Jones, Jr., and Felix Trinidad. This is more of a *now* crowd than in the old days. In Griffith's years in the sixties and seventies, we would not have forgotten our heroes of the thirties to the fifties. But now the new fight crowd, if that's what it was, seemed to have forgotten or never knew about Griffith's illustrious past. I had an urge to stand up and shout, "Hey, you're giving this silent treatment to one of the great welter/middles, who fought eleven title bouts in the Garden, and never a dull moment!" Cheering Trinidad and falling silent for Emile Griffith was like hailing Jay McInerney and ignoring Scott Fitzgerald.

Two recently retired champs, the ringwise Buddy McGirt and the tough Iran Barkley, also got the silent treatment, making me think again of the Four Seasons of Success and how quickly the winter chill sets in after the fall. A big hand for Joe Frazier—his trilogy with Ali now the stuff of legends—but the biggest hand at the intros was reserved for an overnight sensation called Butterbean (real handle, Eric Esch), an undefeated three-hundred-pound curiosity who was coming to the Garden with fifteen stirring victories over tomato cans, on his way to becoming a cult figure and media darling.

I was fortunate to have as my seatmate Stephanie Arcel, whose distinguished husband Ray was one of the great trainers of the century, starting with Charley Phil Rosenberg and Benny Leonard, later Ezzard Charles and what seemed like a covey of the Bomber's opponents, then all the way up to Roberto Duran and Larry Holmes. In Ray's sensitive and gifted hand, the Game was truly Sweet Science, and that spirit was clearly reflected in Stephanie, who watched the first clumsy moves of Butterbean, in there with a journeyman last-minute substitute, Mitchell Rose.

"Oh my God, no skill! No skill!" she cried out. And as the fat toughman brawler walked into punch after punch, his white face coloring red and leaking blood, my knowledgable companion turned to me and said, "A travesty of an art form."

In less than two rounds, the undefeated Butterbean was exposed for the sideshow freak he really was. And there had been talk of putting him in with the windless "Hurricane" Peter McNeeley in the next show. In the bad old days, Frankie Carbo, Eddie Coco, or Blinky Palermo would have had a little chat with Mr. Rose. Mr. Butterbean might have gone all the way to the top a la Primo Carnera. So please, dear Madison Square Garden, spare us the Butterbeans. But thank you for Oscar De La Hoya.

Whether young De La Hoya will reach Armstrong's level of accomplishment depends on the matches ahead. There's talk of a jumbo fight down the road with Julio Cesar Chavez. In December the smaller Jesse James Leija, a nice little junior lightweight from San Antonio, was clearly in there as a supporting player, not unlike Buster Mathis, Jr., in his honest effort the following evening in Philly to smother in flab the still wild and rusty Iron Mike Tyson. If both fights were mismatches, nobody cared. Leija put in his two rounds as an opponent, one more ornament on De La Hoya's year-round Christmas tree. There's genuine talent in the kid. He passed the Stephanie Arcel test: "You feel the style in him, a seriousness. An approach to the job. He can punch, in bunches, accurately, with an instinct for closure."

Behind the flash of De La Hoya, I saw the ghosts of all those lovely lightweights who used to thrill the Garden—Beau Jack, Bob Montgomery, Ike Williams . . . nights when you forgot the sleaze that corrupted the game, nights when you went back to Toots Shor's exhilarated, your hope for mankind somehow reaffirmed. And the welterweights! The night our nonpareil Sugar Ray Robinson fought oh-so-tough Tommy Bell for the vacant title. Ray was down but boxed his way to the crown. Or the night our classy Billy Graham was jobbed out of the championship because Mr. Carbo had made it abundantly clear that he preferred Sr. Gavilan.

Everybody in the Garden knew that Billy was the uncrowned champ, just as almost twenty-five years later, in Ali-Frazier I, we knew we had seen an unforgettable contest for the true Championship of the World.

I had been in Ali's corner that fabled night, in the limo with him driving to the Garden, then crouching at the ring apron with Angelo Dundee, Dr. Ferdie Pacheco, and "Blood" Wali Muhammad. Oh, that furious fifteenth round when Ali was down but refused to stay down, as he somehow managed to float and sting again as the first act of the Ali-Frazier trilogy closed with a roar that rose layer on layer of emotion from the capacity crowd.

To be fighting in the Garden was to be anointed in those days. When the heavyweight fighting out of my barn in Bucks County, Archie McBride, beat up everybody in Trenton and Sunnyside Garden, I remember the excitement when we got the semi-windup in the Garden. More than the fifteen hundred dollars, a semi in the Garden was one step away from fistic heaven. There was a feeling of muscles tightening around my heart when Archie was in there (for seven rounds) with Floyd Patterson. And I remember another Archie on another night, the venerable Archie Moore, finally getting his shot in the Garden at age forty, and putting away a class light heavyweight contender, Harold Johnson, in the fourteenth round.

The Garden was truly a Mecca then, and if the mismatches, faked ratings, and manipulations of greed can be avoided—a big If—we'll have our Mecca back again. Certainly, following De La Hoya with Roy Jones, Jr., in there with a toughie, Merqui Sosa, and then Foreman's farewell perfomance against enigmatic Michael Moorer, are hopeful signs of Friday Nights in the Garden for '96.

Thank you, Caesars Palace, we'll take Manhattan. . . .

[1996]

II. The Guessing Game: De La Hoya-Whitaker

BOXING—God love it and God save it!—is the only sport I know that can leave a major event like the recent De La Hoya-Whitaker fight without a manifest winner, or in the case of the puzzling

Golden Boy-Sweet Pea encounter, without a satisfactory conclusion.

I mean, if you look at any other sport from football to Ping-Pong, points are scored for all to see. We see the ball going into the end zone. With our own eyes we see the kicker nailing the ball cleanly between the goal posts. Three points unarguable. Just as no one can argue with the electrifying swish of Michael Jordan's signature jump shot. When Cuba's giant bird, Sotomayor, clears eight feet in the high jump, there are officials to measure it to the fraction of an inch. When our human running machine Michael Johnson dominates his world-class rivals in the 200 and 400, there are the wonders of state-of-the-art high-tech electronics to record his times to the 1/100th of a second.

Alas, no such precision attends the decision in a crucial contest of championship boxers. With De La Hoya-Whitaker, for instance, ringsiders who consider themselves experts in the arcane art of judging a contest of fisticuffs will be arguing the round-by-round scoring of their bout until both those performers with 180-degree contrasting styles are ready for their Social Security benefits well into the next century.

No one truly knows who won this anti-climactic, sometimes lackluster, but technically interesting twelve-round engagement. The three judges, those official but somewhat Vegasly suspicious arbiters, awarded only three rounds to the peerless Pernell, which was roughly half the total the aging, still crafty champion earned from this corner. Most reporters at ringside had it by a single point, most for Whitaker, but with some competent votes for the now slightly tarnished Golden Boy. Our own score reflects the subjectivity of scoring fights. Not able to make the Vegas scene, this time, with nose pressed against the screen and notebook in hand, first I had it for Oscar by two. Yes, he was tentative, and as Larry Merchant complained, "robotic," especially compared to Whitaker's weirdly frustrating style, but he seemed to be pressing the fight (if you could call it that) and landing the harder if fewer punches.

But replaying the tape next day, and maybe at a kinder hour, I found that Whitaker had improved considerably overnight. Oscar was extending his left hand too far forward to be able to jab with it effectively. Pernell's jab was furtively incessant, and though the young challenger would flurry in the last thirty seconds of almost every round, provoking his passionate rooting section to standing ovations, there were so many more misses than hits in these attacks that you had to admire Sweet Pea as probably the smoothest master of defense since Willie Pep. And since the Whitaker style is to feint and sucker opponents into attack and then counterpunch from unorthodox angles, Oscar's more conventional aggression was often being smothered as he fell victim to Whitaker's unexciting but efficient game plan.

So this time I had the old champ up by one. With the score now tied one to one on my cards I ran the rubber match, and now there was no doubt in my mind. It wasn't the "blow-out" the super-confident Whitaker insisted he had won—"10 out of 12 rounds—I toyed with the kid." Nor was it—except officially—the glorious night the De La Hoya Boys were ready to celebrate. Even if the self-satisfied Whitaker waltzed the last round, his big eleventh was the convincer for me. When asked why he urgently wanted a rematch after pulling out the controversial decision, Oscar replied, "Because next time I know I would do much, much better. I will not be satisfied until I dominate Whitaker's style."

Still, it was a close, technical, beglowed debate, a learning experience for the preppy kid who's more Madison Avenue than Barrio now, and who moves on to easier nights with less talented names such as David Kamou and over-the-hill fighters like Macho Camacho. In the good old days it might have been called a draw, too close to take the belt away from this unique practitioner of the Sweet Pea science; a champion since the late eighties, who rose to the occasion the other night but who fell to the whims of the WBC "judges."

To his credit as an honest man in a sport rather underwhelming in integrity, here's how Promoter Bob Arum's new mega-million-dollar meal ticket sums it up for us:

"Boxing is all politics, it's all money. What the WBC sees is that I'm a young fighter. If I win the title I obviously make more money for them than Whitaker or anybody else. It's more sanctioning fees for the WBC. That's the way it goes."

As for the rematch, despite Oscar's professed good intentions, let's not hold our breaths. The last thing the very practical Mr. Arum would like to see at this moment is a detour in the De La Hoya run on the mint. "Who the hell wants to see Whitaker again?" Arum filibustered after the fight. Just us fight fans, we might answer, but who listens?

"Show business with blood," we've always called the fight game. There wasn't a lot of blood to De La Hoya–Whitaker, just a few flecks from an unintentional butt, for which Pernell was penalized an undeserved point. But plenty of emphasis on business, especially the business they gave our erstwhile nine-year-champion of the world, Master Pernell Sweet-and-Sour Whitaker.

[1997]

III. The Oscar Express Rolls On

IN THE OLD DAYS, the big fights eclipsed the buildup. When you talk about "Opposites Attack"—the catchy title for Oscar De La Hoya's most recent star turn (with Macho Camacho in a supporting role)—you remember the real thing. In Louis-Conn I, opposites *attacked*. There was the ever-stalking Brown Bomber and the nimble-footed, nimble-fisted Pittsburgh Billy. I flew across the country for that one, and my reward was a thirteen-round classic, the cocky 169-pound challenger ahead after twelve. Moving in and out, side-to-side, attacking. And opposites attacked again when the original Sugar Ray (Robinson) finally caught up with Raging Bull LaMotta in another thirteen-round unforgettable.

Opposites attacked when the raw power of Rocky Marciano finally chopped down that cutie who knew every move in the book and ad-libbed a bunch of his own, Jersey Joe Walcott. And again when the street dog from Panama, Roberto Duran, cut off the ring on Sugar Ray Leonard in Montreal. There was attacking on both sides when Leonard, a boxer-puncher, met Tommy

Hearns, a puncher-boxer. And attack-counterattack defined Marvelous Marvin's reception for Ray Leonard in the first and by far the best of Sugar II's multi-comebacks.

Since we go to the fights for the personal drama not to be found in any other sport, we are invariably intrigued with the matchup of boxer vs. slugger. All the way back to Sullivan-Corbett at the turn of the century and on to Dempsey-Tunney, Ali-Foreman. Could the boxer defuse the puncher? Could the puncher crash through the craft, as craft almost won the night for the wily Archie Moore (vs. Marciano), who finally went down like a fighting ship with all flags flying?

Everyone of those rivalries played out even more dramatically than they were scripted. So for De La Hoya–Camacho, why not dust off the old slogan "Opposites Attack" and blazon it all over the roller-coaster town of Las Vegas and all over the world for the benefit of PPV? You saw it on billboards, posters, and marquees. You saw it on the ubiquitous TV teasers, you saw it on T-shirts, peaked hats, and sweatshirts. Give yourself a few days in the razzle and the dazzle of Suckertown and the repetition of "Opposites Attack" begins to stitch a tattoo in your brain.

Of course we're not only talking boxing styles now. Macho Camacho, in his seventeenth year as a pro, with only three losses in sixty-eight fights (and none in his first eleven years), was as slippery as an eel. And some would say he had all the charm and personality of a coral snake. But give this little snake from Spanish Harlem his due. I remember him as the Boy Wonder of the Golden Gloves. Hands *muy rapido* (with the speed and grace of a dancer who could win salsa contests). I caught him in the Garden as a teenager in the early eighties and he was electrifying. Brilliant. Quite simply the best junior lightweight I had ever seen. (Footnote: I missed Kid Chocolate, and a little Mexican born the same year as Camacho, Julio Cesar Chavez, was knocking down other little Mexicans like bowling pins, but only in his hometown of Culiacan.)

Meanwhile, Macho sparkled like the glitzy bangles that dangled from his neck. He won world titles and beat champions who could put serious hurt on you, like Bazooka Limon, Boza-Edwards, and Edwin Rosario. He actually had people saying, "This could be the lightweight Muhammad Ali." He could be magically elusive like Ali; and on occasion, when he did get caught, he had a chin like Ali's. Before the Golden Gloves he had trained as a gang fighter in the mean streets of Harlem, and he had a very tough streak in him, hidden in an adolescent flamboyance, a theatrical extroversion that made people wonder if he didn't spend more time working on the outlandish costumes with which he was wont to enter the ring than in serious training. A cutup, a show-off, what we used to call a wisenheimer, a tasteless self-promoter, he didn't know how to make his rare gifts and his TVish theatricality work for him as Ali, even in defeat (Frazier, Norton), reached out to people who made him their champion.

We defenders of boxing like to point to the ghetto kids who could have wound up lost to the slammer but who found salvation through boxing. Alas, the career of Macho Camacho is a marker for the other side. Winning and successfully defending his WBC 130-pound and 135-pound belts did nothing for Macho's character. Not just *vino y mujeres y salsa* was where Camacho was spending his Macho Time. Throw in *drogas* too. There were years when he seemed to have more fights with the fuzz than he had in the ring. He was driving down streets the wrong way with no license. Literally. A pocket-sized Leon Spinks.

When Julio Cesar Chavez pounded on him for twelve rounds like a bongo drum five years ago, he earned a begrudging respect for the kind of courage expected of the true professional. For all his goofiness and all the squandering of gifts lesser athletes would kill for, he hadn't lost that Nuevo Yorkin pride. You couldn't knock him out. Chavez couldn't do it. And the undefeated J.C. was still in his prime five years ago. But Macho Time for the irrepressible scatterbug was now half an hour past midnight: the "Lightweight Ali" of the eighties had become the glorified welterweight "opponent" of the nineties, in there for a paynight and the chance to fatten the record of a Chavez or the new boy on the block, Felix Trinidad.

The year Macho was taking his lumps from Chavez, a new star was rising out of Little Mexico's East L.A., Oscar De La Hoya, the Golden Boy of the '92 Barcelona Olympics. Here's where the "opposites" apply. While Macho, who might have been called the Golden Boy of the eighties, pissed everybody off with his outrageous behavior, young Oscar was turning everybody on with his preppy manners and his golden smile.

A truly promising lightweight who could lick name fighters like John-John Molina, Rafael Ruelas, Genaro Hernandez, and an over-the-hill Chavez, Oscar was made for prime time. In a time of Celebrity Madness, Oscar could not only light up the ring (though the "W" over Pernell Whitaker has quotes around it), he could light up the money tree of television and bring a new constituency of fans to the fight game, the teeny-boppers whose grandmother had squealed for Frankie, whose mothers had fainted for Elvis and the Beatles, and whose older sister screamed for Mick Jagger.

While true fight fans welcome a legitimate new talent like De La Hoya, it's these cute little screamers, by the thousands and counting, who follow Oscar around like wild-eyed handmaidens and throw themselves under the wheels of his golden chariot. At the tumultuous weigh-in at Caesars Palace the day before the fight, Macho not only had to strip down to his teeny-weeny black bikini but then drop even that to get a rise out of what looked like a high school cheering section. All Oscar had to do was flash that nine-million-dollar smile at them, and they were his.

Each decade seems to have a way of developing the perfect role model for reflecting the spirit of its time. In this era of high-tech, high-celebrity cultism, Oscar De La Hoya has what my old man's movie discovery, Clara Bow, had in the 1920s . . . "It!"

After the squealy weigh-in came the usual pre-fight seminars in which self-appointed experts spend the waiting hours in profound ringwise analysis of the respective chances of the combatants. There was general agreement that Macho was in the best shape he had been in since his lightweight years—"Maybe ever," his trainer, Pat Burns, was earnestly assuring us at lunch that day. "Believe it or not, Hector had never done a sit-up in training before. The other day, on a dare, he did thirteen hundred! Unbelievable. I know he has a reputation for not working hard, but this time he knows he'll never get a shot like this again. He may be in the twilight of his career, but he's ticked off about those odds [8 to 1] and I tell you, it's turned him into a monster."

And Macho had his serious face on when he said, "After tomorrow night, we'll see who's the Golden Boy. I'm going to surprise him the way Ali surprised Foreman. Let's see if he can really fight a real fight. Hit, get hit back. Get hit, hit back. A real fight, like the way I beat on Sugar." Of course the Ray Leonard he took out in five was forty years old and came in with a gimpy foot. If he had been a horse, he never would have been allowed in the starting gate. Still, Macho's weight—147, compared to his 158 for Leonard six months earlier—seemed to confirm Pat Burns's claim that Macho was in the prime shape of his life and ready to make the fight of his life.

Meanwhile, Oscar's trainer, the eminent Emanuel Steward, was telling us that he had trained Oscar to be far more aggressive than he had been in his less than spectacular performance with tricky Pernell Whitaker. Golden Boy was going to put relentless pressure on Camacho. Call it six rounds or less. Oscar was slightly more generous. He saw the possibility of Macho's hanging in until the seventh. I listened quietly to all the predictions, including one distinguished boxing writer's picking Camacho by KO in seven, and then quietly placed a modest wager: De La Hoya by decision. If Limon couldn't do it, I figured, if Rosario couldn't do it, if Chavez and Trinidad couldn't do it, an in-shape Camacho could draw on the experience of those seventeen years (plus all those amateur rounds) and sixty-eight fights to devise escape routes and survive.

Twenty seconds into round one, I was getting ready to tear up my "W-Dec." chit. Oscar came roaring out of his corner as if his own bet was "KO-1" and smashed a left hook to Macho's body that sent a powerful message: "I own you, man!" Any serious intention Macho may have had of actually winning this fight was instantly a thing of the past. By the end of round one the fight was all but over. Poor Macho wasn't going to be the Ali of the nineties any more than he had been in the eighties. The only suspense left was how long Macho could take those hooks to the body, fierce uppercuts, and straight rights to the head without obliging Oscar with the knockout victory the TV star from East L.A. had predicted. To frustrate his oppressor, the sixteen thousand in the Thomas & Mack Center, and all the PPViewers around the world, Macho changed the title of the "fight" from "Opposites Attack" to "One Opposite Attacks, the Other Opposite Backtracks."

Like a wily general who knows he's outmanned and outgunned, Macho knew it was time to run so he could run another day. He backed this way and that way, anyway he could find to escape. If there had been a closet in the ring, Macho would have slipped into it and locked it from inside. And where there was no room to run, Macho moved forward, not to hit Oscar—that would be foolhardy—but to wrap his arms around him and hold on for dear life.

The crowd booed, as they booed Macho's entrance into the ring in his silly Darth Vader mask and his glitzy silver-festooned Romanesque loincloth, split seductively at the sides. Boring rounds of running and clutching, until the frustrated attacker finally put Macho down in the ninth for only the second time in Hector's singular career. But somehow Macho survived. That's what he does for a living now. In the eleventh he was on his way down again. But the instinct to survive sent him lurching forward, grabbing his tormentor around the waist and pulling Oscar to the canvas with him, like a pass rusher sacking the quarterback. Often the sacker is back on his feet before the sackee, as happened here as well. Oscar took his time getting up. All that punching and chasing was taking its toll. Meanwhile, Macho the survivor was ready for more. More run and grab and grab and run found him still on his feet at the final bell, knocked about but still never knocked out.

At the press conference a barechested, still cocky Camacho was almost exultant. There had been talk of a side bet: if Oscar knocks him out, he gets to snip off the irritating spit curl, a Macho trademark he affects on his forehead. But if Macho's still there at the final bell, Oscar deals him $200,000. So for Macho, it's a moral victory—plus a few hundred grand for those gold chains and diamonds. I watched him strut off the stage, oblivious to the boos, and my notes scribbled on the spot read: "There goes crazy Macho, maybe for the last time(?). No contusions and no illusions." *Sic transit*. Golden Boy, Class of '80, makes way for Golden Boy '97.

The winner and still champion of the WBC welterweights takes his time coming out for his press conference, as befits the poster boy of pugilistica. He holds a cold cylinder to a left eye swollen from Macho's defensive jabs, but he's all smiles and youthful enthusiasm and becoming modesty and that articulate way of talking as if he's just returned not from a fight but from his elocution teacher.

His promoter, Bob Arum, who is wreathed in his own smile and money, introduces Oscar as "The greatest fighter in the world today." That may be a slight exaggeration, but hey, asking a promoter with a hot ticket not to hyperbolize is like asking a rooster not to crow. Golden Boy '97 puts it in perspective. His goal is to be one of the greatest fighters who ever lived, up there with Louis, Robinson, and Ali. But he realizes he's not there yet. "I still have a lot to learn in the sport of boxing."

Meanwhile there's the business of boxing, which is a very different animal. The welterweight / junior middleweight field is full of talent—Felix Trinidad, Ike Quartey, Terry Norris, Pernell Whitaker—but Trinidad is with Arum's rival, Don King, and HBO's rival, Showtime. Quartey is the WBA champion. "Why should we pay those exorbitant sanction fees of the WBA? We don't need the WBA. The WBC is treating us fine," said Arum, walking out of the fight with us. Trinidad is with King and Showtime. Whitaker is a logical rematch, but Pernell is a far craftier and better southpaw than Camacho. A good reason to avoid him. The other potential money fight is with WBC super welterweight champion Terry Norris, who's suing Don King and signing with Arum. Emanuel Steward acknowledges that "Terry is still too big, too strong" (and too good, he might have added). "This is Oscar's first year as a welterweight," he points out. "He's going to be one of the great ones, but give him time."

"The greatest fighter in the world today" needs time to develop his skills and "learn more about the sport of boxing."

The sport of boxing and the business of boxing are on their usual collision course. The undefeated champion is willing to take on all comers. Arum smiles. "I'm not afraid of Trinidad, or anybody," De La Hoya says. The kid is willing to learn on the job. Arum smiles some more. He'll go where the money is.

Oscar gave himself a nine, and deserves an eight, for pitching a shutout against Camacho. In the old days of McLarnin and Robinson, later Leonard, Hearns, and Duran, he would not have been a four-time champion with only twenty-six fights. He'd have been a very good prospect with good hand speed, power, and intensity.

But while we're being critical and technical, the young champion with the rock star charisma is leaving the stage, and all those girls are screaming and swooning and squealing "Oscar! Oscar! Oscar! . . ."

It warms the cockles of Bob Arum's heart and bank account. Trust him to find a way to wind the business around the sport. The De La Hoya Express rolls on.

[1997]

IV. The Welters Are Coming! The Welters Are Coming!

WITH THREE of our erstwhile heavyweight champions—Tyson, Bowe, and McCall—in the hoosgow, and the anti-climactic Holyfield-Lewis "unification" leaving us with bifurcation, investigation, and frustration, boxing diehards are finding relief is spelled D-E L-A H-O-Y-A and T-R-I-N-I-D-A-D.

In a sticky season when once again the hounds forever snapping at the heels of our Sweet and Sour Science are thrown too many bones by wrongheaded decisions and cynical power plays, the old game gets a shot in the arm—and not a moment too soon: Here come the welterweights!

On back-to-back mid-winter Saturday nights, we had the four top welters of '99—two champions vs. No. 1 contenders—Oscar De La Hoya vs. Ike Quartey, Felix Trinidad vs. Pernell Whitaker—in lively if not epic twelve-round contests that gave us a taste of the glory days of Barney Ross, Jimmy McLarnin, Henry Armstrong, the original Sugar Ray, Emile Griffith, Ray Leonard, and Tommy Hearns.

But for now, here comes Oscar the Golden Boy, so called for his four belts in four different divisions, his $75 million in earnings, his movie-star looks, and enough miniskirt groupies to arouse the envy of Leonardo Di Caprio. They know nothing about the art of boxing, but they know what they like: the sweet, seductive smile of their young, undefeated hero with the bod of a twenty-six-year-old Adonis, a begloved, near-naked Woody Harrelson.

And the kid can fight a little bit, too. Though he showed his inexperience, and for much of the match his excessive caution, before coming on big to knock the talented, hard-punching Ike Quartey down and almost out in the final round. Inexperienced? After twenty-nine fights in five years, four titles, and wins over marquee names—Julio Cesar Chavez, Pernell Whitaker, Genaro Hernandez, Jesse James Leija, Macho Camacho? Hard truth is, the chic Chicano may have been more carefully groomed for his role than the Prince of Wales. He was getting rich and famous knocking over smaller champs like Hernandez and Leija, and shot fighters whose future was behind them, like Chavez and Camacho. Now, for a $9 million paynight, he was in with his first real test, the undefeated Quartey from Ghana, the West African nation where Dr. Azumah Nelson presides. For more than half the fight, the beautifully conditioned challenger with the stinging jab was giving Golden Boy a boxing lesson, punishing him for his mistakes with stiff right hands short and accurate that were beginning to make a bloody mess of that pretty face. Quartey was moving nicely, fluidly, in total control, and Oscar was flat-footed and tense, the gold turning to tin. Like the latter-day Tyson, he seemed suddenly bereft of skills, the jab listless and of lateral movement, none. After eight rounds, maven scorer Harold Let-

terman had Nelson's compatriot ahead by three. Oscar's Machiavellian promoter Bob Arum must have been plotzing. His cash
cow was blowing the big one. The nasty tomato under the left eye
looked ready to pop. The multi-millionaire from East Lost Angeles was accepting his punishment gamely while his boxing professor would give him a double D, Dumb and Dumber.

And then, as if written by the hand of the playwright who
knows how to drive the work to a climax, the show took a dramatic turn. As he had in his last encounter, with Jose Luis Lopez
sixteen months ago, Quartey ran out of gas. Seizing the opportunity, De La Hoya set the pace for the first time, his confidence
growing as Quartey's seemed to fade. He stormed out for the last
round as if he had to knock Ike out to win, as indeed, on the card
of one judge, was the case. A score of unanswered blows drove
the almost defenseless Quartey into a corner where referee Mitch
Halpern seemed ready to step in and call it a night. But, suddenly,
like a flash storm, Oscar was spent and Ike survived, losing a split
decision he bitterly protested.

At the press conference De La Hoya iced his wounded eye as
a badge of honor. Scorned as "Chicken de lay Hoya," accused of
lacking the fighting heart Mexican battlers are famous for, his
last-round fury was a rite of passage. He wasn't just a pretty face.
At last the Mexicans who doubted him would give him his due:
Mucho Corazon!

Our verdict: More will than skill.

Meanwhile, the other undefeated champion, Felix Trinidad,
may be the ultimate welterweight as we cross that bridge to the
twenty-first century. In the once unhitable Pernell Whitaker, a
six-time champion, he faced an old master who had given De La
Hoya fits years ago, with his now-you-see-me-now-you-don't
style—the most elusive boxer since Will-o'-the-Wisp Willie Pep.
But fourteen years in this cruel sport, and the booze, the nose
candy, the enforced layoffs, had taken their toll. "Sweet Pea"
("Snow Pea," meanies called him now) came out flat-footed but
full of fight, taking the first round and silencing the Puerto Ricans
rooting for their "Tito! Tito!"

But not for long. The ring magician who had managed to avoid three of every four punches thrown at him by experts in an illustrious career was getting nailed by more than half the punches the classy Puerto Rican boxer-puncher threw at him. Whitaker was knocked down. He was bloodied. His jaw was broken. There was a glorious last hurrah in the seventh, when the tricky old pitty-patterer actually shook the front-running IBF champion. But from there on it was all downhill. "I thought I won—he never hurt me," the proud ex-champion spoke those familiar words of gladatorial denial through his fractured jaw on his way to the hospital.

"I'd love to see him retire," said his tough-looking, softhearted manager, Lou Duva, who's been with him since his Olympic Gold Medal days. "I don't want to see this kid get hurt. If he was my son, I'd tell him to pack it in."

Sweet Pea, hold on to your money. Stay out of the switches. Maybe you can teach a new kid the art you perfected. Now you see me, now you don't.

So, we're ready for the welterweight showdown of the decade. De La Hoya vs. Felix Trinidad for all the marbles. McLarnin-Ross time. Robinson-Tommy Bell. Gavilan-Graham. Leonard-Hearns. We should get so lucky. All it needs is Don King and Bob Arum to get together. That very odd couple. And HBO and Showtime. And Trinidad wants parity dollars with De La Hoya. And Oscar says, "no Way." It's Holyfield-Lewis wheels-within-wheels all over again. Let the one-upmanship begin! But there's an old saying in boxing, "If there's enough money in it, they'll find a way." Money-honey makes arch enemies instant best friends.

[1999]

V. De La Hoya-Trinidad: A Tale of Two Champions

ONCE UPON A TIME, in the golden age of boxing, every division was competitive. The top ten were a formidable band and the next ten not too shabby, either. Now the No. 1 contenders come in the form of Henry Akinwande, Ricky Frazier, and John Ruiz. Contenders cum Pretenders. Once the proud domain of Joe Louis, Marciano, and Ali, the heavyweight picture has degenerated to the point where even the heralded, undisputed title fight—Holyfield vs. Lewis—ends in controverted fiasco. Convoluted negotiations for the rematch no true fight fan is panting to see.

Light heavies set off sparks in the days of Jack Delaney and Paul Berlenbach, again in the time of Billy Conn and Gus Lesnevich, as later with Michael Spinks, Dwight Qawi, and Saad Muhammad. Today Roy Jones, Jr., is so far ahead, he can look over his shoulder and laugh all the way to the bank. As for middleweights, well, there're Bernard Hopkins and William Joppy, but if Otis Grant, the Canadian scholar, is No. 4, and the top two can't get on each other's dance card, that once feisty division is drifting on a windless sea.

But, as noted recently, not only are the welters coming, they're here, beckoning us to a level of creative intensity that comes along once in a decade. Not only have we enjoyed a unique, back-to-back semi-final, involving Oscar De La Hoya / Ike Quartey and Felix Trinidad / Pernell Whitaker, the top four 147-pounders in the world, now we're going to the final. We thought lions and lambs would lie down together sooner than Don King and Bob Arum, Showtime and HBO, WBC and IBF. In the fractured world of Fight Game '99, these contending entities are usually more difficult to get together than Milosevic and the Kosovo Liberation Army. But this time money didn't merely talk, it shouted, it screamed, it begged on its cynical knees, "Please, fellas, this is too big to miss! This is so fat we'll all get rich!" So Felix Trinidad and Co. settle for a mere $9 million to the Golden Boy's $15 million, Showtime bows to arch rival HBO, and those two unloved Machiavellis of PPV waltz together around the money tree.

There's good reason to call the Chicano kid from East L.A. the Golden Boy, even if he's more accurately Golden Boy II, for those of us who cherish the original, my dear old chum and best man at my long-ago wedding, Art Aragon. Art was my hometown's all-time box office winner until Oscar came along. But he never led the charmed life of his successor. From the moment he took the gold at the '92 Olympics, young Oscar has been a crossover star unequaled by any boxer in the history of what my estimable colleague Hugh McIlvanney rightly calls "the hardest game." With his movie-star looks, his elocutionist diction, and his flashy style, he was attracting as many groupies as Limp Bizkit's Fred Durst. They came squealing to his fights and his press conferences in such numbers as to make him the richest sub-heavyweight in the history of this show business sport. In a handful of professional years he had scored $50 million without taking any genuine risks, as his crafty pooh-bah Bob Arum had him in there with smaller champions with marquee names—Rafael Ruelas, Jesse James Leija, Genaro Hernandez—or famed veterans over the hill, like Julio Cesar Chavez and Macho Camacho.

In his first real test, with Pernell Whitaker two years ago, I'm still not sure he won it. It was too close to lose a title on, as did Pernell that night. But all my life I've seen the judges go with the money. Oh, I'm not talking anything as brash and uncouth as bribery. Oscar is golden because he sells the tickets, he brings the crowds, he generates the buzz, and the most any opponent can hope for, even a longtime world champion like Pernell Whitaker, is Best Actor in a Supporting Role. Nobody has to grease the judges. The tilt is toward Oscar. Is there any other major sport open to such subjective deliberation? The judges may not even be trying to curry favor with the promoters who pay them. The roar of the crowd provokes a subconscious reaction. Pernell would have had to knock Oscar out to win, or win decisively. Oscar was lucky to eke it out. His inexperience showed, for the trouble with an undefeated record like Oscar's is how easy it's been. You make a lot of money bowling over the Jesse James Leijas and the Patric Carpentiers, but you're still in fistic grammar school. You don't learn much from beating up old Julio Cesar, either. You can listen to Emmanuel Steward or Gil Clancy all you want (if Oscar's really listening), but you go to college in the ring. That's where all the great ones matriculated—Sugar Ray Robinson, Willie Pep, and Archie Moore.

Oscar is a gifted kid, with a nice jab, punching power, and the appetite for taking punches essential in this relentless sport. But watching him against Ike Quartey last spring, I was reminded again how much this begloved multi-millionaire still has to learn about this activity he's mastered financially but not fistically. (If his groupie shrikes are reading this, I'm in trouble, but chances are they're not—able to read, period.) Against the toughest opponent he's ever faced, Ike Quartey, he seemed puzzled and tentative through many rounds, planted in front of the dangerous African who was outjabbing him and scoring right hands. In the sixth round of an often lackluster fight, Quartey was down for a short count but stormed back to deck Oscar and have him in trouble. After eight rounds, Gil Clancy, who managed a great welterweight champion in Emile Griffith, was telling Oscar, "You're stuck in the mud." Oscar was giving the sharp and dangerous Quartey no side-to-side, no in-and-out. After five years and twenty-nine fights, with only Whitaker to test him, inexperience was telling.

Yes, he made up for a less than golden performance in the final round by abjuring his abundant but errant boxing skills and becoming no longer the cutie who had moved out of his Chicano ghetto to the white burbs. He wasn't following his corner now, or his head. Under the pretty-boy face was a fighting heart, and as he traded punches for a wild sixty seconds with the dangerous Quartey and almost took him out, we remembered Toluco Lopez and Chucho Castillo and all those indomitable Mexican warriors, inspired by punishment, refusing to lose.

Whether aided by judges or his macho demons, Oscar reminds us that Somebody Up There Likes Him, and that, for all his aberrant ways, he finds ways to win. The boxing mavens with whom I've discussed this favor Trinidad to put the first "L" on Golden's undefeated record. Maybe even "by KO." If Oscar thought Ike Quartey was tough, he's going to find the Puerto Rican champion even tougher. This could be the Leonard-Hearns of the nineties. Trinidad may have the niftier jab, the crisper right hand, the more self-contained style. But if Oscar remembers to

move, throw combinations instead of solo hooks, and if he fights
through pain as he's shown the will to do, he could find a way to
win the defining fight of his magical career.

When I was in Zaire for the Ali-Foreman fight, I was phoning
home to bet the house on the underdog, Muhammad. This time
I'm still waiting for a signal from my little fistic bird. I wouldn't
bet the doormat, much less the house. The logic says Trinidad.
The magic says De La Hoya.

And remember, if they both get up from knockdowns, and it's
still close at the end, they're fighting in Las Vegas.

[1999]

VI. Mosley-De La Hoya: My Hometown

FROM THE MOMENT they made the match, Mosley vs. De La
Hoya was on my mind. For the first time since Ali-Norton, almost
thirty years ago, a mega fight was coming to my old hometown,
our freeway-spangled, glitzed-up, and smogged-up City of the An-
gels. When I was still in grade school, I was at the Hollywood Legion and Downtown Olympic Auditorium with my father, cheering on our local heroes, Jimmy McLarnin and Fidel La Barba,
Mushy Callahan, Ace Hudkins, Jackie Fields, Henry Armstrong,
Baby Arizmendi, Archie Moore. If Madison Square Garden was
the Mecca of the Manly Art, our Los Angeles rings, with their parade of world champions, were Mecca West.

Hollywood was a fight town almost as much as it was a movie
town. Ringside at the Legion on a Friday night looked like a
Who's Who of Tinseltown. My old man, as head of Paramount
studio, enjoyed the royal prerogative of sitting front row in the
press section. He would arrive in style, bowed to his seat by obsequious ushers, greeted by famous faces, and waving his formidable Upmanns like a scepter to fellow moguls. And to the marquee names, Al Jolson, Maurice Chevalier, Jack Oakie, Adolph
Menjou, George Raft, Jimmy Cagney, and the racier pair of Marx
brothers, Chico and Zeppo. . . .

I remember the Mexican sexpot Lupe Velez, in a tight red dress in case no one would notice her, in the first row, so close to the corner she could stand up and touch the fighter on his stool. He happened to be a good-looking Mexican kid called Rojas. Between rounds the irrepressible Lupe would shout instructions to which he seemed to pay considerably more attention than to his manager and trainer. Since his vantage point, as she leaned forward to advise him, afforded him an inviting view down the plunging neckline, this was understandable. Rojas was doing pretty well until round four when Lupe called to him with urgent advice. As he turned his head to look at her, he took a crushing left to the jaw. Lupe sobbed as her nino took the count.

Fast forward to Mosley-De La Hoya: I have my ticket for a nonstop to LAX, I have my press credentials, and my folder of pre-fight clippings. I am almost as ready as the two gifted boys who will make L.A. shine as a fight town again.

And then, as if Oscar had landed that hard left hook to the heart (mine), I'm under the knife for a four-way bypass. On the night of The Fight I'm not back in L.A. ready with pen and paper to cover the fight. I'm in the hospital, remembering the long-ago night when our local heavyweight, Turkey Thompson, knocked Bob Pastor down seven times in round one. Pastor kept getting up. And finally, six rounds later, he chopped Turkey down. So there was hope. All I had to do was Pastor myself back into the fray. How would I cover Mosley-De La Hoya? My twenty-year-old Benn, who had been coming to Garden and Vegas fights with me in the Schulberg tradition since age twelve, would be out there in my place covering the weigh-in, the fight, and the press conference, faxing his notes and phoning in his take on everything that came down at Staples Center. Meanwhile another family expert on the Game, my seventeen-year-old Jessica, would tape the fight and I'd score it from my hospital bed. All I had to do was close my eyes, rev up my imagination, and I was on the scene.

As I waited for the bell I found myself listing my most dramatic memories of hometown rings. I was twelve years old the night my father took me to Vernon, where that hoary arena adjoined the slaughterhouse, its sickly sweet aroma, as from an invasion of skunks, following us to our ringside seats. There we rooted for our local boy, Mushy Callahan, sporting the six-pointed star of our Hollywood tribe, as he doubled up his jabs and danced forward to take the belt from the junior welterweight champion, Pinkey Mitchell. Mushy gave me the gloves he won the title with, and for years they hung reverentially above my bed.

There was our classy little flyweight, Fidel La Barba, who moved on from Olympic Gold to fight Jimmy McLarnin three times in his first six fights, a vest-pocket prodigy. A handful of fights later he was outfoxing the clever champ, Frankie Genaro, conqueror of Pancho Villa, with only one loss in sixty fights. Can we really pull these milestones back into memory seventy-five years later? Maybe it's because after Fidel retired, following a hairbreadth loss to Kid Chocolate in the Garden and a disastrous fight two weeks later in Chicago that cost him half his right eye, he had ambitions to become a writer and came to me to look over his stuff. Over the years we talked writing and fighting, and re-fought the Genaro victory that launched his notable if finally ill-fated career. Forty years after I'd first seen him in there with McLarnin, he was a co–best man at my marriage to Geraldine Brooks, along with the original Golden Boy, Art Aragon, who could lick all the local boys, if not Carmen Basilio.

I have only to shut my eyes and put my mind into rewind to watch again the nonpareil Henry Armstrong in with one of my all-time favorites, the inscrutable Baby Arizmendi. They had similar styles, in close without clinching, nonstop attack from two resolute little bulls. Baby had won the first two in Mexico City, but in the three I saw, each time a little more so, the Armstrong fury mounted until even Arizmendi's diehard Aztec resistance had to give. Armstrong came to Arizmendi V after thirty-six KOs in forty fights, and the only four who managed to go the distance were Barney Ross, from whom, as an overgrown featherweight, he had won the welterweight title; Lou Ambers, from whom he won the lightweight title; Ceferino Garcia, against whom he had defended his welterweight belt; and, of course, Baby Arizmendi, off whom punches seemed to bounce as if he were made of rubber. I see them still, in perpetual motion, and I knew back then I was in the presence of the greatest fighter I had ever seen.

A year later at L.A.'s Wrigley Field the incredible Armstrong, little more than a junior welterweight that night, was in there again with Ceferino Garcia, who had just won the middleweight title with an explosive knockout of tough champion Fred Apostoli. Ceferino had size, height, and reach on Henry that night, but there was Armstrong on the attack backing up Garcia in a furious fight called a draw, enabling Garcia to keep the title that I thought the little guy won.

I found myself personally involved in the next Garcia ballpark fight. Through the screenwriting Epstein brothers of *Casablanca* fame I had met Paul Moss, who had managed the boxing team at Penn State, where the Epsteins' teammate was Billy Soose. Billy turned pro with Paul still in his corner. I was with them the night Soose took the middleweight crown from clever Ken Overlin in the Garden. Paul and Billy liked having me around because my first novel, *What Makes Sammy Run?*, was an unexpected success critically and in the stores, and as someone having been banished from Hollywood for writing it, I was enjoying Eastern celebrity. I was with Paul in Toots Shor's when a phone call came in from L.A. with an offer for Billy to defend his title against Ceferino Garcia.

"It's a good money fight for us," Paul said. "Garcia's over the hill. Overlin licked him and so did Steve Belloise. And he's still a big draw in L.A. He's got the right style to make Billy look good."

Billy, Paul, and I stayed with my father at his big house in Windsor Square. For the hell of it, I went down to the Main Street Gym to watch Garcia train. Hard to tell with aging fighters, but he didn't look over the hill to me. After the workout, Garcia's manager, George Parnassus, whom I had known in my years on the L.A. scene, invited me to a drink at Abe Attell's bar next door. "Whatya think, my guy's lookin' good, huh?" I wondered where he was going. George was an operator. Beware of Greeks bearing gifts. "He's in shape, but you know, he's had a hundred and fifteen fights, we figure he's getting ready to pack it in. I figure you'll be talking to Paul . . ."

Uptown I delivered the unspoken message: Parnassus is looking to make a deal. Paul thinks a moment. "Who needs it? Garcia didn't look that good a year ago. Billy will box rings around him."

At Wrigley Field for seven rounds it goes exactly as Paul predicts. Billy's a nifty boxer, never a great puncher but playing skilled matador to Garcia's brave bull. But with seconds to go at the end of the round, a desperate Ceferino leapt in with a charge that opened an ugly cut in Billy's eyelid. Was it a crushing right hand or Garcia's head running interference?

Between rounds, with blood streaming from Billy's sliced eyelid, nothing could be done to close the wound. "I'm not going out," I heard Billy say. "Nothing's worth losing my eye." The bell for round eight found our dejected fighter still on his stool. Garcia's Hispanic cheering section in the cheap seats erupted in celebration. Ceferino by TKO! But referee Abe Roth saw it differently. The cut was the result of an illegal butt, he decided. Under California rules, a technical draw. Billy keeps his title. Enraged Latinos charged the ring, broke up the seats, set fires, and started beating up the flour-faces they assumed were Soose's people. On my way to the dressing room for the postmortem, I was so shaken I actually didn't recognize my father for a moment when he stopped me to commiserate.

Given the short-fuse or no-fused emotions of our Chicano fans, riots triggered by controversial decisions were an occupational hazard. The mega-millionaire and megalomaniac Jack Kent Cooke worshiped his Inglewood Forum like a cathedral. Some thirty years ago I was invited to be his guest for Lionel Rose's defense of his bantamweight title against the Mexican idol Chucho Castillo. The going was intense, all fifteen rounds, the sold-out Forum deafened with the chanting of "CHU-CHO! CHU-CHO!" At the final bell Castillo danced to his corner waving to his confident rooting section. But the decision went to Lionel Rose.

Another explosion. Worse, if possible, than at Wrigley Field. Raging Chicanos tore down the elegant Roman orange curtains my host was so proud of, and set them on fire. Seats were torn apart and piled up for bonfires. Cooke was screaming for more police! More firemen! Retreating to the club, we heard the mob was turning cars over in the parking lot and setting them on fire. I tried to call home to explain the delay, but the wires had been cut. We were under siege. A memorable postscript to the mayhem was the picture of the two little warriors—the polite Australian aborigine Lionel and the charismatic Mexican Indian Chucho talking quietly together at a small table while the battle involving them raged on outside.

"What possible language could they be talking?" someone asked me.

"Fistish," I said.

Back home, put back together again, I was ready to rerun the Shane and Oscar Show, recalling the glory days of L.A.'s classic welterweight title fights from McLarnin and Armstrong to Mantequilla Napoles and Pipino Cuevas.

The prologue was all Oscar, who made his old friend Shane wait fifteen minutes until he finally made his grand entrance, heralded by rousing mariachi music, a fireworks display that anticipated the 4th of July, and a deafening majority of the twenty thousand fanatics chanting his name. But Sugar Shane, the 13 to 5 underdog who had never faced a real welterweight test before, seemed serenely unperturbed. Through the long stage-wait he had kept smiling, looking confident and self-contained. And there was none of the customary "feeling out" in round one as he went at his famous rival with energy and style, with nifty jabs and straight right hands, one of which bounced hard off Oscar's sturdy chin.

Oscar was being outsped and outmaneuvered but not discouraged. He fought back with jabs of his own and, scoring with the main weapon, the big left hook to the body, he was regaining control. Between rounds four and five, an anxious Jack Mosley reminded his son, "You waited your whole life for this! Don't slow down!"

Still, in the next two rounds it was Oscar who kept the pressure on, backing Shane up, snapping his head back with the jabs, and scoring one-twos, one-two-threes that frustrated Shane's rhythm.

But in the seventh, it was as if Mosley had suddenly shifted from third gear to overdrive. Heeding his father's earlier advice, he was the aggressor now. Dramatically picking up the pace, moving in and out like the great ones of old, he was making Oscar's head a target for straight, rapid and punishing right hands. A turning-point round in what was developing into a fight living up to all the hype.

All but four of the twenty-five "experts" quoted in the program crystal-balled Oscar as the winner. Two dissenters were this writer and our prescient Benn, who filed this for me at the weigh-in: "I like Shane's confidence, his calmness on the eve, and I also like his speed against the slower De La Hoya." Shane was rewarding our faith, trailing by a few points but coming on. The exchanges were furious now, but Oscar was tiring and Shane was stronger and faster. Suddenly turning southpaw to defuse those left hooks to the body that Oscar had been scoring with earlier, he was confusing the champion. Then deftly turning back, he imposed his will with crisp jabs and arrow-straight right hands.

Winning round after round now, Mosley had wiped out Oscar's early lead. Going into the twelfth, there was good reason for Oscar's trainer, Roberto Alcazar, to warn his client, "You need this final round, but be careful."

But the last three minutes of this rouser of a fight were pure Sugar. At least ten right hands thrown with great accuracy and power rocked the very game but very tired De La Hoya. At the bell the almost 3 to 1 underdog had outpunched his bigger rival three-to-one. If this had been the old fifteen-round days, Oscar might have been down and out for the first time in his magical career.

In the ring, having blown his title, Oscar was civilized and gracious, acknowledging Shane's gifts, pleased that they had given the public a great fight, and agreeing that it called for a rematch.

Answering post-fight questions, Oscar was a banged up, weary, and schizo interviewee. Now he thought he had won by one point but wasn't given the decision because, in the cynical ways of the fight game, this would generate more money for the rematch. "To take it away from me was an injustice."

But retirement rather than revenge seemed to be Oscar's focus now. "I'm going to rethink my whole game plan in life. I'm thinking about my health and my life. I'm a businessman. I want to take care of my money and my health. . . ."

He had "enjoyed the slugfest," he said, but "not getting a knockout was not having my dream come true." In truth, take-out power had been absent from all his fights against top welterweights. Forty-eight rounds with Whitaker, Quartey, Trinidad, and Mosley.

If Oscar moves on to his singing career, his acting, architecture, managing his unprecedented millions, and all the other options he likes to ruminate about, I'll remember him not as the best L.A. Chicano fighter I ever saw, just the first to take on the aura of a rock star. And by light years the richest.

Meanwhile Shane Mosley, who credited "soul searching" for his overwhelming performance in the final rounds, is up there with the golden boys at last. Without Oscar's distractions, he's eager to prove he's more than a good fighter like De La Hoya. Maybe one of the great ones up there with legendary welterweights like the two Sugar Rays, Robinson and Leonard? Dream on. Stay tuned.

[2000]

P.S. Alas, I was searching for heroes in the mode of the great ones of old, from Barney Ross and Henry Armstrong to the lightweight version of Roberto Duran, unbeatable at 135. And believing I had found a twenty-first century model in Sugar Shane. And then he comes apart against a latter-day entry, Vernon Forrest, who in turn is taken out by the primitive Ricardo Mayorga, who is soon exposed as a mindless punching bag by Felix Trinidad, who then loses every round to the defensive marvel with the wicked right jab, Winky Wright. Our trouble today is that the top performers don't have enough fights to establish a creditable average. In the days when boxing was more of a mainline sport, the best fighters fought several times a month. They were gaining experience our best boys today will never know. Good God, while winning the featherweight title in 1937, Henry Armstrong fought twenty-six times. And after winning the world lightweight and welterweight titles in 1938, he fought fourteen times; in the following three years, after winning the welterweight title from Barney Ross (the greatest Jewish fighter since my old man's hero, the Great Benny Leonard) our little buzzsaw from L.A. defended his crown twenty times, finally losing it to Fritzie Zivic when he was beginning to slow down at last after one hundred fights, in there with a score of immortals and so many other toughies whose names still ring a bell with long-memoried old-timers.

A grand master in chess doesn't win a world title his first or second time out. He learns by playing other masters. Our chess game with blood is no different. If Sugar Shane had been fighting sixty or seventy years ago, he might have learned from a Vernon Forrest defeat how to cope with that type of fighter. Learning on the job, even when losing, was par for the course in those busy old days. But in today's fifty-to-a-million-dollar HBO or Showtime extravaganzas, to lose a mega-match, often that once-a-year PPV night for all the marbles, is to find yourself in virtual eclipse, if not retirement. Great fighters, indeed Hall of Famers, often lost their share. Kid Gavilan. Billy Graham. Jake LaMotta. Emile Griffith . . . a distinguished list. Because the quality of the opposition was so high and they fought so often. But today, with a lovely boxer like Shane Mosley (and three or four others come to mind), instead of three, it's one strike and you're out. Either you're a multi-million-dollar baby or a bum. I look before and after, and pine for the days when boxing was as frequently competitive as big-time tennis.

[2000]

VII. Mosley-De La Hoya, Act II

A FAR MORE COMPLICATED SPORT than most people realize, boxing is fencing, only with pain involved. It's a chess game in which the board is the body and face of the opponent. Jose Torres, the literate and notable ex–light heavyweight champion, calls it "the art of lying." What separates able boxers from merely tough fighters is their ability to outthink an opponent, feint him out of position in order to score. It can be done with gloves, shoulders, head moves. Now you see it, now you don't. The old wizard Willie Pep comes to mind, and the ancient heavyweight cutie Jersey Joe Walcott, who knew so many feints he was said even to be able to feint with his eyebrows.

The best two junior middleweights in the world, and two of the very top fighters in the game, Sugar Shane Mosley and Oscar De La Hoya, aren't quite in that Houdini class. But they put on a remarkable exhibition of boxing at its almost best in the turbulent Las Vegas MGM Grand Casino Arena last Saturday evening. A million PPV buys made it the second richest nonheavyweight event in history (just behind De La Hoya-Trinidad) and the home viewers, noisy and partisan live audience, and sold-out closed-circuit theaters all over Las Vegas got their money's worth. They saw a close, smartly boxed contest that lacked the fireworks of their first meeting as they boxed through all the opening rounds with so much respect for each other that the great beast (the crowd) that lurks in the dark around the ring and up to the rafters began to boo for more action. But the boys boxed on. They knew each other almost too well from their first encounter when De La Hoya, the 3 to 1 favorite, was unable to match Mosley's blazing speed, or his stamina in the late rounds, and lost for what he thought of as the first time in his life, having questioned with some reason his controversial loss to Trinidad.

This time—as fans flooded in from all over the country and Mexico for the rematch hyped as Revenge for De La Hoya, and Redemption for Oscar (but also for Shane after his two unexpected

Oscar De La Hoya (right) fighting Arturo Gatti in Las Vegas, 2001. (Pat Orr)

defeats at the hands of Vernon Forest), Oscar was boasting that his new trainer Floyd Mayweather, Sr., had taught him how to neutralize Shane's speed. The loudmouthed ex-fighter, ex-drug addict Floyd had almost come to blows with Shane's quiet-spoken father and trainer at the pre-fight press conference after Oscar's man had read some dreadful, sub-Ali doggerel to the effect that "after Oscar meets Shane, your boy'll never be the same."

For all the braggadocio, Oscar seemed to be following the new game plan as he doubled and tripled up on his jab to keep Shane off balance in the first half of the bout and scored with straight right hands. But Shane maintained his poise, bobbing and weaving and patiently waiting for an opening, losing close rounds that seemed more one-sided than they really were because the rabidly pro-Mexican crowd roared every time the favorite's punch landed—and sometimes when it didn't—and fell silent when the classy underdog scored his own jabs or dug punishing left hooks to the body. Meanwhile those watching on television had their vision of the fight colored by the HBO ringside team, Larry Merchant, Jim Lampley, and Big George Foreman, who sounded more like a De La Hoya rooting section than objective commentators as they described a fight so different from what the official judges (and these eyes) seemed to be watching.

After four careful and technically interesting rounds, the action began to heat up in the fifth, which built to a furious exchange at the bell. The De La Hoya rooters were so loud that it was hard to hear oneself think, but I gave the round to Mosley. Oscar might have been winning the Compustat totals, but I felt the power in Mosley, and Oscar must have been feeling it too. Body punching is something of a lost art in modern boxing. It's not as flashy as punches to the head, but it can prove more deadly. Body punches wear a fighter down and slow him up in the later rounds.

It was still intangible, and Oscar seemed to be winning the fight, but that's exactly what was happening to him. After six rounds I had him leading four rounds to two, but Oscar's questionable stamina was about to be tested again. Slowly the tide was turning. Two of the three judges gave Mosley the last five rounds, and I had him winning five of the last six, hurting Oscar with so many fiercely thrown left hooks that the partisan crowd grew eerily quiet and the underdog rooters began chanting MOS-LEY! MOS-LEY! Oscar was able and willing but soooo tired. The unanimous decision, 115 to 113 in favor of the new and now redeemed champion, put the Sugar back in Shane and struck this corner as exactly right. The pained silence of the disappointed throng seemed a reluctant agreement with the judges. But the HBO trio were outraged. They denounced the verdict as highway robbery. George Foreman even went so far as to charge that it was a fix or conspiracy against promoter Bob Arum. By odd coincidence, I happened to come out from the arena with George, who is an old friend all the way back to Ali/Zaire days. He was surprised that I had seen the fight so differently from him, and when boxing historian Bert Randolph Sugar chimed in on my behalf, he made a face and said, "Wow, if you two think Mosley won, maybe I went too far!"

Bob Arum and his $20 million meal ticket showed no such grace. At the post-fight press conference the overheated Arum was posturing that he would never promote another fight in a state that allows gambling on boxing. Apparently after having promoted scores of fights in Vegas, he had just discovered that betting on fights was legal in Nevada. Oscar took up where his promoter left off, insisting that he had won the fight and threatening that he had the resources to hire the best lawyers and seek a reversal of the decision. He wasn't doing this for selfish reasons, he insisted. Not at all. He was doing this for the good of boxing, to clean up the sport. Give us a break, Oscar. With your purse of $23 million (to the winner's measly $5 million) you're not only crying all the way to the bank but shamelessly raining on Shane's victory parade.

From the *Los Angeles Times* to all the New York papers and on to the BBC and the clear-eyed Steve Bunch, the working press called it as we did. So did Hitman Tommy Hearns and Lennox Lewis. And when ace trainer Teddy Atlas reran the tape silently he found that without the HBO spin he had to reverse his decision. So add one more knowledgeable vote to the Mosley column. Instead of fighting it out in court, Oscar should be looking to fight it out in the ring. The rematch deserves a rematch. But let's not hold our breath. Despite his protestations, we doubt Oscar wants to get back in the ring with Shane, even for another twenty mil.

De La Hoya is still a very good fighter, but his dream of ending up as one of the all-time greats in the company of Louis, Ali, and Robinson is dashed by that nagging lack of stamina. If he were a racehorse he would be a great miler and might even win the Derby, but he'd never win the Belmont. The thoroughbred Mosley would always run by him at a mile and a half.

See you at the next one, George. And don't be too upset about our friendly disagreement. You know what they say about great champions. They can do everything—except pick a winner.

[2003]

VIII. The Real Main Event: Arum vs. King

WHAT OPTIMISTS like to call the Information Age may be more accurately identified as the Misinformation Age. With the verbal Niagara of the internet and the magical leap through the wires of the fax machines, the force of the old-fashioned P. T. Barnum pitchmen has been multiplied, magnified, and amplified ten thousand times ten thousand.

How else to explain the astronomy of the hype that kept building Oscar De La Hoya vs. Feliz Trinidad to heights never before reached in the history of boxing's nonheavyweight championships? It was to be, the latter-day hypesters assured us, nothing less than the "Fight of the Millennium."

That modest claim alone should have put us on guard against letdowns and anti-climaxes. If our two young, undefeated welterweights were really to create together the fight of the last one thousand years, where would that leave Louis and Conn, Robinson and La Motta, Leonard and Hearns, not to mention Mendoza and Humphries, Cribb and Molineaux? Or Hamilton and Burr?

A millennium used to mean one thousand years, but in the quick-talk of the hypester it's become a fancy mouthful for 1999, which seems to work fine because the memory of Generation X doesn't seem to reach back much farther than that. Remembering Emile Griffith's classic series with Benny Paret and Luis Rodriguez or the Robinson-Gavilan-Billy Graham-Basilio days, we wondered how Trinidad-De La Hoya could qualify as the Fight of the Century much less all that millennium jazz. Indeed, the overcautious encounter, with Oscar sticking and moving and Felix chasing and missing for nine boring rounds, followed by an out-of-gas Oscar running for his life in the last three, with the desperate Felix finally loading up on those chopping right hands, didn't even make it the Fight of the Night. There was more emotion in the cruiserweight semi-final as Dale Brown (who he?) stood his ground against the Kazakhstan Terror, Vassily Jirov, only to take a devastating blow to the belt line that left the tan kid from Calgary gasping for breath and momentarily paralyzed.

The most dramatic moments in the Trinidad-De La Hoya dance were left to their respective promoters, the fight game's artistically juxtaposed odd couple, Don King and Bob Arum. If words could score knockdowns and draw blood, Arum would have been in danger of having the press conference stopped to save him from further punishment. Through months of bitter negotiations on how to cut up the biggest boxing pie in welterweight history, Arum had held the upper hand with De La Hoya his crossover star eclipsing Trinidad, whose following was limited to Puerto Rico and hard-core fight fans. King and his boy had to settle for half of Arum and Oscar's $21 million guarantee.

But the unexpected split decision had created a dramatic turnaround. Waving his little Puerto Rican flag, the teflon Don, who's got more lives than a litter of cats, actually broke into a victory dance while the usually articulate Arum was choking on silence, his complexion reddening to the point where reporters wondered if it might presage a heart attack.

"Good has triumphed over evil!" King announced, with that championship *chutzpah* that has made him the despair of his army of detractors. "The lights have gone out in Arumsville! The air is out of the balloon! Felix Trinidad is the greatest welterweight in the world! He ran down the rabbit! Viva Felix Trinidad! Viva Puerto Rico!" The Rs became more Hispanically accentuated as Don rose to the occasion, the once and future king.

My notes read: "Press conference much more exciting than fight. Don screaming. Bob sweating. The Don-and-Bob show. Don ecstatic. Bob tortured. 'You look like your mother just died,' a Latin reporter twists the knife." Bob tries to remind the press corps that twenty of twenty-four of those polled at ringside had Oscar winning, with only two for Trinidad and two scoring it a draw. But Don was in his element now, spewing the eloquence he mastered in the prison library.

What a delicious contrast, these two: Arum, the Harvard Law School graduate recruited for Bob Kennedy's Department of Justice, and King, the prize student of the University of the Street who earned his Masters in Self-Promotion in the Ohio penitentiary.

Only in Fight Game America could this pair from the opposite ends of the social spectrum be brought together to co-promote their incredibly enriching but artistically disappointing spectacle.

Like the other major fight of the year, Holyfield-Lewis, this had ended in the kind of split-decision controversy that inevitably leads to talk of a rematch. Strictly on points, De La Hoya had a thin edge, but tired and overconfident, convinced he had enough winning rounds "in the bank," he had passively surrendered to Trinidad at least the last three rounds. If Oscar won the contest, he blew the fight.

"I want to be one of the great legends of boxing," he keeps saying. But all the great legends we've seen, from Armstrong to Ali, fought the last round as if their lives depended on it. Oscar "fought" this one as if his profile depended on it, as he took great pains to protect that for the movie offers that could be in the offing.

So, will there be a rematch? Back to the Don-and-Bob show. "I have no problem with the rematch," King chortles. "I would say 'immediamente' in Spanish, 'immediately' in English and 'right now!' if you speak street. Nothin' to negotiate. Just take the contract we had 'n turn it upside down. Put my name on top 'n yours on the bottom." "That'll be the day," the outmatched, outvoiced Arum tried to interpose. But Don is all over him, throwing more punches than Oscar and Felix in their twelve rounds of inaction. "Short-time pain for long-term gain!" King gloats. "Oscar's shining star has dimmed! He's no longer the Golden Boy, he's . . ." For a moment the volume drops. Don's mike is dead. "Shut the hell up!" Arum had suggested, before deciding to do that for him by pulling the plug.

But Bob Arum should have known that Don King carries his own built-in amplification system. From his numbers-running days in the mean streets of Cleveland, he had known the power of the human voice, and now he only had to notch it up a few decibles to accuse: "You see, censorship! Can you believe this in America? A clandestine conspiracy! Sabotage! I thought they only did this in Russia! Or Red China! They can't stand the truth! Can't accept that Tito [Trinidad] is the greatest in the world! Viva Tito! Viva Puerrrto Rrrrico!"

And then, finally, this contemporary, improbable Black Tex Rickard was off to the victory party and Bob Arum and his disappointed and disappointing champion were left at the podium with $21 million worth of egg on their faces.

Would I fly across the country again to see Trinidad-De La Hoya II? Not if they boxed with as much mutual self-respect as they did the first time. But it might be worth it to catch the rematch between the canny Harvard barrister Bob Arum and the born-again Puerto Rican patriot and Ohio slammer's gift to pugilistica, the self-acclaimed champion of Good over Evil, Maestro King.

"I've been to the mountain top," Martin Luther King said, "and I've seen the promised land." Don King's style is to buy the mountain. And as for the promised land, Don'll tell you he's got options on it.

[2000]

After an eighteen-month layoff following his knockout loss to Bernard Hopkins for the middleweight crown, Oscar took on the Nicaraguan Dirty Mouth, Ricardo Mayorga, for the WBC 154-pound title, and added one more championship belt to his collection. So what's next for the Golden Boy? He could hang 'em up after the most remunerative career by a non-heavyweight in the history of the sport, and devote the rest of his life to his successful boxing promotions and investments. Or he could hold to his dream of a farewell fight on Mexican Independence Day, September 16. The only problem is, with Felix Trinidad in retirement, the logical rivals are the defensive marvel Winky Wright, or Floyd Mayweather, Jr. If I were Oscar, I'd stay home with the gorgeous wife and kiddies, and all those businesses working for him. He doesn't need the twenty mil. He's done more for the popularity of boxing than anyone since Muhammad Ali. That should be honor enough, as instead of Winky and Floyd, he takes on Arum and King, in his new role as head of Golden Boy Promotions.

[2006]

11

Lennox Lewis:
The Reluctant Dragon

I. Lewis-Golota: The Bigger They Are . . .

THERE ARE TIMES when the theatrical titles of major fights carry more entertainment punch than the event itself. After the recent epidemic of disastrous evenings in pursuit of the heavyweight championship of the world—the Tyson Bite Fight, Oliver McCall's nervous breakdown in his loss to Lennox Lewis, and Henry Akinwande's impersonation of a frightened octopus in his hapless challenge to the recrowned Lewis—the public was assured that next time Lewis went in there, things would be different. Wasn't Andrew Golota the Polish assassin? For the first time since Rocky Marciano in the fifties, and the brief reign of Ingemar Johansson in '59–'60, a new heavyweight on the scene was given a serious chance to become the first white heavyweight champion in forty years.

True, his twenty-eight victories were amassed over the usual collection of "opponents," with the possible exception of Samson Po'uha whom he butted and bit and finally knocked flat in five. Still, in his two DQ losses to Riddick Bowe, Golota had badly punished and outclassed the rich and enigmatic former champion, and done it with a lively jab, power punches that had Bowe reeling, and impressive speed for a man as big as an NFL linebacker at 6 feet 4, 240-plus pounds. If you took away the mindless low blows that cost him the Bowe fights, Golota was essentially undefeated, which is virtually the way the oddsmakers saw it as they made Andrew (Foul Pole) Golota even money against the far more experienced WBC champion who had lost only one fight (a quick knockout at the hands of McCall) in his somehow lackluster eight-year campaign to convince the American public that he was a worthy and legitimate heavyweight champion.

In more than thirty fights after winning Olympic gold (and defeating Bowe), Lewis had demonstrated explosive take-out power with straight right hands that had destroyed Mike Weaver, Razor Ruddock, Frank Bruno, and Tommy Morrison. But a tendency to lose concentration and drift marked his fights to decision with Tony Tucker and Ray Mercer.

So it was Golota and not the British-born champion who had caught the imagination of the crowd, that great beast who lurks in the darkness of the arena and now in living rooms and bars on every continent.

Much of the support for Golota was nasty racist. For all the gains of the civil rights movement, with African Americans now looming as gridiron heroes rather than pariahs at Alabama, Mississippi, and Georgia universities, the serpent of prejudice still slithers across our American landscape. No one would actually come out in public and call Golota the Great White Hope. But in a sea of black heavyweight champions and top contenders, he was the only Caucasian game in town, and a lot of suppressed resentment of black domination of the fight game triggered the prolonged ovation for Golota when the Lewis fight was first announced.

So, "The Bigger They Are, the Harder They Brawl" seemed an appropriate teaser for the proposed toe-to-toe between the 6 foot 5, 250-pound Lewis and an opponent of almost equal height and weight.

Feeling in the sold-out Convention Center on the Boardwalk of Atlantic City was running high. Indeed, that is understatement. It was boiling over. Especially in the cheap seats in the balcony where the large and rowdy Golota rooting section, waving Polish flags and swilling beer, found a ready opposition in the British boys flashing their Union Jacks and matching the Poles bottle for bottle and taunt for taunt. The atmosphere recalled the notorious soccer wars that have taken the lives of overwrought fans from England to Italy. This seemed to be a case of The Drunker They Are, the Harder They Brawl as fights broke out all over the upper tier. There was a hairy moment when a couple of Golota supporters with faces decorated in the colors of the Polish flag were dangling over the edge of the balcony a struggling Brit draped in a full-size Union Jack. Security officials, who were all over the hall this time (in contrast to their insufficient numbers and failure to control the ethnic riot in the Garden for Bowe-Golota I), saved Lewis's man from a fifty-foot swan dive into the crowded five-hundred-dollar seats below.

By the time "God Save the Queen" had been played, and the seemingly endless Polish national anthem, patriotic allegiances had been whipped to fever pitch. Everybody was ready for battle, it seemed, except one of the combatants, or should we say, the supposed-to-be-combatant. Andrew Golota, the hulking tough from Warsaw by way of Chicago, who had talked so boldly for the TV cameras about his readiness to achieve his dream of becoming heavyweight champion, had been whistling Dixie, or whatever they whistle in Warsaw to summon bravado to cover up fear. In truth, hours before the fight, Andrew had suffered a severe anxiety attack. Be it fear or stage fright, the giant Golota's behavior suggested that he had just heard that the death penalty was about to be enforced in the State of New Jersey. His crime? Presuming to contend for WBC's baroque heavyweight belt without being emotionally prepared to mount the stage. Instead of riding to the arena in style, Golota decided to walk from Caesars Palace to the ring site about a mile down the tawdry pawn shops and delapidated liquor stores of Tennessee Avenue.

Professional fighters get to the grounds about two hours before fight time to rest, prepare themselves mentally, and warm up for half an hour. But Golota arrived just thirty minutes before his ring appointment, to veteran cornerman Lou Duva's consternation.

Attendants noticed that he was pale and cold. As referee Joe Cortez gave the traditional instructions, Lewis reminded me of a revved-up thoroughbred entering the starting gate. You could almost feel the power and confidence radiating from him as he stared—not into Golota's eyes, because the challenger in refrigerated anxiety could not bring himself to look at his executioner.

I had wondered about Golota's state of mind the evening before in the Caesars Palace version of Planet Hollywood, where the usually upbeat Lou Duva had joined us for a few minutes. He was sky-high on his kid in the eight-rounder opening the telecast, Fernando Vargas. "I'm in love with a beautiful blond," he quipped, "a dynamite kid, a coming champion." But when I asked him about his entry in the main event, I was struck by his failure to accentuate the positive. I don't remember when I've heard a trainer or manager predict less than convincing victory for his corner. In Vegas for the De La Hoya fight, Camacho's trainer Pat Burns told me he was so high on Macho that he wouldn't be surprised if he won by KO. So much for the credibility of trainers' predictions. Now in the gaudy, starstruck café, Duva was saying, "I don't know. We'll see. He's a funny kid. Strong as hell. But you never know what's going on in his head. We'll just have to see tomorrow night."

Not exactly an overwhelming vote of confidence, I noted at the time.

Now they were coming out of their corners for round one, Lewis breaking smartly from the gate like Cigar, and Golota like the blindfolded nag of the picador already sensing the punishment in store.

With the first ticks of the ring clock, the bravado title "The Harder They Brawl" was obsolete. A series of quick jabs and fervent right hands to the unprotected Caucasian jaw and Golota was doing a Peter McNeeley, down and nearly out before some of the Fancy had found their scalper-priced fifteen-hundred-dollar seats. Cortez allowed the massacre to continue a few more ticks as the now semi-conscious Golota stumbled into more overhand rights than he needed to convince himself, the now-silenced

Poles, and the boisterous Brits that the "Brawl" was just another ignominious first-round-over-and-out.

In Lewis's career, 1997 will be remembered as the year he defeated an emotional wreck, a clutch artist, and a self-destructive anxiety freak. As Lewis himself put it neatly if not so kindly at the press conference, "I just wanted to get rid of all the misfits in the heavyweight world."

Back in his dressing room, misfit No. 3, trying to work up nerve to meet the nosy press, suddenly pitched forward, his body shaking in convulsions, in danger of swallowing his tongue. According to Gary Hope, an ex-boxer friend of mine in the Golota camp, no paramedic or doctor was immediately available (a strange oversight given Golota's condition on leaving the ring). A quick-thinking assistant trainer shoved his leather wallet in Golota's mouth to save him from suffocating on his own tongue. For at least ten seconds his heart had stopped completely, as if God was counting him out along with Joe Cortez. But next morning he was released from the local Medical Center with no brain damage indicated on the CAT scan. In other words, whatever brains Golota brought to Atlantic City he still retained when he returned to Chicago, to brood on his next career move. The honest WWF might be a suitable venue. In that world of theatrically packaged violence, our chopped-down Pole could bite, aim for the wedding tackle, and employ those other endearing tactics so cherished by the Neanderthals who actually seem to believe what they're seeing at their wrestling "championships."

Meanwhile, on the high road and taken seriously at last is the now focused and very determined Mr. Lewis, who may be as good as the British boxing fraternity have been trying to tell us. "If he had been an American fighter you would have had him up there with Holyfield and Tyson long before this," a London correspondent complained in the press room. "He's the best in the world right now. He'll knock out Holyfield."

Lewis vs. the winner of Holyfield/Moorer is the logical title fight come spring '98. If this were Wimbledon or the U.S. Open, these would be the mandatory finalists. But expecting logic in the Byzantine world of boxing is like expecting Fidel Castro and Jesse

Helms to sign a mutual admiration pact. Lewis punches people for HBO and the WBC. Holyfield/Moorer, by hook or by crook, is a Don King promotion now, on the rival cable's Showtime, with WBA and IBF titles as the bait. Getting these disparate elements together takes a bit of doing. Like getting Iran and Iraq to join in a co-production of "Yankee Doodle Dandy."

But for the sake of unity, clarity, and sanity in pugilistica (well, we can dream, can't we?), let's join our British cousins in hoping Lennox Lewis gets the opportunity to move on from the misfits to meet the best heavyweight left standing in 1998. And thus restore to the much-abused championship of the top division its traditional mystique.

[1998]

II. The Emperor Has No Clothes

SO ONCE AGAIN Lennox Lewis—in his five-round TKO of the latest pretender to the crown—proves himself to be the Rodney Dangerfield of the heavyweight division. Yes, he is the champion of the world, at least in the myopic eyes of the WBC. And yes, he has lost only one fight in ten years (albeit an embarrassing knockout at the hands of embarrassing Oliver McCall). And yes, three heavyweight champions—Riddick Bowe, Mike Tyson, and now Evander Holyfield—have managed to avoid his persistent challenge, in which he says, in his own soft, English-accented voice, that he is indeed "the greatest heavyweight in the world today."

Maybe. But if so, after defending his title successfully against the only man ever to keep him down (McCall) and the Carnera-sized contender (Akinwande), and then the conqueror of George Foreman (at least officially), Shannon Briggs, why did Lewis once again leave the ring with the rude booing of unimpressed fans pursuing him to the dressing room while their cheers were reserved for the bravehearted but still obviously inexperienced loser, young Mr. Briggs? Why is this elegant black man built to epic proportions at 6 feet 5 and 245 pounds—the only British-born boxer to win a heavyweight belt since Bob Fitzsimmons a hundred years ago—vocally disrespected at every performance?

While it may mystify the thirty-two-year-old Lewis, who could attribute it to anti-British feelings that go all the way back to our eighteenth-century Revolution (and manager Frank Maloney doesn't help matters as an over-the-top patriotic fashion plate in his tailored Union Jack), still this old ringsider has seen enough of Lewis's appearances to understand why our fans continue to be underwhelmed and make those rude noises despite his string of KOs.

Take round one of the recent Briggs encounter. Lewis came out like a champion determined to impose his will, jabbing and moving forward, a game plan that worked very nicely for all of thirty seconds, when the strong but raw challenger found he could tag Lewis solidly with a left hook to the jaw. Follow-up blows were soon driving the WBC champion backward. An excited Shannon Briggs was moving forward now, tagging the panicked Lewis again and again. Instead of beating a strategic retreat, moving away from danger, or knowing how to stop suddenly and tie his man up, Lewis literally turned his back and cowered against the ropes. Yes, he was an Olympic gold medalist (indeed, stopping talented young Riddick Bowe), but this defenseless behavior as Briggs drove him back against the ropes, with only those strands saving him from a possible knockdown, reminded us that after more than thirty professional fights a Lewis in serious trouble could revert to the sorriest kind of amateur mistakes.

If the round had been twenty seconds longer, or if Briggs had had a tick more ring savvy, the 12 to 1 underdog might have won an unprecedented one-round victory. In the press sections all the "experts" (which included everyone I polled before the opening bell) who saw Lewis as an easy one- or two-round winner, looked at each other in self-bemused shock. We were beginning to question Lewis's chin, remembering that Frank Bruno had him ready to go. And the McCall thing. A very serious demerit for a heavyweight: chin trouble.

To his credit, Lennox was able to regroup for round two, reestablish his jab, and move forward, though he's not exactly a

Larry Holmes, or even a Holyfield, when it comes to aggressive forward rhythm. He won the round but with a mouth sucking for air. A front-runner again but with the ugly first round having taken its toll. He was wanting in stamina.

In the next two rounds Lewis was winning the jabbing debate and throwing his specialty, crossing right hands that knocked Briggs down so hard that it now became a question of how many times the gutsy but unsophisticated challenger could get up. But to everyone's surprise, and especially Lewis's, he not only struggled to his feet but swung wild, desperate blows, some of which landed. And each time he did, Lewis was shaken again. Even against a dazed, wide-open opponent, he was unable to slip, defect, or duck the punches coming at him, deficiencies that made for an exciting fight rather than proof of Lewis's (and trainer Emanuel Steward's) claim to being the world's No. 1 heavyweight.

Round five. Lewis was tired, but not too tired to knock the battered Briggs down again. Once more the former model climbed that ten-story ladder back up off the canvas. This time he swung so wildly and futilely that the momentum carried him back to the floor. A grateful Lewis, breathing hard, saw the merciful referee move in to save the exhausted challenger from ineffectual heroics.

So the heavyweight championship circus rolls on, the flawed and vulnerable WBC champion to meet the unproven Croatian, Zeljko Mavrovic, while WBA-IBF champion Evander Holyfield takes on Henry (The Octopus) Akinwande, who qualified for the honor by getting himself DQ'd for hanging onto Lennox Lewis like a life raft in a storm.

So we're saying again that the only contest that deserves billing for the "Heavyweight Championship of the World" is Holyfield vs. Lewis. After watching Lewis use his left jab erratically, alternating crisp with tentative, throwing straight right hands a la Holmes, but unable to stay in focus three minutes a round, one would think Evander might lower his asking price from $20 million to a modest $16 million to unify the titles.

But this isn't the fight game; it's the boxing business where the champions, managers, promoters, and cable guys will keep on giving fight fans the business until a stand-up commissioner—a Senator John McCain, if you will—imposes order and reason on a fascinating sport mired in greed, galloping egos, and anarchy.

As the first boxing editor of *Sports Illustrated*, fifty years ago, I founded a mythical organization called APPPFF, the Association for the Protection of the Poor Put-upon Fight Fan. After watching the champions and their sponsors loop around each other in the Gimme Gimme Waltz, maybe it's time to call the old boys back into action again.

[1998]

III. Lennox Lewis: A Want of Passion

THERE WAS A TIME when I regarded the heavyweight champion of the world with a reverence just this side of religious fervor.

I never met the early heroes of the century, Jim Jeffries and Jack Johnson. But when Jack Dempsey came to our house in Hollywood in the mid-twenties, courting my mother's friend, actress Estelle Taylor, I remember worrying that the hand that was shaking his was damp with awe. My father had told me of his explosive knockout of the Argentine wild man Luis Firpo.

In the Golden Age of Babe Ruth, Red Grange, Bill Tilden, and Bobby Jones, the heavyweight champion of the world was still the greatest of the great. He walked with Epeus, whom Homer hailed in his blow-by-blow description of a classic KO of Euryalus, who "Beneath the ponderous arm's resistless sway / Down dropped he nerveless and extended lay."

From Homer to Mailer, we have revered our undisputed champions. We think of Louis and Marciano, Foreman and Ali, our gods of the heavyweight mystique. We think of the special hush that comes over us as we tense forward in the darkness of the arenas, with millions more plugged into television, the whole world holding its breath as the announcer intones those magic words: "Ladies and gentlemen, for the heavyweight championship of the world . . ."

The heavyweight champion was no mortal man but stood with Lancelot and Galahad, no longer merely a splendid fist fighter but a legendary hero. Even those people who disdain boxing as a brutal sport had to acknowledge the magic and symbolism of the heavyweight championship.

When Jack Johnson won it some ninety years ago, white America was so affronted that it had to pass a special law to entrap the black champion and drive him from the country. And the only way he could return was without that precious belt.

When Joe Louis destroyed Max Schmeling, millions of Americans who had never seen a boxing match cheered him as the defender of democracy against fascism, a victorious portent of the war to come.

And when Ali returned from his exile in the Vietnam years, he became a hero of Greek proportions to the Bob Dylan generation. Whether he faced Frazier or Norton or Foreman, he seemed to be fighting not only for black pride—somehow succeeding in making his noble black rivals "white"—but for some mysterious universal principle.

Which brings us up to—or rather down to—the first undisputed champion of the twenty-first century: the Jamaican-Canadian-Brit, Lennox Lewis Esq.

A marvelous physical specimen at 6 feet 5, 250 pounds, the first British-born heavyweight to hold the title in over a century, alas our new standard-bearer has neither magic nor mystique.

For someone so physically well endowed, he is curiously and annoyingly lacking in fistic passion. He is not a fighter who throws caution to the wind. Indeed he seems to embrace that doubtful quality like a seductive mistress. He has, at times, an exceptional jab. But instead of snapping it consistently, like the excellent Larry Holmes, at least half the time he is content to paw with it, not so much careless as lazy. He has power in his right hand, but again, unless there's an easy opening, he keeps it cocked without firing, like a sniper who doesn't fire because it will expose his position.

Lewis (right) meeting Holyfield for the first time in Madison Square Garden, March 1999. (Pat Orr)

In the first go with Holyfield, on my scorecard he won nine of the twelve rounds but had to settle for a suspicious draw. Lewis was facing what looked like a very old warrior, piling up points with his jab. But nothing reflects character more nakedly than boxing, and Lewis's comes across as smug, self-satisfied, and lazy. He does enough to win, in a style frustrating and boring. You want to send him reruns of Larry Holmes's fights so he could see what a series of swift jabs and straight right hands can accomplish. Holmes had skill and will. Lewis has skill and won't.

In the rematch last November, Holyfield showed he's finally on the cusp of fistic senility. But at least this time he tried to jab with Lennox and to move in under that eighty-four-inch reach. In the middle rounds he was finally scoring, wobbling Lewis with old-fashioned right hands. But that was to be the high-water mark for doughty old Evander, who kept walking into trouble in rounds eight through eleven.

And that's where Lewis showed his curiously passive fistic character. Instead of taking advantage of Evander's visual fatigue, he kept on with his lazy jabs and only occasional combinations. In the twelfth and final round our new champion borrowed a page from Oscar De La Hoya. With only three minutes to go he had obviously scored the bout in his head and figured he didn't need the round to win. He let the old man take it by default. By not trying hard enough.

Even so, we had Lewis up by two. But we couldn't get mad at ringside colleagues who saw it for the Holy man from Atlanta. Give him an "A" for a valiant last stand.

So now, at last, we have a champion who's got all three belts—or is it half a dozen? But flying home from the clang and clatter of Las Vegas, we couldn't help comparing this largely lackluster fight with the great ones we've seen.

Heavyweight history: the 169-pound Billy Conn going into the thirteenth round ahead on points and wanting to knock Joe Louis out; Rocky Marciano, battered and bloody, taking out Jersey Joe Walcott with a savage and historic right hand in another unforgettable thirteenth; the inspired Ali taking Foreman's best shots and then stopping Big George in the mesmerizing eighth on Conrad's fabled Congo River. . . .

That's what we fly across continents and oceans to see.

But, as my old friend, AP veteran Eddie Schuyler, said to me as we were comparing notes on the new champion's chess-game performance, "They don't have great fights any more . . ." At least in the heavyweight division.

So, do we pass on the next heavyweight title fight? To be a fight fan is to be a cockeyed—or is it black-eyed—optimist, with hope everlasting.

On the roll call of challengers, Michael Grant still looks green. David Tua is strong but predictable. Maybe if they got Ike What's-his-name out of jail. . . . Or reinvent rusty Iron Mike . . . ? Somewhere on this planet there must be a heavyweight who brings passion and intensity to a heavyweight division now ruled by a reluctant dragon.

In the name of Epeus, Daniel Mendoza, Joe Louis and Ali, *please* bring back the heavyweight mystique.

[2000]

▪ 12 ▪

Roy Jones, Jr.:
The Pensacola Pinwheel

I. Genius at Work

LAST JUNE I went down to Atlantic City to see for myself just how great a fighter was Roy Jones, Jr. He was in there with Vinny Pazienza, once a crowd-pleasing lightweight champion, now blown up to 168 pounds or more. Paz looked strong as a bull, and he fought like a bull, at least the brave ones, coming straight at you and eating punishment.

That was made to order for Jones, whose classy left jab seemed permanently attached to Vinny's unprotected face. At one point my notes showed: "Six piston-like jabs, split seconds apart, ripping Vinny's eyes." Roy was so fast, the futilely aggressive Pazienza literally couldn't see those jabs coming, nor the punishing left hooks and straight right hands that Roy throws from gloves carried unconventionally low, like the Ali of old. That's a dangerous stance unless you've got the lightning speed to bring those gloves into punching position—no peekaboo for Jones—he's got the speed, and he's got what very few speedsters ever have, the power.

This was not so much a fight (except on Paz's side) as a bravura performance by the Pensacola Pinwheel. Halfway through the first round the handwriting wasn't written on the wall, it was written on Vinny's pugnacious but shock-absorbing face. Vinny would lunge at him and try to throw his punishing but not finishing punches. Roy would avoid them with his dancer's

140

Roy Jones, Jr., found Vinny Pazienza's style made to order for his speed and power. (Pat Orr)

mobility. Every time the willing Pazienza committed himself, Roy made him pay the price.

The Pazienza style, in supper-club-fighter tradition, is to move forward and intimidate opponents with strength and aggression. That has worked well enough to beat all but a handful of top boxers ringwise enough to neutralize aggression. He was not the best of the super-middleweights, but had earned the shot by twice beating a ring-geriatric Roberto Duran, who should be home rocking on his porch in Panama City, enjoying his scrapbooks on his triumphs in the seventies.

Still, nobody had ever knocked out the durable Pazienza, and there were even smarties like Angelo Dundee and Emanuel Steward who saw it as a hard fight that would go the distance. Going in, I saw it like the inimitable Bert (The Hat) Randolph Sugar: "Vinny is so overmatched, all I want is the ambulance concession."

Thank the Lord of Boxing, this time there was no Jimmy Garcia or Gerald McClellan tragedy. When the ever-willing but hopelessly outclassed Pazienza was knocked down twice, eyes cut, face swollen, gasping in exhaustion, Roy Jones was ready to call it an evening. He put his arms out straight and made eye contact with referee Tony Orlando to move in and avoid his having to hit the helpless opponent again. But the brave Orlando foolishly let it continue. Jones hesitated a moment, then brought up a devastating uppercut to what was left of Vinny's face, caught the reeling Vinny in a flurry of punches too rapid to count, and the end had come none too soon for the valiant but mismatched, colorful but essentially defenseless Pazienza.

Roy Jones had his twenty-fifth knockout in an undefeated string of twenty-nine fights. Having already defused the best of the super-middles, James Toney, Jones is out there so many lengths ahead of the field, like Secretariat, that the question for boxing buffs is: Just where would you place him in the pantheon of all-time greats? Having watched nearly all the great ones for some seventy years, I found myself cornered by younger boxing writers (including fifty- and sixty-year-olds) to evaluate Roy Jones against the best of the fighters I've been fortunate enough to ringside since the mid-1920s.

Though such lists are instantly controversial, my mind's eye has settled on eight "genius" fighters (with a score of others pressing close behind): Henry Armstrong, Willie Pep, Joe Louis, Sugar Ray Robinson, Carlos Monzon, Roberto Duran, Archie Moore, and Muhammad Ali. True, these fighters had hard fights with great fighters: Willie Pep with the freakishly strong Sandy Sadler, Robinson with tough welterweight Tommy Bell and oh-so-tough Jake LaMotta, Archie Moore with a dozen great black fighters no rated Caucasian would want to be in the same town with, Joe Louis with Billy Conn and Jersey Joe Walcott. And Henry Armstrong . . . in one incredible half year (1938–1939) our nonstop featherweight took the welterweight title from Barney Ross, the lightweight title from Lou Ambers, successfully defended his welterweight crown against Ceferino Garcia and then against another of our favorite Los Angeles fighters, Baby Arizmendi. Armstrong and Arizmendi fought each other like fighting cocks. I saw the last three of their five fights, a genius (Hammerin' Henry) in there with one of the best little fighters of his day. In '37 Armstrong had almost thirty fights, knocking out all but one, and we're not talking tomato cans but tough little cookies like Varias Milling, Mike Belloise, Wally Hally, Lew Massey, and finally Petey Sarron for the featherweight belt.

What I'm trying to say is, when you see an Armstrong, you spot the genius right away. Just as you spot it in Roy Jones. But Armstrong, like Ali and Moore and the others, was tested and retested by strong opposition. I saw Armstrong with his irrepressible energy almost take the middleweight title from a bigger, physically stronger Ceferino Garcia. And so for Roy Jones, who can dance like the vintage Ali and punch like the vintage Duran, the only question is, how would he stand up under heavy pressure? Seemingly invincible in his own weight class, and likely to stop a nice but light-hitting 175-pound champion like Virgil Hill, how would he fare against the heavyweights he now talks about fighting? Billy Conn scaled 169 for the 200-pound Joe Louis, who could take you out with a six-inch punch from either hand. Ali, after his three-year exile from the ring, fought wars with Joe Frazier and Ken Norton, not to mention Ernie Shavers and Oscar Bonavena.

Every great fighter, no matter how slick his defensive skills—Benny Leonard, Willie Pep, Ali, Alexis Arguello—gets nailed sooner or later. It's how you shake off pain, or fight through blood like Robinson in the second Turpin fight, that separates our genius fighters from the merely great.

The first (and best) Sugar Ray had seventy fights before he won the welterweight crown, and another fifty fights before whipping Jake LaMotta for the middleweight belt. His opponents included scores of great fighters, some of them in the Hall of Fame.

Sugar Ray was marvelous to watch when we first saw him out of the amateurs. But he improved like heady wine, knowing so much and still learning on the job.

After only twenty-nine fights, Roy ranks among the truly gifted boxers I've watched from '25 to '95. But in the fragmented world of today's fight game, with Don King's champions separated from Bob Arum's, and WBA champions able to ignore WBC's and IBF's, with HBO and Showtime presiding over rival title fights, things aren't as simple as in the days when little Henry Armstrong challenged Barney Ross, or Billy Conn took on Joe Louis. It's a political minefield in which HBO's Roy Jones may never get the opportunity to put his gifts to work against the challenges that will hone his skills and prove his genius. Sam Langford, Mickey Walker, and other great middles fought the best around, month after month, including top heavyweights.

If Jones can reach beyond the boring mandatories (and more mismatches) and get the chance to stretch his talents, even move among the heavyweights, I'd like to be there for the razzle-dazzle of the niftiest box fighter I've seen in years. Maybe up there with Robinson and Ali. So far, so good. . . .

[1995]

Jones vs. Griffin: Pretty Boy Loses Ugly

A FEW MINUTES before Roy Jones answered the bell to defend his newly acquired WBC light heavyweight belt, a young sportswriter at the press table at the Taj Mahal challenged me. "Hey, your piece on the 'genius' of Jones. Would you really put him in a class with Sugar Ray Robinson? Up there with the best you've seen since the thirties and forties?"

He has the potential, I said. The fastest hands since Ali. Speed and power is a rare combination, and Jones has speed to spare and hurts you from funny angles. Only trouble is, an intriguing prospect like Jones isn't being tested as Robinson was when he had to fight eighty fights before finally getting a chance to win his first championship (against very tough, now very forgotten Tommy Bell).

By that time Robinson had been through wars, no less than five with Raging Bull LaMotta, and had honed his skills in battles with Fritzie Zivic, Henry Armstrong, and the rest of the best. He knew how to outbox the boxers (Sammy Angott) and outpunch the punchers (Artie Levine).

Roy, on the other hand, had only thirty-four fights in eight years, all of them as one-sided as the victories over Toney, Pazienza, and Merqui Sosa. That kind of leisurely career encourages complacency and stagnation, and that's what Jones seemed to bring to the ring against a stubborn, determined, unorthodox, and savvy Montell Griffin. We've described Jones in these pages as being "as far ahead of his field as Secretariat," but the Griffin fight forces us to get a tighter grip on our hyperboles. Maybe the Cigar analogy is a better fit. The invincible Cigar came back to the pack and got himself beat on his way to retirement.

Round one was all about Jones, a trademark combination catching Griffin early, leaving the squat challenger from Chicago wobbled and troubled. "Sosa all over again," somebody said, remembering Jones's two-rounder in the Garden last fall.

But Griffin came out for round two with other ideas. To our surprise, he was sending the overconfident Jones a message: I'm not going quietly. With an awkward southpaw stance and a crafty plan, he bulled Jones into a corner and flailed away with both hands to the body. A more experienced champion—say a Robinson with Kid Gavilan—would have known how to spin his man around and get out of that corner. But Jones seemed trapped and suddenly vulnerable in a way none of us would have imagined.

And our astonishment grew as the now-energized Griffin established a pattern that Jones seemed unable to break. Jones's jab, so dominant in the Toney and Pazienza fights, was tentative, even feeble. Only stinging jabs, the kind that had painted a grotesque mask on Pazienza's face, could discourage Griffin's aggression, and Jones seemed curiously to have left that essential weapon at his home gym in Pensacola. He was fighting Griffin's fight, his back reddening with rope burn as Griffin, shorter and stronger, kept him pinned in a corner where Jones's speed of foot and boxing skills were nullified. Griffin was using the classic under-and-over style of a ringwise brawler, varying the bruising body shots with an occasional looping right to the jaw. "At least Roy takes a punch," we concluded as we watched the 10 to 1 underdog take it to him into the middle rounds.

This was a wake-up call for Jones, and in rounds five, six, and seven we could feel something click in his head: I can't box and showboat this dude. I've got to fight 'im. And to Jones's credit, refusing to be bullied into corners at last, he fired back with those fast hands, but setting himself to punch harder now. There were furious exchanges, a fierce round six, and even a flash knockdown of Montell in the seventh, but the challenger was standing his ground. He was giving Jones the first competitive fight of his charmed (and too easy) professional life, and at the end of eight our scorecard had it dead even.

Round nine began as had so many others, with Griffin backing Roy up again and landing hard rights to the head. But Jones was firing back now, and suddenly Griffin was in trouble, reeling around the ring like a barfly who's had one too many. Down on one knee, and beginning to look like a beaten fighter who had pushed himself to the last gasp, Griffin was waiting for referee Tony Perez to show up and begin the count when midnight madness set in. A confused, frustrated, or overwrought Roy Jones blew the fight it had taken him a long night of catch-up to get even. With Griffin down and Sr. Perez somehow failing to signal Jones to a neutral corner, the mindless champion landed a right hand, and then as hard a left as he had thrown all night, flush on the fallen fighter's unprotected head. Griffin crumpled with his face pressed against the canvas as if in Muslim prayer.

Unaccountably the usually professional Perez continued to count. It looked from ringside as if Commissioner Larry Hazzard had to remind him that the last two punches were not only illegal but unquestionable cause for disqualification.

After Oliver McCall's nervous breakdown against Lennox Lewis and Andrew Golota's fouling out twice against Riddick Bowe, bizarre climaxes to major fights are getting to be the rule rather than the exception. Griffin-Jones goes into the record books as Roy's first loss (by DQ), and Montell goes back to Chicago a little woozy in the head but with the WBC light heavyweight belt around his steely thirty-four-inch waist.

"What a rematch!" The fight crowd was already looking forward to the next one. And since Griffin's crowding tactics had made Roy Jones look something less than the "genius" I had hastily nominated for all-time greatness, there's a bonus to the messy ending. It brings new life to the light heavyweight division, where the personable WBA champion, Virgil Hill, meets the German with the Polish handle, Dariusz Michalczewski, next month, and the winner of Jones-Griffin II becomes a candidate for that longed-for unification bout.

"I thought I was looking him in the eye when I hit him," said the erstwhile No. 1 pound-for-pounder, not quite as apologetically as ring moralists might expect. "Looks like he's been training with midgets," a cynical fight reporter (is that an oxymoron?) described Jones. Maybe the trouble is that he's so gifted, he thinks of his opposition as midgets. At 34 and 0, he was on cruise control. Now, if he really wants to be up there with the Robinsons and the Alis, he may have to give up basketball games on the days of his fights. Maybe it's time to study film on the solid, forward-marching toughie who backed into the light heavyweight championship but who said to us at ringside after it ended ugly, that next time he's ready to prove he can win it on his feet.

[1997]

III. The Mouthpiece Hamlet

A PUNCHER who can box, a boxer who can rattle your cage with a left hook and take you out with a straight right hand is the kind of fighter you wait for. He justifies your sitting through all the letdowns, the disappointments of watching too many coulda-beens or never-woulda-beens. There's nothing more boring than mediocrity, in the ring, on the page, on the screen.

When Roy Jones roared in from Pensacola three years ago, ready to take center stage, the heavyweight division was in the doldrums, with venerable George Foreman as linear champion; Riddick Bowe as champion of what I called the Overweights; Michael Moorer a reluctant tiger; and Mike Tyson preparing to load up on rollovers. There was an unprounounceable light heavyweight over in Germany, and East Los Angeles' gift to Madison Avenue, Oscar De La Hoya, lighting up the lightweights. But timing is everything, and when the speedy, still needy Jones boy outclassed the previously undefeated James Toney, stopped the formerly unstoppable Vinny Pazienza, and made short work of another reputed ironhead, Merqui Sosa, we were ready to nominate him for the genius club, that inner circle reserved for Louis and Robinson, Moore and Ali.

Wasn't it nice to watch a fighter with the fastest hands since Ali, who seemed to know the dance, and with all that flurry and grace, could punch with the authority of that great light heavyweight champion of the sixties and seventies, Bob Foster?

Of course Roy's nomination to the inner circle came with a warning: the original Sugar Ray had to go through some seventy fights, against scores who could hold their own with the De La Hoyas, Whitakers, and Trinidads of today. His skills had been honed, his defenses developed, his chin and his stamina and his heart had been tested by the Jake LaMottas and the Fritzie Zivics when he was still a baby-faced kid of twenty or twenty-one. The great ones of the past weren't given their chance at the gold ring nearly as quickly as young Roy Jones. The television hunger for headliners and heroes rushes our promising boys into their megafights before we know, or they know, how they'll stand up to all the hype, the pressures, and sometimes even whether they can take a good punch to the chops.

So the first Jones-Griffin fight made me wonder if, in my eagerness to find class among all the brass, I had overpraised Mr.

Jones as he ascended from the super middles to the light heavies and seemed to reign supreme. For a "genius" he certainly allowed the aggressive but wily Montell to bull him into a corner time and time again, without spinning himself out of that corner as any seasoned boxer should know how to do. By the time he began turning things around in the ninth round—before his mindless combination to the head of the floored Griffin DQ'd him, he had taken far too many body shots to maintain his credentials in high fistic society.

But in the rematch earlier this month at that glitzy Indian aberration, the Foxwood Casino, Roy reinforced his claims to the "pound-for-pound" title with a one-round destruction of the same Montell Griffin who had been beating on him for eight of the scheduled twelve rounds the first time around. This time a motivated and focused Roy Jones reversed gears and brought the fight to the startled Montell in the first ten seconds. In less time than it takes Michael Johnson to run two hundred yards, Griffin was down. An aroused Jones, fighting as he can when the mood suits him, never let Griffin back into it. In two and a half minutes Griffin was on his way back to Chicago a battered millionaire, and the ecstatic Roy Jones was bopping around the ring, once again anointing himself as Numero Uno and modestly offering to "save boxing" by challenging Evander Holyfield for what we used to call "heavyweight championship honors."

But it's time for a reevaluation of the once-again WBC light heavyweight champion. He feels unappreciated because he doesn't draw the crowds or money of a Tyson or De La Hoya. And yet he does nothing to burnish his image. He stiffs or walks out on press conferences. He disses boxing, sometimes so bored with the sport that he devotes his afternoon to a professional basketball game on the eve of a title fight. He takes control of his career from the Levin brothers, who are not fight guys but attorneys in his hometown, Pensacola, who supported and befriended him in his amateur days and through the difficult time when he was breaking with his overbearing father and original trainer, Roy Jones, Sr.

Avenging the only blemish on his record by disposing of Montell Griffin as quickly as Sonny Liston overpowered Floyd Patterson, Roy might have challenged the undefeated WBO champ, Dariusz Michalczewski, and unified the title before moving up to heavyweight. Three of the best light heavies I ever saw, Billy Conn, Archie Moore, and Bob Foster, all tried moving up and for all their skill, punching power, and heart, were still unable to weather the for-real heavyweight power of Louis, Marciano, and Frazier.

Roy Jones should be ecstatic about Griffin II, but, alas, he seems caught up in the mega-fame and windfall millions that infect so many young star athletes in the '90s. The genius of Archie Moore was never displayed in Madison Square Garden until the Old Mongoose was forty and had fought and licked a hundred fighters (seasoned warriors like Harold Johnson, Curtis Sheppard, Jimmy Bivins) tougher than Griffin. Now that's what being unappreciated really means. But Archie didn't mope and blame the press. Old Man River kept rolling along until finally in middle age he got those major paynights in the ballparks that had been denied him in his youth.

It's a generational thing. Ivan Rodriguez says he's "insulted" when he's offered only $38 million for five years when he really deserves $43 million. Instead of being King Roy of the light heavies for a year or so, and then testing the waters with some top ten heavies, it's "I want Holyfield." I want the $30 to $40 million the Holyfields are getting. And I want it now. One mega-money fight and then back to the basketball court and the chicken fights.

Roy Jones is Hamlet with a mouthpiece. To be or not to be the greatest fighter of the '90s? Cus D'Amato used to say boxing is 10 percent skill and 90 percent character. The way Roy took Griffin apart proves again he's blessed with skills. But like the sadly deposed Mike Tyson, he seems pursued by the demons of his life and times. For his sake, and the sake of the fans who welcome his gifts, we hope he wins the big one. Not against Evander. Against Roy Jones, Jr.

[1997]

IV. A for Ability, B for Bored

MY FATHER, B.P., dividing his nights between sneak previews of the movies he produced and going to the fights at the Olympic Auditorium in downtown L.A. and the Hollywood Legion Stadium (whence came my education in both art forms), gave me early lessons on light heavyweights.

Before he came west as a Hollywood pioneer, he was a habitué at the old Garden (the real *old* Garden) and would hold forth on the excitement of the light heavy round robins: the power punching Paul Berlenbach against the clever Jimmy Slattery; Young Stribling; durable Jack Delaney; Mickey Walker, the toy bulldog; boxing master Tommy Loughran, busy every month against the best of his day—Harry Greb, Mike McTigue—and, when he had cleared out the division, taking on the heavyweights and beating three champions, Max Baer, Jack Sharkey, and Jimmy Braddock, plus half a dozen top contenders and going fifteen rounds for the heavyweight championship against Primo Carnera, a head taller and a hundred pounds heavier.

B.P. had a sharp eye for talent, discovering Cary Grant and bringing Shirley Temple, Gary Cooper, and Marlene Dietrich to the screen, or picking the Gene Tunney–Harry Greb series as the most stirring championship bouts he had seen. It was his contention that, barring a superstar like Jack Dempsey or Joe Louis, the light heavies provided more sporting entertainment because they had the speed of the smaller men, the middles and welters, and the punching power of the big 'uns.

A perfect example of my father's ideal should be the reigning WBC-WBA unified light heavyweight champion, Roy Jones, described in this corner after his destruction of the never-previously-knocked-out Vinny Pazienza as being the only fist fighter of genius on the contemporary scene. No one, all the way down to the bantams, has faster hands or can match his footwork, his unpredictable surges of offense, and his elusive offense when he is in focus. But his recent outing with the erstwhile WBA champ,

Lou Del Valle, which gave him the unification bout, ten rounds to two, won no new friends for the Pensacola prodigy.

There's a reason why the world's No. 1 pound-for-pounder, above De La Hoya, Prince Hamed and Holyfield, fails to catch fire with the general public, or even with hard-core boxing fans who admire his skills but are turned off by his . . . what is it, exactly? Why is this singular champion, fighting a local Brooklyn boy who had lost only once—and that a questionable decision to then champion Virgil Hill—unable to fill the small Madison Square Garden Theater, let alone the main arena? There were barely 3,500 of the Fancy and the not-so-fancy attending the affair at the minor Garden venue on a normal Saturday night in mid-July, and they were largely there to root home the local boys, the Bronx underdog Del Valle, and, on the undercard, the popular little ex-champion from Queens, Kevin Kelley, rematched with Jones's nimble stablemate, "Smoke" Gainer, in what was probably his farewell performance in a notable career highlighted by his coming *this* close to stopping the little beast of Britain, Prince Hamed, in his previous New York engagement.

So here we have a light heavyweight we're ready to compare with the best we have seen—Billy Conn, Archie Moore, Bob Foster, Michael Spinks, not to mention Dick Tiger, Jose Torres, and John Henry Lewis—and the ticket window for a Jones title fight against a winning Puerto Rican New Yorker turns out to be a very lonely place. When Jose Torres joined me at ringside, I was reminded of his light heavyweight title fights with Dick Tiger, when nineteen thousand filled the Garden for those electrifying contests and almost tore it apart when Torres lost controversial decisions.

Of course it's not all Jones's fault. Boxing was still a major sport in New York thirty years ago. Before the Don King–Caesars Palace days, the Garden was truly the mecca for the world of pugilistica. It's lost its continuity now, and its local ethnic patriotism. If the Kevin Kelleys and the Lou Del Valles were fighting every month against competitive outsiders, winning or losing but pleasing as in the glory days of Jimmy McLarnin, Barney Ross,

Tony Canzoneri, Lou Ambers, and Henry Armstrong, it might be different. Now it's one big-money shot at a time, half a year apart—if we're lucky.

No, the meager gates and the want of media attention can't all be red-checked against Roy Jones. There's also the problem of his running out of competition. He destroys the best light heavyweights around: Montell Griffin in one round, Virgil Hill in four. He's so bored, he dreams of moving up two weight classes to fight Evander Holyfield. And that was the trouble in the Del Valle fight. The current nonpareil (shades of the original Jack Dempsey) was bored. When he wanted to avenge his DQ loss to Griffin, he was all business and fused his vaunted skills with intensity. But with Del Valle there were the now familiar flaws: posturing and loss of concentration. At times he carried his left hand so low he seemed to be aiming for Del Valle's kneecaps. At times he went southpaw. To confuse his opponent? Partly, he said at the curious post-fight conference. But also because he was getting bored and tried the southpaw stance for the novelty. In all my years of fight talk, this was a first: a boxer in defense of his title admitting boredom in the ring.

Jones's boredom was temporarily relieved in the eighth round when the earnest, conventional, unbored Del Valle followed a right jab with a corking left hand that not only put Jones down but had him dazedly wandering back to his corner when he finally got up. The 20 to 1 underdog was too excited or too inexperienced to finish the job and, in the ninth round, instead of jumping on Jones and going all out—for what did he have to lose?—he let Jones be Jones again, setting his own erratic pace and getting bored again. Roy boxed in flurries, as if to say, "You see, this is what I could do to you if I really wanted to." The speed is astonishing, the eccentric angles from which he's able to land punches truly unique.

But once again, as in a previous report, I must describe him as the Mouthpiece Hamlet. The only excitement of the night, the dramatic knockdown, was provided by the loser. Ringsiders came away with two impressions. Any talk of pitting Jones against Holyfield was premature, if not idle speculation. If Jones could not even wobble a willing light heavyweight, how could he put any hurt on the heavyweight champion? So his dream of promoting himself into the heavyweight picture is on hold, at the very least. And what makes things more interesting now is that the Del Valle fight proves Roy Jones is vincible. Gifted but hittable. If Del Valle has him hearing Chinese bells, maybe Reggie Johnson can do it, or that Kraut with the Polish handle: Michalczewski.

Bored fighters make boring fights. In my dictionary a bore is a nuisance, a tiresome person, a dullard, a twadler. Roy Jones is bright and quick-minded, as well as quick-fisted and quick-footed, when he wants to be. Please, Roy, don't be a twadler. Don't get bored on us. Push to the utmost the talent you've been blessed with. Think of Michael Jordan, Ali, Jack Robinson. They never indulged the curse of boredom in themselves. They worked and played to banish it in others.

Isn't that what boxing, or any sport, or any artistic endeavor, is all about?

[1998]

V. Move Over, Ruby Bob— Here Comes Roy Jones!

ON MY WAY to the weigh-in for Roy Jones's challenge to John Ruiz for the latter's WBA heavyweight championship, I found myself with a television camera in my face and an eager TV reporter asking me a familiar question. Why did I find boxing so fascinating? What is it about the "Sweet Science"—as the stylish A. J. Liebling called it—that captured the imagination of William Hazlitt, George Bernard Shaw and A. Conan Doyle, Jack London, Hemingway, Nelson Algren, Norman Mailer, and Joyce Carol Oates?

In the midst of one of the most raucous weigh-ins I've covered in half a century, with Jones's trainer knocking Ruiz's trainer off the platform and sending him on a stretcher to the hospital, I tried to clear my thoughts. On your way to a major prizefight there is a tightness in your throat, a kind of chill on your skin. We all have our favorite teams in every sport, but they are *teams*, and if they lose an important series this year, they'll be back next year. Writers identify with fighters because, while the former have agents, editors, and publishers, the latter have promoters, managers, and trainers; but when the bell rings they are in there alone, under the bright lights, naked and alone. Yes, tennis also sets up dramatic contests of one on one, but if Leighton Hewitt or some other top racketeer blows a five-set match to Andre Agassi in Australia, chances are he'll face him again at Wimbledon or at the U.S. Open. The revolving door of Grand Slams. Only in boxing is there one defining night when history is made and dreams and careers go rattling down like bowling pins. To the tenth and last frame. Game over. Only this isn't bowling. This is one night that may decide how you will be remembered. Take a bow, you're the champion of the world! Or—Get lost, ya bum!

The latest example of the roller coaster every title holder and contender rides was Roy Jones's attempt to become the first former middleweight champ to win a heavyweight crown since the broad-chested, spindly legged Brit Bob Fitsimmons KO'd Jim Corbett in the fourteenth round with the famous "solar plexus" blow he buried in Corbett's belly. One hundred and six years later we still talk about it. Of course the human body, like the world, has changed since Ruby Bob starched Gentleman Jim in 1897.

As the heavyweight king, Corbett weighed in at a dapper 183. Fitzsimmons came in as what we now call a super-middleweight at 167, just sixteen pounds lighter. Jones was facing what many experts saw as a far more daunting task. Even beefed up to 193, the undisputed light heavyweight champion would still be giving away almost 35 pounds, not to mention eight inches in reach and three inches in height. He was also bucking the tides of light heavy vs. heavyweight championship history. For deep into the twentieth century a parade of legendary light heavyweight champions had tried to win the ultimate crown. Call the roll of reigning light heavies who tried so hard and fell even harder. Philadelphia Jack

O'Brien . . . George Carpentier . . . Tommy Loughran . . . John Henry Lewis . . . Billy Conn . . . Archie Moore . . . Bob Foster . . . these splendid light heavies were 0 for 11 until finally, late in the century, 1985, a resculptured Michael Spinks weighing 205, giving away 18 pounds to Ali's worthy successor, Larry Holmes, won a razor-thin decision to finally score one for the little guys.

Jones came to his challenge with Ruiz with a curious history. He made the big time ten years ago with the quickest hands, swiftest feet, and slickest moves since Sugar Ray Robinson. When he humiliated the undefeated middleweight champ James Toney, won another middleweight belt from the formidable Bernard Hopkins, and knocked out the heretofore unknockoutable Vinny Pazienza, I found myself hailing the "genius" of Roy Jones. At last we had not just the newest "pound-for-pound" champion but a candidate for All Time. And then a curious thing happened to him on the way to the Hall of Fame. He got bored. He was so good he toyed with opponents and practically yawned in their faces. He could razzle and he could dazzle, he could feint you out of position with a glove, a shoulder, or even an eyebrow, and he could hurt you when he wanted to with a short left hook you never saw coming. But he could also coast and showboat and carry a covey of incompetent pugs into late rounds. Stiffing the press and boring the public, the gifted but reluctant warrior faced a rated local boy, Lou Del Valle, and couldn't even fill the smaller arena, the theater tucked away in Madison Square Garden. I went to that fight with a dear friend who once held the light heavyweight title, Jose Torres, and as he looked around at the sparse crowd he remembered when he and Dick Tiger sold out the Garden. Twice. Because both fought with skill and passion while Roy was what I called the "Mouthpiece Hamlet."

In a pre-fight piece for a New York paper, I wondered how Jones would be remembered. As a curiosity with a boring reign as light heavyweight champion who couldn't take the lumbering punch of the strong but awkward "assistant heavyweight champion" John Ruiz? Or was he ready for membership in the exclusive club of Fitzsimmons, Conn, Moore, and Spinks? I didn't quite make it to Carson City for Fitzsimmons-Corbett. I was minus seven. But I was there for the other three. The Oscar goes to Billy Conn, who really weighed only 169 when he faced a 204 Joe Louis in the prime of his time. The wily promoter "Uncle" Mike Jacobs had his foot on Billy's scale at the weigh-in and managed to sneak five pounds from Joe's as he feared the true discrepancy would put a damper on the box office. Billy fought the fight of his life that night, sticking and moving around the Brown Bomber until at the end of round twelve his corner was telling him, begging him, "Stay away, run, coast in and you're heavyweight champion of the world!" Billy's answer is part of our boxing lore. "Hell with that, I'm gonna knock 'im out." Trading punches with Louis until he finally fell on his face, and scolded by his manager for being so stupid, Conn came up with his classic: "What's the use o' bein' Irish if ya can't be stupid?"

In becoming the first former middleweight champion since Fitzsimmons to win a heavyweight title and only the second winner for a 175-champ against the big 'uns in fourteen subsequent tries, Roy Jones gave us a performance that may now become his legacy. Ruiz was big and rough, and even though his corner kept pushing him to fight harder, he was doing his lumbering best to press a man who could outbox him, outthink him, and finally even outfight him. The big question had been: How will Roy react to being hit by the first heavyweight punch of his career? Answer: Roy hit him back. Roy took more chances with this erstwhile heavyweight champion than he ever took with the bogus No. 1 light heavyweight contenders who were moonlighting from their day jobs as cops or bus drivers. Several of my British friends at ringside scored every round for Jones, but more generously, I gave Ruiz four. He rushed from his corner to make a fight of it at the opening bell, and after four rounds Ruiz's strength against Jones's speed promised an interesting evening. But as Jones asserted himself with those dazzling skills and Ruiz began to thrash around in frustration, with blood pouring from his broken nose, it began to remind me of those bullfights I used to shudder at but watch in Mexico City, where the bull rushes in the arena ready for the kill, and halfway through the ordeal, as he slows down and suffers, he begins to realize that it is he who's to be on the receiving end of the killing.

In the twelfth and final round Jones was doing what Conn's corner had begged Billy to do. Coast in. With thirty seconds to go, Roy began to showboat and smile and then raise his hands to award himself the one-sided decision that would soon come officially from the three judges.

So that's what we fly across a continent to see: defining moments. For Ruiz, always more of a clincher than a puncher, it's the end of the line. Nowhere to go but down. An asterisk to heavyweight history. While Jones can only go up. Whatever he chooses to do next, he's up there in the history books with Bob Fitzsimmons. There's talk of his staying in the heavyweight division and fighting venerable (or should we now say vulnerable?) Evander Holyfield, or Evander's recent pitty-patting conqueror Chris Byrd. Whatever road he takes, and he's going to take his own sweet time while attending his fighting cocks and pitbulls (his next big fight could be with the ASPCA), he made a convert of this once-critical ringsider. When our "Mouthpiece Hamlet" finally decides TO BE rather than NOT TO BE, he's awesome.

Okay, Sugar Roy?

[2003]

P.S. That was then. This is now. Roy could razzle and dazzle with the best of them. Almost as hard to hit as Will-o'-the-Wisp Willie Pep. Through his career he boxed like someone obsessed with the idea that getting hit was an unacceptable affront to his dignity. In the ring against the best in the division he was immaculate. Some of us wondered what would happen if an opponent finally broke though that elaborate defense and smacked him one. Now we know. In the twilight of his career he faced the new light heavyweight champion, Antonio Tarver, and was belted out. Even more devastating was the one-round knockout he suffered from the former champion, Glen Johnson. As the once elusive boxer we thought of as unhitable lay unconscious on the canvas for several minutes, we held our breaths. Please, Lord of Boxing, not another death in the ring. When the fallen icon was finally back on wobbly feet, we knew the curtain was going down on a remarkable career. But any comparisons with old Bob Fitzsimmons were misplaced. Ruby Bob, a middle-weight who fought the top heavyweights, took a helluva punch. Ask the shades of Jim Corbett, Jim Jeffries, and Tom Sharkey. Now we'll remember Roy Jones as the classiest boxer of the modern era, but also with the glassiest chin.

[2006]

▪ 13 ▪

Evander Holyfield:
From the Real Deal
to the Sad Deal

I. Holyfield-Bowe:
Act III (The Rubber Match)

AS I SAT CLOSE to Holyfield-Bowe, Act III, on a chilly early November evening in the arena behind Caesars Palace, I wondered: Is boxing a metaphor for life? Do those fervid minutes under the glare of the lights over the squared "ring" represent the deepest efforts of human beings to impose their will in their lifelong battle of win or lose, life or death? Their first two fights had been close and exciting, and both a trusting public and a cynical press had been caught up in the excitement of the rubber match, with a touch of the anticipation surrounding other notable heavyweight trilogies, the legendary Ali-Fraziers, the bitterly contesting Ali-Nortons, and the rivalries of Jersey Joe Walcott and Ezzard Charles, and Marciano's dogged doubles against Walcott and Charles.

In fighters' careers I see Shakespeare's Seven Ages of Man, with Evander doing his inspired turn as Everyman struggling up out of the cradle, leaving his mark on the world in the fullness of his maturity, and then surrendering to the inevitable weaknesses of mortal flesh as his power deserts him, when he can no longer deliver stiff jabs and follow with straight right hands against his final opponent, still undefeated, the Undertaker.

The heavyweight muddle or mess, with five sanctioning bodies marching off in five different directions, contributed to the growing support for Holyfield-Bowe. Neither man held one of the gaudy but essentially meaningless belts, and yet they were by consensus the two best heavyweights atop the sorry list that passes for champions and designated challengers. In that disorganized and dispirited atmosphere, we accepted Holyfield-Bowe as a legitimate contest for bragging rights as Best Heavyweight, Vintage '95.

And if the promotion needed an extra shot of adrenalin, it came from the somewhat rusted Iron Mike Tyson, scheduled to meet Buster Mathis, Jr., the very night of the Holyfield-Bowe festivities. Apparently (some thought, conveniently), on the Monday before the fight, Mike broke his thumb in training. Curiously, he held his first public sparring session on Tuesday, calling it quits in the third round and holding up the wounded digit as proof positive. So our poor little rich boy was out of fighting and into shopping. On the Saturday afternoon of Holyfield-Bowe, he was sighted in an expensive shop in Caesars, which was closed off to would-be customers so Mike could spend $75,000 on badly needed items for his growing and glowing circle of intimate friends. In Las Vegas, Tyson "sightings" had replaced "O.J. and Elvis sightings."

The only place somebody's "No. 1 Contender" would not be sighted was in the ring at the MGM Grand, where Showtime and King Vision were holding a wake while across the street, rival HBO-TVKO and Caesars were celebrating what was now being hailed, with good reason, as the "People's Championship." The heavyweight belts had finally fallen with a sickening splash into the multi-boxing commissions' alphabet soup.

Bowe had won the first one because he had talent and strength and had worked hard enough to get down to 235. He had blown the second because he'd ballooned to 246 at the weigh-in and looked over 250 in the ring that night, trying to pull his sail-sized trunks up to hide a Santa Claus belly. Evander was his usual gym-dandy-body muscular, blue-collar worker, obediently giving his all.

Old-fashioned virtue had won. Hard work and a little skill over superior skills laced with laziness.

This time, round one gave us a sense of the old, reliable Holyfield, jabbing, throwing combinations, taking a punch from a lumbering Bowe but fighting back when hit, as we'll always remember him.

Bowe took command in the next few rounds, using his jab and his strength and scoring inside with short uppercuts. He was also scoring with body blows, some of which were obviously low but for which Bowe was warned but not penalized. There were furious exchanges, punctuated by holding and pushing, and we were close enough to hear both men already breathing hard as they went back to their corners.

Bowe was back to his good-bad habits in the fifth, outjabbing Evander—who was growing older by the minute—and missing with looping right hands that left him wide open. A younger, better Holyfield might have seized the advantage, but Bowe landed another hard right hand and then a punishing blow so low that finally referee Cortez signaled a point penalized, and gave Evander a breathing respite. We watched his face, pained and tired. Hurt and game. The many times he had stood toe to toe, eschewing self-defense, were writing the same old boxing story on his face.

But what separates champions from couldabins? The unique ability to reach down when the body and the mind seem too weary to fight on. Evander came out for the sixth and reached with a lightning left hook. "Big Daddy" Bowe was down, for the first time in his life, and not only down but looking glazed, three ticks from coldcocked. The end of the Riddick Bowe Show . . .?

Somehow he was on his feet, but barely, still out of it, his mind no longer interested in defensive tactics. There for the taking. Then came the inexplicable, the mystery that will make the moment one to remember. What did competitive Evander do? *Nada.* Absolutely nothing. He looked at his helpless foe, almost without interest, and pawed listless left jabs at him. With more than two minutes to go!

One punch away from his third championship of the world, something had stopped in Holyfield. Something had died. The punch never came. In the Seven Ages of Fighters, ironically in round six, Evander had reached his Sixth. When he went back to his corner, with a 10 to 8 round and a one-point lead, the golden moment had slipped away.

Character carried him through the seventh, with Bowe recovering and the aging Evander still trying, and in the eighth there was even a last, desperate Holyfield flurry, and Bowe still a target to be hit. But as a slowed-up and maybe ill Holyfield moved in, almost accommodatingly, he offered his chin to Bowe's chopping right hand, and down he went, so hard it was frightening to those who knew his courage. Somehow he was back on his feet, in the Seventh Age now, a very old man as fighters go. Joe Cortez should have helped him to his corner, to regain his consciousness and consider the blessings of retirement. Instead the brave Cortez seemed to shove dazed Evander back for the coup de grace. He allowed the luckily triumphant Bowe to land an unnecessary right-hand crusher that could have moved bravehearted but sometimes dim-witted Evander from the Seventh Age to that undefeated Undertaker that awaits us all.

As for Tyson vs. Bruno, come March 15, 1996, and maybe People's Champ Bowe against the softest money touch Rock Newman can find (Andrew Golota, etc.?), stay tuned. Big George needs money. He's made only half as much as Holyfield's 100 mil and counting. He's only 47. And, hey, Ron Lyle won in Denver the other day. He's 53, but commission doctors and the Mayo Clinic tell me he's in even better shape than Evander Holyfield.

Take care, Evander. Three seconds away! You gave us a lot of good, honest years in a sport that could use more of them.

[1996]

II. Reenter Evander: A Big Night for Him and HIM

OUTSIDERS SEE BOXING as two brawlers swinging on each other until the weaker falls.

But we keep describing boxing as a chess game with blood: was this ever more apparent than in Real Deal Evander Holyfield's unreal defusing of Mike Tyson in the most astonishing comeback of a heavyweight champion in the history of the division?

Anyone who had seen Holyfield's clock seem to stop in the last Riddick Bowe fight would tell you that the old warrior from Atlanta should be retired to his rolling green pastures. And if there was any doubt, there was his sorry showing in a sloppy win over the blown-up light heavy Bobby Czyz, who took a brief sabbatical from his articulations for Showtime fights.

Match the brave but used-up Evander with merciless Mike Tyson, whose iron fists had terrified giants like Frank Bruno and Bruce Seldon? Opening at 25 to 1, the only question was whether poor old Evander would suffer serious injury.

"I hope they stop it fast," was the prevailing opinion going in. "Evander's a decent man. A true Christian. A good father. Always gave his best. Even when he lost to Moorer and Bowe. An A for work ethic. A credit to boxing. But put this washed-up thirty-four-year-old in there with angry Mike Tyson? Puh-leeze!"

"You really want to fly across the continent to see another three minute massacre?" people kept asking me.

One-sided or not, it's another page in the Mike Tyson Saga, I tried to explain. And anyway, I didn't think it would be another one-round fiasco. Drawing on my three score years as a boxing maven, I assured my friends that Evander was no rollover, beaten before he climbed through the ropes like the gutless wonders who preceded him. My crystal ball showed a determined Evander standing his ground in round one, caught and stung in round two, then courageously and ever so reluctantly giving way in round three.

At that, I gave Holyfield one more round than did fellow boxing writers I respect: Dave Anderson of the *New York Times*, knowledgeable Jerry Izenberg in Jersey, Colan Hart of the London *Star*. Wallace Mathews, one of the best, couldn't see the old man making it through round one. And the "Fight Doctor" Ferdie Pacheco, the silver-tongued Showtime analyst, also gave it one round, concerned that Evander's characteristic stoutness of heart would expose him to danger if the referee was not merciful and prompt.

But arriving at the MGM Grand I call the green monster, I fell in step with Emanuel Steward, the maestro of the famous Kronk Gym in Detroit, mentor of Tommy Hearns and other champions, including Holyfield for a time. Emanuel's take on the fight was an interesting antidote to us well-meaning doubters.

"You know why I give Evander a real shot in this fight? You know what Cus [D'Amato] used to say—boxing's a battle of wills. It's the power of the mind that wins the fight. The mental discipline you bring with you to the ring. I expect Evander to come in with the real confidence. He's not afraid of Mike. He's a far more intelligent fighter than Mike. He won't be unfocused as he was for Czyz. He's been wanting this challenge for five years. I wouldn't sell him short."

The tension building to fight time is almost unbearable. All serious heavyweight championship fights are Super Bowls cum World Series, intensified by the terrible possibilities of one on one. The live audience of almost seventeen thousand has made Evander their underdog hero. You can almost feel their neck cords tighten and the belly butterflies flutter as the crowd gives off something between a roar and a howl at the opening bell. Tyson bolts from his corner like a fighting bull from the chute, throwing fierce but wild hooks. Evander catches a few but keeps his cool. He introduces himself to Tyson with a nice one-two, and then, smothering more wild swings from the headlong attacker, scores again, and again. It's more than just a very good round for Holyfield. Just as Emanuel Steward had suggested, mind is asserting itself over matter.

When the pattern continues into the second round, with Tyson punching ponderously and often aimlessly, and the clearly unintimidated Holyfield boxing with serenity and an unmistakable sense of purpose, we know we are watching a totally different fight from the one- or two-rounder we had dreaded but had to see. When Tyson lands, Evander doesn't swoon like Mike's sacrificial lambs. He shakes off hard shots to body and head, actually outstrengths and pushes Mike off in the clinches. He is the thinker and the doer out there, and the erstwhile, invincible Mike Tyson is manifestly vincible, floundering and confused. Through seventeen thousand mouths the great beast in the arena is chanting "HOLEE-FIELD! HOLEE-FIELD!" and the old battler is responding with the performance of a lifetime, a kind of anthology of the Best of Holyfield.

Already trailing on the scorecards, Tyson comes on in the fifth, with one-punch-at-a-time desperation. For a moment there's a hush in the Holyfield crowd as their man seems to back off for the first time and Tyson puts some of the pain on him that Mike's oafish corner had promised in the pre-fight hype. Well, we console ourselves, if this is as far as it goes, Evander's imposed his will on Mike for almost half the way, and whatever happens now, we've got a heavyweight championship fight worthy of the name.

But wait, miraculously fresher and more self-contained than his younger nemesis, Evander absorbs Tyson's aggression, regroups, advances in style, beats on Mike with speed of hand, and as in a slow-motion scene in a Hollywood fight movie (*The Harder They Fall*), Tyson is down, dazed, bewildered, and diminished. Never again the Baddest Man on the Planet he thought he was for the fifteen-months of the McNeeley-to-Seldon show, he struggles to his feet, an ordinary fighter now. An energized Evander moves in for the kill.

It doesn't come in the seventh when the bloodied and tiring Tyson is unable to avoid the indignities being imposed on him, or in the eighth or ninth when a superbly disciplined Holyfield is hitting Mike with every punch in the repertoire. But by the end of the tenth Mike isn't down, quite, but the Fat Lady is warming up her larynx. A battered Tyson barely makes it back to his corner, and in a 100 to 1 turn of events it is the mindless Mike who must be saved from serious injury as referee Mitch Halpern signals an end to his misery a few ticks into round eleven.

The Tyson Express has hurtled off the tracks. In a reasonable world, Don King's stranglehold on the heavyweights would be

Holyfield surprises Tyson, who's "down, dazed, bewildered, and diminished." (Pat Orr)

broken. Evander's promoters, Don's bitter rivals, Lou and Dino Duva, would be calling the shots. But this is the fight game. Just as our Teflon Don walked in with Frazier and walked out with his conqueror Foreman when George took Joe's title in Jamaica, so Don came in with Tyson and somehow walked out with promotion rights to future Holyfield title defenses. To the winner belongs—Don King.

At the press conference a chastened Mike Tyson, now a gracious loser, perhaps mellowed out in unexpected defeat, reaches out for the hand of his conqueror, giving praise where praise is due. With dollar signs dancing in his head, unsinkable Don King is already hyping the rematch he will now co-promote. Not exactly a tough sell. As a morality play, it's a little over the top. Tyson, the prince of darkness vanquished by Holyfield, the prince of light. Who said "Nice guys finish last"? Some of the good guys are back in business, with a say on who runs the bigs. A breath of fresh air after the Seldons, Brunos, McCalls, and trash-talking Team Tysons. The King is dead. Long live Evander.

This may be the best thing that's happened to the game since Joe Louis sent the battered Max Schmeling back to Nazi Germany, or maybe since the Supreme Court exonerated Muhammad Ali and restored his right to practice his profession. In an age of cynicism, the Holyfield miracle gives hope to the lost and last. People poured out of the arena exhilarated, refreshed in spirit, bathed in optimism.

If Holyfield could come back from the fistic graveyard to dominate the dominator, we were in Dr. Pangloss's best of all possible worlds. A cripple could throw away his crutches and climb Mt. Everest. Ray Charles could read Proust without using his fingers.

Evander Holyfield is the only fighter I've ever seen who went into the ring with a biblical inscription on his robe, "Philippians 4:13," directing us to the lines: "I can do all things through Him, which strengthens me." Throughout his press conference he spoke not of left hooks and uppercuts but of the power of his Lord Jesus to inspire him in battle. "I prayed in training, I prayed in the dressing room, I prayed in my corner, and I even prayed during the fight," Evander preached. He may have done more for the Christian faith in eleven rounds than Billy Graham in eleven months of Sundays.

It was a big night for him and a big night for Him. And, at least for the moment, God seems to have replaced Don King as the Supreme Ruler of pugilistica. To Philippians 4:13, add TKO-11.

[1997]

III. Evander the Holy: The Once and Future Undisputed King

AFTER A SERIES of commedia dell'arte PPV frauds contrived to devaluate the mythological power of what once had been the most coveted title of all sports—Heavyweight Champion of the World—Holyfield and Moorer finally gave back something to reassure us that all was not rotten in the shaky state of the heavies, at the end of the twentieth century.

From Sullivan and Jeffries to Dempsey and Tunney, from Louis and Marciano to Ali and Larry Holmes, the undisputed heavyweight champion walked in seven-league boots, a ruler of the universe. Presidents and kings wanted photo-ops. He played Pied Piper to children in the streets. A figure of awe, in retirement Dempsey had only to sit at the window of his Broadway restaurant to draw the tourists. Forty years into retirement, Joe Louis was still a magnet to a new generation moved to touch the flesh of a legend. And Ali? He seems to travel the globe as the adored Pope of Fistiana.

After three consecutive heavyweight title fights lost by DQ (McCall, Akinwande, and the eerie Mike Tyson), fight fans bought into Holyfield-Moorer II with a sense of unease. From 1992 to 1996 Evander had lost three out of four to Bowe and Moorer, and in surrendering his title to the phlegmatic Moorer three years ago, he had fought like an old man, with a sore shoulder and a troubled heart. A lackluster performance against the semi-retired Showtime commentator Bobby Czyz made those who admired him for his character and his piety wish he'd retire to his pastoral estate and his ministerial calling before he caught the old boxers' disease of thickening speech and stumbling step. But Evander had risen like Lazarus to intimidate the intimidator in destroying the 20 to 1 favored Mike Tyson.

If I remember my Scriptures (and Evander is certainly doing his part in calling us back to the Book), Jesus gave brother Lazarus only one shot at rising from the grave. But Evander is beginning to make a habit of it. Behaving unlike any other heavyweight champion I've ever followed, just forty-eight hours to fight time he was holding a passionate revival meeting for some fifteen thousand disciples in an outdoor ballpark and giving alms to the homeless. The next night he was at Bally's Casino watching his trainer's young heavyweight Michael Grant quickly dismantle the falling tower of pizza, Jorge Gonzalez. And on his way to the ring the following night, it was not to the usual hard rock or rap but to Evander's favorite gospel song—and singing it all the way down the aisle. He may lack the charisma of Ali or the gutter appeal of Tyson, but anyone who can preach the mercies of his Lord Jesus one night and live up to the "Warrior" inscription on his trunks the next is his own kind of original.

In his fight with the younger "other champion," Evander's first round was cautious and thoughtful, Moorer winning it with an unsettling right to Evander's always-solid chin. Moorer had an edge in round two as well, but without establishing the nasty right jab he had going for him in their previous encounter. Still, he was winning round five, until Lazarus struck again. Right hands from Holyfield executed with destructive and serious intention sent Moorer in a backward jitter step to the canvas. He was up at nine, game, but the bell was tolling and defeat was in his eyes.

To his credit he made a fight of it, but Evander was growing stronger, with the mass chant of HOLY-FIELD, HOLY-FIELD urging him on, varying the overhead rights with spirited uppercuts that put the vulnerable southpaw down, and then down again. It was simply a question of time now, and the only surprise was that in defeat Michael Moorer was winning first-time friends with what our early-nineteenth-century mentor Pierce Egan called "Bottom" and sometimes "gluttony." Never before identified as a fighter of great heart, Moorer lived up to the cruel, sometimes enobling demands of the sport by getting up, even at the end of the eighth when he was dazed and foggy-eyed but willing to continue an engagement that was over in the view of the ring doctor who signaled "Enough!"

After twenty-four minutes of spirited but increasingly one-sided action, Holyfield was two-thirds of a heavyweight champion for the second time. Now the final prize, Undisputed Champion of the World—as he had been in the early nineties—is within his reach.

The logical move pits him against WBC Champion Lennox Lewis for all the heavyweight marbles. Bigger and younger than Evander, Lewis looked overpowering against Andrew Golota, and he seems to have a new attitude to go along with his reachy jab and big right hands. At ringside he was belittling Holyfield's winning effort and assuring everyone within earshot that he'd take out Evander in three rounds or less. Restricting his pugnacity to the ring, Holyfield spoke with trademark dignity: "I'm looking forward to matching skills with Lennox."

If logic prevails, a match in the Spring of '98 should produce an undisputed champion for the first time in half a dozen years.

But Evander's Lord could be back for the Second Coming before logic comes to the fight game. In the fractured world of professional boxing, Don King has one more promotional shot with Holyfield, while the Duvas and Main Event are Lewis's promoters. Lewis is a Time/Warner–HBO property while of course King is Showtime/King Vision and all that other jazz. Then there are the rival commissions with their sweet sanctioning fees to worry about. And, finally, that always sticky wicket—how much will Holyfield and Lewis, or their team of lawyers/negotiators demand? Will their overweening demands "ice" the one heavyweight championship fight the fans really want to see?

It's no secret that both the Lewis-Golota and Holyfield-Moorer were box office lemons. So whether HBO or Showtime wins the toss, it may all come down to what it always comes down to in our flawed and fascinating sport, MON-NEE. . . .

Holyfield and Moorer put on a refreshing eight rounds of old-fashioned milling. But it's going to take many more rounds of wheeling and dealing by a gaggle of crafty manipulators with egos even larger than the two willing and able combatants if we are to hear those golden words, "Winner and New Undisputed Champion of the World!" ring out in '98.

[1998]

IV. Evander's Homecoming and Going

HERE'S WHAT the Holyfield-Vaughn (Don't Call Me Butter) Bean encounter in Atlanta reminded me of: They're throwing a humongous welcome-home party for the big kid on the block who's been out there in the world getting rich and famous. He's passed the hundred-million-dollar mark in purses, and he's grabbed the headlines up north, out west, New York City, Las Vegas, and now it's Atlanta's turn to show off its hometown boy and bask in his glory.

But once they bring out the party cake, big enough to satisfy the 41,000 celebrants in the Georgia Dome, and their favorite son, Master Holyfield, gets ready to blow out all those glittery candles, out of the blue an imposter—a roly-poly kid who somehow ootzed his way into the party—blows them out instead. And instead of getting mad, the record number of hometown fans who paid dearly to pay homage to the guest of honor go fickle on Evander and cheer the 10 to 1 underdog: "Way to go, Vaughn!"

Expected to last three or four rounds at most, Bean ignored all the dire press predictions of his early demise, actually took the fight to a suspiciously tiring champion in the middle rounds, and kept throwing looping right hands at Evander's head. Even when Bean was knocked down, controversially, in round ten, being pushed into the ropes and not quite clear of them when Holyfield landed his chopping right, he proved the kind of determined survivor that fight fans admire—even the biased hometowners who sang, along with Evander, "Spirit of Jesus" as he led the fanatical parade to the ring under the promotional banner, "The Champ Hits Home." Except for the flawed knockdown, this was a contest wanting in passion, and Evander's failure to deliver the fireworks set off in his Tyson fights swung his fellow Atlantans against him. When Bean had the audacity to press the action and win the twelfth and final round, the 41,000 who had come to cheer the local hero had transferred their fickle loyalties to the outsider who had lost a unanimous decision but won their respect.

So the Holyfield Express hits a bump or two as it pauses at its local station on its way to its professed destination—the undisputed Heavyweight Championship of the World. A year ago, when Holyfield dispatched melted-Iron Mike Tyson a second time and fought like a true champion in dismantling the brave headcase Michael Moorer, boxing fans were ready for the logical shootout with Lennox Lewis to rescue the true championship from the WBA-WBC-IBF-WBO alphabet soup. It's still the only meaningful contest in the confused and corrupted heavyweight division. It's the fight Evander says he's been seeking as a fitting farewell to his notable but curiously roller-coaster career. Disposing of one mandatory challenger in Bean, the WBA-IBF champion was to face another manipulated No. 1 in Henry Akinwande, the reluctant warrior who "fought" Lewis like a frightened octopus.

In theory, giving the No. 1 contender the right to challenge for the title before the titleholder meets a lower-rated boxer seems the sporting thing to do. But given the cute little ways of the fight game, in practice it is cynically misused. Once a promoter-manager winks his boy up to No. 1, he's in line for that million-dollar "mandatory" paynight. No self-respecting fight fan wants an Akinwande in Holyfield's path to the Lewis unification bout, just as no one took seriously a No. 1 IBF rating for Zeljko Mavrovic—a household name only in the Mavrovic household—without a single credible opponent on his dance card. So, instead of Lewis-Holyfield last fall, we had Lewis-Mavrovic in a lackluster defense of the black Brit's gaudy belt matching Evander's methodical but uninspired victory over the overweight but underestimated Bean.

The good news is that these phony mandatories may now be put aside and that Evander's ready to sign a real deal for $20 million, even if it comes from HBO, the Lewis outlet, rather than from Showtime, for whom Evander's been beating on people ever since Teflon Don King glaumed onto him via the Tyson fights.

Lewis-Holyfield—one world, one champion—can't come soon enough for Evander fans who begin to wonder how long the Holyfield engine can keep chugging along. We've said goodbye to him too many times now. When he looked spent and sick in losing to Moorer four years ago. Then, a year later, when he had Riddick Bowe ready to go, stood there admiring his handiwork and a round or two later, went down so hard we thought he'd never get up. We said goodbye to Evander that night again. Thank you, Mr. Holyfield, you've been a credit to the game, but now go home and enjoy those multi-million-dollar purses. Enjoy your life and take care of all those kids in and out of wedlock. The slow dance with Bobby Czyz in the Garden two years ago confirmed our conclusion that Evander should be put out to pasture.

But Evander the Bible student took a page from Lazarus when he shocked the world with his total domination of Tyson. And he still fought with disciplined passion in avenging his loss to Moorer. But in rising again, Lazarus didn't have to take all that head-thumping Evander's taken from Bert Cooper and George Foreman, from Bowe, Ray Mercer, and Moorer.

A workhorse for conditioning, Evander has been able to surprise us in the sunset of a career that has tied him with the legendary Ali as the only heavyweight to win the title three times. But as we noted in our requiem for Roberto Duran, "Good Night Sweet Princes," there comes the night in the life of every great fighter when he's breathing hard after four rounds, when his timing is off and he's sucking up punishment that will haunt him in later years.

Who wants to see that happen to Evander, who's had his problems outside the ring but has been an exemplary practitioner of the cruel science inside the ropes?

As that feisty little referee in Las Vegas says, c'mon Evander, if you must face Lewis, before another year slips away, and time further erodes the engine, "Let's get it on!"

[1999]

P.S. Well, they got it on, in Madison Square Garden, when the won't-quit Evander was thirty-seven in 1999. Lewis was the clear winner, but Evander was gifted with a sentimental draw. The rematch left no doubt as to Lewis's superiority, and this time the judges had it right. Evander was aging fast, but in his warped mirror he was still a fistic Dorian Grey. His jaws were singing the old blues, "Oh, Lawdy, you been a grand old wagon but baby now you done broke down." He was hitting forty now, with enough money to live on as country squire on his expensive estate out-

side Atlanta. But the conqueror of Larry Holmes, George Foreman, and Mike Tyson trudged on. After three lackluster fights
with the king of lackluster, John Ruiz, he was outfoxed decisively
by Chris Byrd, knocked out by old James Toney, and lucky to get
a draw with boring journeyman Larry Donald. The Real Deal of
the eighties and the nineties, one of the last of the true heavyweight champions, keeps coming up with no cards to play but refuses to leave the table. When the New York State Athletic Commission withdraws his license to box, for his own protection, the
final humiliation in a sport he dominated twenty years ago, instead of departing in dignity to that long-overdue retirement,
Holyfield contests the decision and insists he'll go on fighting in
other states. He's tied Ali's record as Champion of the World
three times, but stubborn as ever in his fistic senility, he still
dreams of a fourth. His speech is slurring, he's forty-four years
old, and his last three fights have been painful embarassments. If
only he had hung 'em up after destroying Mike Tyson, what a legend this gritty old man would be, instead of winding up like too
many other roundheels. For the sake of the sport of boxing, and
for the sake of the grand old warrior you were, old gander Evander, go home. For God's sake, go home.

[2005]

14

Mike Tyson:
From Wonderboy to Has-Been

I. The Softer They Fall

LONG AGO, in the novel *The Harder They Fall*, I imagined a giant heavyweight, Toro Molina, who looks as if he should be heavyweight champion of the world. Only one drawback: he can't fight. Big muscles, broad shoulders, no skills, no punch. But the mob boys who own him aren't worried. They puff his record with enough roundheels to go 30 and 0, with 28 KOs . . . and Toro's ready for the six-figure paynight that meant real money in the 1940s and '50s.

Fast forward to the nineties: we've got multi-million-dollar TV fights on pay-per-view and the ante's soared from million-dollar gates to $70 million, the record set last August 19 for the "Tyson's Back! Coming Out Party" (out of the slammer!) at $1,500 a pop if you wanted ringside to smell all the excitement, and fifty bucks if you chose to be a TV couch potato to watch "the biggest sporting event in the history of the world," as promoter Don King did his modest best to describe his King-size spectacle.

In the paragraph above, smell is the operative word. In front of a live audience of seventeen-thousand and millions of jaundiced eyes from Texas to Thailand, write in the name Peter Mc-Neeley for my Toro Molina, and you have another major fraud perpetrated on a bamboozled public by our master of bamboozlement, Don King.

Deafening were the cheers for Mike Tyson as he moved menacingly down the aisle, Tyson Redux, emerging dramatically from a cloud of blue smoke to a soundscore of thundering drums. Seventeen thousand delirious voices chanting "Mike! Mike! Mike!" as he stalked the ring in his now familiar all-business black trunks, black shoes, no socks, a plain towel with a hole in it for his stolid head. Then, only a few minutes later, just as deafening were the BOO . . . s, those seventeen thousand voices now chanting "Bull-shit! Bull-shit! . . . !"

In just eighty-nine seconds "the greatest sporting event in the history of the world" had become "Brute farce! The most farcical sporting event in the history of the world." It came as part of King Vision's three-minute special, with Johnny Gill's eccentric rendering of our national anthem sucking up two-thirds of that time.

There can be no question that "Hurricane Peter" came to fight. That is, he made all the right moves. He checked in at the MGM Grandiose. He showed his muscles and blew kisses at the weigh-in. He obliged with some po' white poetry (Robert Frost, forgive me) a la Ali: "I'm Peter McNeeley from Medfield, Mass / And I'm here to kick Mike Tyson's ass. . . ." He bopped down the aisle in his robe of Irish green, waving bravely to the waiting crowd. He fell to his knees in pious prayer, perhaps praying that his mentor, Vinnie Vecchione, would save him from bodily harm. He didn't make a wrong move until the bell for round one, when he barged out of his corner like the Boston Bull (minus the other syllable) that King & Co. had trumpeted him to be. Six seconds later he was down from what looked like a glancing blow to the inviting Celtic chin. He got up and charged again, throwing wild punches like a barroom brawler after one too many. He grabbed the rusty Iron Mike and, in the only effective attack of the brief, unsightly night, suddenly lifted his head and butted Mike. Meanwhile Mike was missing with awkward left hooks that made one think back wistfully to the young destroyer who took out a legitimate professional, Michael Spinks, in less than a round seven years ago.

That was a memorable performance. This overblown thing was, put simply, a mess. His timing off in wild hooks that left

Mike wide open, able pros like Bowe and Holyfield, maybe even Moorer, Foreman, or Lewis, would have spotted vulnerability. Finally Mike managed a professional right uppercut that found the waiting jaw again and took the wind out of the "hurricane." The Medfield Pretender (who could be fined for impersonating a prizefighter) was down again. That's when the fun began. Peter was ready to continue, though not looking overjoyed about it, when into the ring came savior Vecchione. He had seen enough. He was taking his boy home to the safekeeping of Mommy and Daddy. Six hundred thousand dollars richer. Minus Vinnie's third (or maybe half?) and a 100-G kickback to old-time henchman Al Braverman.

Flashing back from the serio-comic ending of this unconscionable mismatch—which we had foreseen as a bad one-round joke—the film writer in me envisioned the following pre-fight scene in the McNeeley home:

MOTHER MCNEELEY: (or Daddy, or the blonde girlfriend who high-fived him when Peter came back to his corner after the "fight"): "Tell me the truth, Vinnie. Is our boy going to get hurt?"

VINNIE: "No problem, Mom. First sign o' trouble, I'll be in there to save 'im."

And of course the boxing writers, those nasty people, those character assassins back in the press room were spreading the rumor that Vinnie had money on Tyson in one.

The post-fight press conference was more King/Visionary than ever. If I had promoted this salami I would have headed for the hills or disappeared into the witness protection program. But there was our unflappable Don flashing his victory smile. Unfazed by the booing and the switchboards clogged with outraged customers wanting their money back, King Don pronounced this a triumphant evening and hailed the unabashed McNeeley as "a magnificent warrior who attacked Mike Tyson like I've never seen any heavyweight do before!" If there is a Chutzpah Award, Mr. Unflappable has won permanent possession.

Unscathed, and now safe from harm, McNeeley could exult: "I talked the talk and I walked the walk . . . he was so friggin' strong

. . . after I got up the second time I twisted my knee . . ." To hoots from doubting Thomases, he fought back, a little harder than in the ring, "Looka the tapes! . . . Looka the tapes!" So he can go back to Medfield with head held high. He wasn't knocked out. He twisted his knee. He can tell that to Peter McNeeley, Jr., when the kid, a fourth-generation "opponent," goes in there for his paynight in 2020. This thing could go on forever. Or maybe they'll get smarter in the twenty-first century.

The cleanest blow of the night came from an anonymous hero who asked, "When is Mike going to have his first fight?"

So after eighty-nine seconds that proved absolutely nada about Mike's ability to compete with the best, the Mike Tyson Show rolls on. But King, Showtime, and the MGM Grand need a summit meeting to decide where it rolls to. If Mike keeps on fighting stiffs, even Don King—who can sell ice cubes to Eskimos and ham sandwiches to Hasidic Jews—may have trouble getting the suckers to shell out a second time, or third. And if Mike goes in against a legitimate heavyweight who may not be Frazier or Holmes but can fight a little, he could be in trouble.

"Show me a hero and I'll write you a tragedy," said our perceptive novelist F. Scott Fitzgerald. There's something about Mike Tyson, when you listen to that squeaky, little-boy voice, that makes you feel sorry for him. Even with his twenty-five mil for a sorry night. Thanks to his sorely missed Cus D'Amato, Mike is a student of fistic history. He's watched the films, from Johnson and Jeffries to Louis and Marciano. Where will he fit into the Grand Scheme? He can be the richest athlete in America, knocking off the Lou Savareses, and maybe Oliver McCall, who's having trouble keeping his finger away from his nose, or the other "Champion," Bruce Seldon, who boxed on the undercard and, with his right hand seemingly chained to his shoulder, jabbed holes in the big, no-talent Indian Joe Hipp.

Mike Tyson—even if no longer the wonder boy he was in the eighties—could run through Don King's laundry list of bogus "heavyweight champions" and keep it all in the family. His jillion-dollar deal with King/Showtime/MGM points him in that direction. Why take a chance with a Bowe or a Holyfield when you can make a mint with South Africa's Frans Botha, the White Buffalo?

Is Mike Tyson going to contribute to the downward slide of the once meaningful heavyweight championship? Or has he come back to redeem it? When Ali came back from his three-and-a-half-year exile, he fought a top contender, Jerry Quarry. When Sugar Ray Robinson came back from self-imposed retirement, he fought a tough cookie, Tiger Jones, and lost. But he got better and better until he cleaned out a middleweight division starring Bobo Olson, Carmine Basilio, Gene Fullmer, and Jake LaMotta.

The twenty-nine-year-old Mike Tyson, riding the American roller coaster of fame, fortune, and notoriety, may not know it but—like the fight game itself—he's facing an identity crisis. Stay tuned.

[1995]

II. Tyson Redux: Act I

WHAT IS THERE TO SAY about Bruno-Tyson? In a thimble, Mike was ready to rumble and Frank was ready to tumble. The once and future king of the heavyweights not only made his intentions perfectly clear in the first sixty seconds of the encounter at the MGM Grand on the 16th of March, he had established his domination of the British Pretender to the throne in those tense minutes in the ring even before the opening bell. While six thousand Brits, overdosing on love of country, queen, and beer, chanted themselves hoarse with their "Bruu-nooos . . . ! Bruu-nooos!," Britain's first heavyweight champion since Fitzsimmons (OK, one-third of one) was standing in his corner with the eyes of a victim about to be strapped into the lethal chair.

I like to sit close enough to watch the eyes of boxers. I've been doing it since the Joe Louis days. If the eyes are indeed the mirror of the soul, poor Frank's eyes betrayed a fighter's most terrible affliction, fear. While Tyson was stalking the ring like a wild thing, but a very self-contained wild thing, was the Black/White Hope of the Empire throwing punches into the air in the traditional mode of the warm-up to the fray? No, he was crossing himself! Not once, but again and again. Meanwhile the beery Brits were on their feet in patriotic delirium, wrapped in their Union Jacks; and somehow we were no longer in Vegas, we were in a rowdy British soccer crowd far across the sea.

But not HRH's Sir Frank. Unlike the British knights of old, this was no Sir Lancelot going forth to do or die. This was T. S. Eliot's Hollow Man, all 6 feet 3 inches and 250 pounds of him, going forth most reluctantly to die. In place of the eerie "Bruuu-nooo" that echoed through the packed arena, the heavy-muscled black giant from Hammersmith was hearing "Oh . . . nooo, oh-nooo . . . Please, Massa King, give me my six million and send me safely home to Mama and the queen."

Interviewed on my way to the press section, I had given my predictions on the assumption that I had seen more heavyweight title bouts than anyone else on the grounds and knew what I was talking about. Wrong again. In the first two rollovers, McNeeley and Mathis, there was rust on Iron Mike, and he was missing with looping punches, his timing and balance well off the high-water mark of the late eighties prior to the Buster Douglas debacle. So it made good sense to think we would only see 50 percent of the vintage Tyson, whereas Bruno might come into the ring with more confidence with the wearing of the gaudy belt. With that logic programmed into this white-haired computer, I had made a modest wager on Tyson by KO in six. We all bring our pre-fight videos to these contests, and mine had Bruno holding him off a bit, with his thirteen-inch reach advantage with the jab and his pride in the eyes of his countrymen carrying him on another round or two. So if he fell in five, six years ago, why not make it in six for '96?

But as Bruno crossed himself for the last time and Tyson came storming out of his corner, wasting no time in going for the kill, I knew I could tear up my chit. Bruno wasn't using those long arms to establish the jab as had Tony Tucker and some of the box-fighters Mike had faced in the past. His arms were thrust forward for only one reason: to clasp them behind Tyson's thick neck and hang on for dear life. The diminutive referee Mills Lane would have to pry himself between their combined 470-pound bulk to separate the two and give Mike room to land punishing lefts and rights before the terrified Bruno grabbed again, hanging on to Tyson like a drowning man reaching a life raft. A committed warrior stout of chin and brave of heart might have made this interesting for a few rounds as further test of Tyson's improvement. For let there be no doubt, Bruno had good reason for his pre-fight trepidations. The Tyson of ferocity, intensity, and ability to punch in rapid, thunderous combinations was back. He had shortened his punches since the first two easygoers of Tyson-Redux, was no longer off balance as he had been for McNeeley and Mathis, and was dealing excessive but disciplined punishment that had the ringsiders ready to restore him again to their all-time litany: Dempsey, Louis, Marciano, Ali. . . .

The Union Jacks weren't waving quite so exuberantly now, and "Bruuu-nooo!" was trailing off to an embarrassed hush. In the second round Bruno's sole means of defense, the desperate holding, was so insistent that Mills Lane seemed ready to present the beleaguered "champion" with the ultimate disgrace, disqualification, for refusing to fight. But early in the third round "Big Frank," as his large and boisterous constituency had been calling him, finally obliged by giving Mike the opportunity to land a series of short and savage left hooks, followed by two quick and devasting right uppercuts. Bruno was still on his feet but listing badly, going down like the *Titanic*. The Bruno Boyz, after surging through the MGM Grand all afternoon, could only drink in sorrow now.

On the way to the post-fight press conference—where of course neither victor nor vanquished showed up—I felt a tinge of sorrow for the wilted Brits who had saved their shillings to cross an ocean and a continent to cheer their standard-bearer. After the abbreviated battle, Bruno had stood in the ring rather forlornly with his battered eye and apologetic countenance, still clinging to a last-gasp chauvinism in slowly waving a Union Jack. And some of his downcast compatriots managed to chant up a few die-hard "Bruno's." "We British are somewhat different about all this than you are over here," said John Rawlings, a British journalist working alongside me at the press table. "You may put greater emphasis on winning. These chaps are still loyal. It's like a soccer match. Their team may lose but they never think of changing sides. They accept Frank as a loyal son who gave a lift to British boxing even if he failed tonight."

What has happened to the British heavyweight? In the bare-knuckle days there were the heralded champions of England, Tom Cribb and "Gentleman" Jackson, Jem Belcher, and Tom Sayers, the middleweight with the heavyweight belt who stood up to the giant American invader John C. Heenan for sixty punishing rounds. Somehow English grit was associated with "Brittania Rules the Waves" and the worldwide prowess of British arms to the turn of the twentieth century. It may be too neat to make a case that with the loss of empire came the demise of heavyweights sporting the Union Jack. It's a pathetic roll call: "Bombadier" Billy Wells and Joe Beckett, who had great difficulty remaining vertical in the twenties, notorious "Phaintin" Phil Scott in the thirties; the game but hapless Don Cockell; porcelain-chinned Bruce Woodcock. . . . The bleery Brits wrapped in their Union Jacks and their faded dreams are so desperately in need of heroes. It's too bad Bruno couldn't have gone down like a game Royal Navy ship with all flags flying and all guns firing.

Meanwhile the Tyson ship is full speed ahead. He was "improving," a suddenly more animated Iron Mike told the "fight doctor," Ferdie Pacheco, in the ring right after the dramatic third-round curtain. And his explanation that he had used a series of uppercuts adopted from the legendary Henry Armstrong style proved that this student who learned his boxing history at the knee of Cus D'Amato (with help from fight film collector and co-manager, the late Jimmy Jacobs) is serious again. Bad news for "sparring partner champions" like Bruce Seldon and Frans Botha. But after Mike cleans up the devalued heavyweight title picture, maybe the conflicting powers-that-be will let us see the real things for a change. Maybe we'll get Tyson-Lewis, Tyson-Moorer, Tyson-Bowe.

Give us followers of this tarnished sport something to cheer about without having to wrap ourselves in patriotic flags waving on hollow men.

[1996]

III. Requiem for a Heavyweight

LAST MONTH it was Mike Tyson vs. Evander Holyfield. This month it's Tyson vs. the Nevada Athletic Commission, and Mike loses again. This time his license to perform in professional boxing rings has been revoked, subject to reapplication a year from now. Cynical observers from the *New York Times* to the *New York Post* see it merely as a twelve-month prelude to Holyfield-Tyson III, with the gross for the next one exceeding the record gross set by this eerie fiasco. But according to the legal adviser to the NAC, "Unless the commission changes its mind, this would be a permanent revocation." And from Mike's former trainer, Kevin Rooney: "Basically, it's a death sentence."

No matter which side of it you come down on in judging the severity of Mike's punishment, I see this as something that goes deeper than any legal decision. Call it Requiem for a Heavyweight. It's time to assess the tragic career of the once-glorified "Iron Mike"—now scornfully put down by his new army of detractors as "Iron Bite."

As a fight fan who hies back to the glory days—Louis and Schmeling, Louis and Conn, Marciano, Walcott and Moore, Ali-Frazier I, II, and III, and Ali's storied destruction of Big George Foreman—June 28, 1997, goes down in my book as the Night of the Ugly and Nasty. A desperately frustrated Mike Tyson, outclassed in the first two rounds and on the road to a second humiliating defeat at the hands of the miraculously rejuvenated Holyfield, seemed to have long forgotten everything his mentor, the unique Cus D'Amato, taught him about boxing and character. Poor Cus was left spin-

Referee Mills Lane stops the fight to examine Holyfield's ear after Tyson's big bite. (© Joey Ivansco/Corbis Sygma)

ning in his grave as Mike abandoned the Marquess of Queensberry Rules he had learned in Cus's gym when the teenage convicted mugger was transformed into a disciplined amateur boxer caringly protected and coached to fame and fortune as the youngest man ever to win the heavyweight championship of the world.

When, to our unbelieving and horrified eyes, the once-but-not-future king of the heavyweights took not a nibble but a mouthful of Holyfield's right ear and gnashed on it like a rabid dog, Mike took boxing back to the cave. Forget all those noble words writers from Jack London to A. J. Liebling to Joyce Carol Oates have used to defend the "Sweet Science." He made veteran sports analyst Dick Schaap wonder aloud if boxing has had it. Lord knows, Oliver McCall, Andrew Golota, and now Mugger Mike have done their worst to give the fight game two black eyes and a missing ear.

When feisty little referee Mills Lane stopped the "contest" to give the ring doctor a chance to examine the cannibalized auricle, the history of the once-noble heavyweight championship had reached an all-time low (and that includes the Schmeling-Sharkey and Sharkey-Carnera performances).

But moments later the Biter of the Ear was at it again, working on Evander's left one now, with the ringside wags already updating Evander's subtitle to "The Real Meal." But this wasn't joke time. This was sick, sad, sordid, and psycho. This was the most revolting moment I had seen in some seventy years of ringsiding. This made Two-Ton Tony Galento's job on Lou Nova look like Boy Scout pattycakes. This put Pittsburgh's Fritzie Zivic in line for the Clean Sportsmanship Award. And in the ugly brawl that erupted in the ring after Mills Lane finally DQ'd the perpetrator, a berserk Mike Tyson reverted from professional athlete to mean street mugger. When less troubled kids had been in school, Mike had been luring old ladies into elevators and scoring clean knockouts to the sides of their heads to cop their groceries and purses. The purses were a little bit larger now, like thirty million, but not only can't money buy happiness, it can't exorcise the demons, and Mike's were buzzing and biting like a shaken nest of hornets on that tainted Saturday night. Spitting out his mouthpiece, Mike exchanged his left hooks and right uppercuts for upper and lower molars as a more direct way of inflicting bloody damage on an opponent who refused to take a backward step and bow down in fear as had Tyson's pathetic rollovers, McNeeley, Mathis, Bruno, and Seldon. In all those mismatches, Tyson had come out swinging wildly, missing as much as he was landing, and learning nothing that would prepare and fortify him for the first unintimidated and thoroughly professional challenger he would face as an alumnus from the slammer. In Tyson-Holyfield I, he came out swinging and missing again, and when he did manage to land, Evander had the audacity to hit him back. The look on Mike's face at the end of that round seemed to say, "No fair, that's not the way Team Tyson tells me it's gonna be: I walk in, I land, they fall down, I go home and count the money."

The first encounter was a major bump on the tracks of the Don King/Mike Tyson Express, but nothing like the major crash on the rematch, when Mouthy Mike Tyson, egged on by an arrogant corner choking on its own hubris, bit off more than he could chew. Adding madness to mayhem, Mike was right there in the middle of the post-fight riot swinging on a couple of the local gendarmes, and not connecting in this extracurricular added attraction, either. It must have been interesting viewing for his parole officer and Judge Gifford if they happened to buy into the $49.95 Pay-for-View entertainment back in Indiana, where Mike had had another off night at that Black Beauty contest in '91.

In a ring that had gone berserk, what I called the Brawl after the Fall, it seemed as if the only island of sanity was the winner-and-still-champion, the self-contained and evangelical Evander. There is a genuine circle of serenity around this man. Whether it is training in the peace and quiet of his native Atlanta, or in Houston where I watched him prepare with quiet intensity for Foreman and Bowe, or whether it is in the ring in the MGM Grand press camp two days before the Tyson fight, where I talked to him quietly on the ring apron, oblivious to all the hype and pressure around him, he is incredibly unchanged. Told that "Mike likes to say he's the baddest man on the planet," his answer was an in-character understatement: "I'm really not interested in being the baddest man on the planet. My only interest is being the best man in the ring."

Now, after the eruptive DQ, Mike was giving a convincing impersonation of the maddest man on the planet, raging around the ring while the Fight Doctor, Ferdie Pacheco, was combining his interview expertise with sound medical advice: "Go straight to the hospital and get that masticated ear injected against infection and sewn up." "If you can't beat 'em, eat 'em," seems to have been the fistic strategy of the poor little rich boy who admitted that he "snapped" after an inadvertent head-butt, abandoning the protective rules of boxing for the more primitive demands of the Brownsville jungle where this son of an absentee pimp and an alcoholic mother was raised in poverty and crime.

The rage to survive by any means possible may have been sub-limated by the saintly/cagey Cus D'Amato when he became young Mike's legal adoptive father and channeled his son's aggressive urges to make him the most charismatic and biggest money fighter of the eighties. Even then, when the fates seemed to be smiling on the reform school alumnus, there were serious lapses, when young Mike would go AWOL, take to the streets of the near-est town, and prey on teenage girls. But there were other times when he was Cus's dutiful son, and I was among those at the me-morial in the ring of the Fourteenth Street Gym with him when he shed real tears for the departed Cus and muttered aloud, "What will I do without him?"

Now in the ring of the MGM Grand in volatile Las Vegas, the answer was all too clear: in the face of intense pressure that you cannot handle, you unravel, come apart, abandon the sport of boxing and revert to mugging. If you can't win fair and square, try to break his arm, knee him in the balls, gouge him, bite him, and if one bloody ear doesn't do it, go for the other.

After a major fight, reporters are trained to interview the principals involved—the boxers, their trainers, managers, cut-men. This was the only fight in my remembered history when the most unlikely of interviewees was someone like MGM Grand underling Mitch Libonati, whose job it was to cut the gloves off Holyfield after the bout. Instead he had the presence of mind to search the canvas of the riotous ring for the missing piece of Evander's right ear. Miraculously—under the feet of all those rioters messing and mugging up the ring, including the masticator and now No. 1 Public Enemy of boxing, Master Tyson—Libonati found the missing mouthful of Mr. Holyfield and turned it over to a paramedic to pack in ice and rush to the nearest hospital where Mitch hoped it might be reattached to the rest of the champion's auditory organ. "I realized right away what it was," the unlikely hero of this loony evening said to me after the melee. "And I hoped it would be helpful. Mr. Holyfield is a very nice man, and I wanted to do everything I could to help him."

As it turned out, the unassuming ring attendant's good deed was aborted, like this mad and manic fight itself. Somehow in the utter confusion of the aftermath, when Molar Mike was being led back to his cage under a nightmare barrage of beer cans, garbage, and spittle, the paramedics lost the missing gristle, flesh, and skin that had been gnawed from the top of Holyfield's ear and then spat out on the bloodstained canvas. "It looked like a piece of chewed sausage about half the size of my pinky."

Plastic surgery will undoubtedly restore Evander's right ear to the cosmetic wholeness it enjoyed before Mike forgot that he had signed a $30 million contract for a fight to be fought with gloves. The restoration of Mike's psyche is a far more lengthy, complex, and maybe even more expensive process. Truth is, Mike has been in free fall for the last ten years, since his disgraceful loss to a mediocre Buster Douglas. He's been losing ever since, to trees, to abused and vengeful women, and to a capacity for self-delusion that's been fed by ex-cons and psychopaths who know nothing about self-defense but everything about self-indulgence.

While we looked to Evander to repeat his performance and stop the retrogressive Tyson again, we can't claim the omniscience of Teddy Atlas, the scrappy little ex-trainer of Michael Moorer, who lived with Cus and Mike in Tyson's formative years and helped transform the thug into the pug. A few hours before the fight, Teddy called it on the nose or—forgive us—the ear: "Mike will foul on purpose and get disqualified. It's in his nature. I can tell Mike is planning it if Evander fights back and doesn't submit." Teddy even mentioned the possibility of biting as Mike's cowardly way out of a situation he couldn't control.

Maybe we should call him Irony Mike Tyson, because as we now look back on his $200 million slide from his fame in the eighties to his shame in the nineties, I remember a charming evening I happened to spend with him back in what seemed like the Golden Days, when he had just reunited the heavyweight championship of the world. Of all the boxers I have known, Mike was by far the most scholarly in terms of heavyweight history. Cus D'Amato loved to talk about the old champions, and co-manager, classy handball champion Jim Jacobs had cornered the market on fight films all the way back to Johnson and Jeffries. Mike had watched them all and talked knowledgeably and lovingly on the defensive skills of Jack Johnson, the devastating two-fisted power of Joe Louis, the ferocity of Marciano, the genius of Ali. There was no doubt in his young mind that night that he walked in the path of their glory and was destined to carry forward the torch previously held by our legendary champions.

But there was a dark cloud hovering over this brooding man-child in a troubled world. On the eve of his title defense against Michael Spinks nine years ago, while predicting a Tyson Kayo in the *New York Post*, I wrote: "So on goes Tyson . . . on to more astronomical gates and astronomical troubles. One can't help feeling that for all his five-million-dollar dollhouse, his Bentley, his Rolls, his women, and his business controllers, the worst is yet to come. . . . The biggest fight of all may still be Tyson vs. Tyson."

Or, as Scott Fitzgerald put it, rivaling Teddy Atlas as a fight prognosticator, "There are no second acts in American lives. . . ."

With all the cynical "Bite of the Century—Bite of the Ear" jokes bandied around the press tent that wretched Saturday night, those of us who still cling to boxing despite its bone-deep afflictions wonder how many more tragedies, scandals, and crocodile bites we can take.

Sean O'Grady, the former lightweight champ and current TV boxing commentator, says "Ban Tyson for life." So do almost two-thirds of the fans. But check out the ratings on the Showtime re-run. Jay Larkin, the Showtime honcho, while giving lip service to Tyson's "totally reprehensible, totally inexcusable" behavior, also calls it "exciting, entertaining, and compelling television." Considering the mindless and gratuitous violence exploited on network and cable every night of the week, Mike's Hannibal Lector impersonation has four-star appeal for sadists and masochists. And, alas, there seems to be enough of them to up the ratings.

But for the purists in the impure world of boxing, it's the pits, and Senator McCain's Professional Boxing Safety Act couldn't come soon enough. Even though it's only a very small beginning.

The grotesque climax to Holyfield-Tyson II, with its one-year banishment for Tyson (and then maybe forgiveness if he's a very good boy?), suggests how far we still have to go.

[1997]

IV. Lewis Takes Tyson to Finishing School

IRON MIKE TYSON had shed his armor. The man millions of white Americans (and some bourgeois blacks) loved to hate has had his comeuppance. There he was, once the unbeatable terror of the heavyweights, hailed in his early twenties as the worthy successor to Joe Louis and Muhammad Ali, staring sightlessly up at the ring lights as the referee reached the fatal count of ten. In less than twenty-four minutes Lennox Lewis—the first British champion since "Ruby" Bob Fitzsimmons 104 years ago—had given Tyson the beating of his life. All week long Tyson and his cornermen had talked a ferocious game. Mike wasn't merely going to knock out Lewis. He was going to crush his skull. He was going to drive his nose bone into his brain. And then, one of the tiresome Tysonites promised in a pressroom filibuster, "We'll throw his body in the river."

For years boxing traditionalists have flinched at the X-rated dialogue. Trash talking has been raised to a fine art on the basketball courts and playing fields of America. But no one has ever attained the psychotic rage of Mike Tyson. In his hysterical outburst at the Sonny Liston weigh-in, the then Cassius Clay had screamed insults at "the big ugly bear." Child talk compared to Mike's variation on Hannibal Lector: "I'm gonna eat your children." And indeed, when they had come together for their press conference to announce this fight earlier in the year, Tyson had lunged at Lewis and actually bitten him in the thigh. The evidence was still there, incredibly, when Lewis stripped for the weigh-in two days before the fight. An angry scar still there on his side. Taking no chances with this money-cow of a battle, for this weigh-in the promoters wouldn't even allow the combatants to be in the same building at the same time. Lewis had arrived at noon so quietly that no one even noticed him until he was on the scale. And then he was gone again, the quiet man in a noisy world. All week he had taken the raving and ranting of Team Tyson with what the American press considered typical British restraint. Confronted with that threat to crush his skull and throw him in the river, Lewis characteristically never raised his voice. "We'll settle this in the ring." he said, in the tone of a barrister saying, "I'll have nothing to say until we're in court."

In the past I had been critical of Lewis for what I called "a want of passion," an overcautious passivity that seemed to diminish him despite his obvious attributes. He has an excellent jab but seemed to use it erratically, and his jolting straight right he used fitfully. It had tended to make boring fights of his two meetings with Evander Holyfield and his challenge from David Tua. "Lewis is boring and Tyson is exciting," said Jay Larkin, the Showtime honcho at a pre-fight party given by the mayor of Memphis, "and that's why we're going over a million (PPV) buys. Nobody cares about Lewis."

That was an in-house exaggeration, of course. The Brits were not in full force because of the World Cup soccer competition. But there were enough of them up there in the nosebleed seats waving their Union Jacks, chanting their "Loo-iss . . . Loo-iss . . . !" and singing their soupy "Walking in the Lewis Wonderland" to drown out the pro-Tyson crowd in the higher priced seats ($2,400 top) below. Sprinkled with celebrities like Denzel Washington, Samuel L. Jackson, Morgan Freeman, basketball's Magic Johnson, and ex-champs Joe Frazier, Evander Holyfield, and Sugar Ray Leonard, the crowd on the floor roared their excitement every time Tyson's familiar bald head was sighted on the big screen over the ring as he warmed up in his dressing room, matched by resounding boos for Lewis as he prepared in his dressing room with the same reserve he had shown all week. One man's "boring" might be another's "professional." In the midst of all this weeklong hyped-up

Tyson-mania, I had rather welcomed Lewis's failure to rise to the bait and join the circus. While I wasn't quite ready to join the toffs in singing "Walking in the Lewis Wonderland," I was beginning to relate him to the first gloved contest for the heavyweight championship back in 1892: the bellicose John L. Sullivan ("I c'n lick every man in the house!") vs. the quiet young accountant from San Francisco, James J. Corbett, who withstood the ranting of John L., kept his poise, and boxed Sullivan's ears off to take his championship belt from that ample waist. For this accomplishment Corbett was awarded a fistic *nom de boxe*, "Gentleman" Jim Corbett.

Watching Lewis fight the fight of his life, belie that "want of passion," show not a hint of fear in facing the raging bull, absorb the characteristic opening-bell Tyson rush, and then take control with punishing jabs, powerful right hands, on-target uppercuts, I began to wonder if Lewis weren't ready for the fistic nickname we reserve our legendary heroes: Jack Dempsey the "Manassa Mauler"; Jim Braddock, the "Cinderella Man"; Joe Louis, the "Brown Bomber"; "Smokin'" Joe Frazier; Cassius Clay, the "Louisville Lip." . . . After his polite demeanor outside the ring and his controlled violence inside the ropes, maybe it's time to dub Lennox Claudius Lewis, "Gentleman Len."

And curiously, there seemed to be something contagious about this gentleman business. Tyson was on record as a bad winner—not only had he knocked out Frans Botha but deliberately broke his arm. In Glasgow, against Lou Savarese, it had not been enough to beat the hapless opponent senseless. He had added insult to injury by taking one more swipe at his victim on the canvas, and then swung on the protesting referees for good—or is it bad—measure.

Followers of the sweet—if sometimes rancid—science have always defended boxing as a sport that civilized fistfighting. Away from the ring, most boxers were devoted pacifists, and in the ring their violence was kept within bounds by rules and referees. No one hits a man when he's down, and if he hits a referee, it should be over and out. But Mike had fought like a throwback to the

early bare-knuckle days, before the good Marquess of Queensberry, when gouging eyes and throttling throats were *de rigueur*.
When Mike the muscular man-child was running the mean streets
of Brownsville, it was strictly survival by any means necessary.
Gouge, bite, blindside, rob—it was all in a day's work. His daddy
was long gone and mama's live-in boyfriend beat her up so regularly that one night in desperation she had poured scalding water
on him. Mike Tyson was a child of violence, violence was the only
school he ever attended, and while other ghetto-reared boxers
learned to trade their street violence for the boxer's discipline,
there seemed to be a permanent rage in Mike that swept away
those boundaries. The bad winner in the Glasgow fight became
the bad loser in the second Holyfield fight, the notorious "bite
fight." He was a walking time bomb in and out of the ring, and to
our common shame, the more outrageous his anti-social behavior, the more tickets he sold. From a family where all three children lived in one fetid room, he had moved on to a twenty-six-
room mansion—and then three mansions—and not one luxury
car but a garage full of Bentleys and BMWs. He had been the fla-
grant flag-carrier for Thorstein Veblen's Theory of Conspicuous
Consumption. But with all the instant fame, success, and money,
the twelve-year-old pickpocket-banger was always there, crouching dangerously inside him, ready to punch out young women,
parking attendants, inquiring reporters, even two old men in
fender-bender clashes. On the eve of the fight in Memphis the
main topic of conversation was, "What will Mike do if he wins?"
And what if he lost?

When he did, ignominiously, the genteel atmosphere projected
by the winner seemed to convert the loser. Tyson? A gallant
loser? Did you say *gracious*? Tyson's inability even to make a
dent on Lewis, the total one-sidedness of the contest, was not the
biggest surprise of the evening. That was reserved for Tyson's gen-
tlemanly reaction to the outcome. Pulling himself together after
the knockout, he made his way to Lewis's corner and, with genuine tenderness, wiped away a fleck of blood from Lewis's face,
telling him through bloodied lips that he loved him, he was truly

a great fighter, the consummate fighter. Tyson has a way of pulling unexpected words out of his head. When he does, I hear the ghost voice of the dedicated old man who took him out of reform school at age thirteen, legally adopted and developed him. "Consummate" is a Cus D'Amato word. Then Mike went on to say he loved Lennox's mother too, and proved it by actually kissing her. Lewis in turn praised Mike for his courage in standing up to all those power punches, eating seven of every ten as Mike just stood there, an easy target, a human punching bag.

So whither goes our erstwhile Iron Mike? "At some point," said his disappointed trainer, Ronnie Shields, "the people who care about him have to say this is it, it's over."

That would seem the logical conclusion. But the fight game has always had an uneasy relationship with logic. With a record PPV gross of $103 million on 1.8 million buys, Mike's purse could reach $25 million. Sounds like enough to retire on. Until you remember that going into this fight, Mike was $13 million in the red to Showtime. Now subtract two-thirds of the paycheck for managers, trainer, and taxes, and the sad arithmetic still leaves Mike $4 million or $5 million in debt. It's the 2002 version of the Joe Louis story. Every time Joe fought, he was deeper in debt. And when he was finally knocked out by Rocky Marciano at the end of his string, the IRS was into him for millions of dollars he could never repay.

So let's not hold our breaths about Mike's taking his trainer's advice and hanging them up before he becomes what the boxing boys call derisively "a trial horse" or, pathetically, even worse, "an opponent." I see him fighting his fellow slugger David Tua for a $10 million purse he's unable to keep. I see an up-and-coming contender like Wladimir Klitschko wanting to add the Tyson scalp to his belt on his way to a title shot. I see Mike touring Europe, the angry bear let out of his cage to perform. Mike Tyson, undisputed king and hero of the late eighties, weighs in as boxing's first tragic figure of the twenty-first century.

Meanwhile the new king, now the heavyweight hero of the current era, has had the defining fight and has claimed the legacy he promised us. Now not just the loyal Brits in the bleachers but everybody is chanting, "Loo-iss, Loo-iss . . ." And eager to know his plans. The heavyweight ranks are so thin that he may decide, aged thirty-seven come September, that it's time for a gentleman's retirement.

Whatever he decides, he will always be remembered as the man who transformed Iron Mike Tyson from a bullying skull crusher to his humble No. 1 fan. One reason so many authors have been drawn to boxing is because its dramatic possibilities are so extreme. In what other sport does a single victory produce a winner for life, or doom the loser to tragic consequences? After the mayhem in Memphis, Lennox Lewis had all the world in front of him, if he wants it, which with his quixotic nature, he may not. And for poor, old, beat-up Mike Tyson, the wonder boy of the eighties, it was all behind him now.

[2002]

15

The Little Prince: Good Hit, No Field

IN ALL THREE Madison Square Gardens, from the early century original to its venerable Eighth Avenue replacement, to the current labyrinthine venue adjoining Penn Station, through a thousand fighters vying for world titles, there has never been an entrance like the disco madness complete with strobe lights, smoke machines, and confetti, starring Britain's most publicized export to America since the Beatles—the eccentric and then undefeated featherweight champion, Prince Naseem Hamed.

In England, where he had won all twenty-eight of his fights (with twenty-six KOs), Hamed's countrymen seemed to be delighted with the Prince's ability to take self-promotion to an all-time level of narcissism. They cheered when the self-anointed Prince leapt toward the ring through a circle of flames. They cheered again when he was borne toward the ring on a golden throne on the backs of half-naked, gaudily costumed "slaves." Then the cocky dance on the ring apron and the theatrically show-off climax of the elaborate pre-fight act, the acrobatic somersault into the ring—it was all there again for Hamed's super-hyped American debut against our veteran featherweight and former WBC champion Kevin Kelley.

The roll call of featherweight champions is an honor roll of greatest fighters in any division, from Henry Armstrong, Kid Chocolate, Willie Pep, and Sandy Saddler to Alex Arguello, Salvador Sanchez, and Azumah Nelson. But all of them together didn't earn what Prince Naseem took down last year—$12 million, with a new contract from HBO for six more fights at $2 million per performance. And since the Arab-Brit was a household name in England but unknown outside of boxing circles in the States, HBO launched an unprecedented $2 million promo campaign on Hamed's behalf. The first thing New Jersey commuters saw as they came out of Lincoln Tunnel to Manhattan was a fifty-foot poster of the Prince in his trademark leopard skin trunks, looking down on his subjects with a sense of haughtiness that could give lessons to his fellow British prince, Charles. Naseem's father is an immigrant from Yemen who became a groceryman in Sheffield, England; but somehow little Naseem, taunted into fighting as a tan-skinned shrimp in a blue-eyed world of public school boys, assumed his own arrogant nobility. It may be an act, pure kitsch, Muhammad Ali on the half-shell, but Hamed has been able to carry it off with his mouthy Beatles insouciance the media happily buys into. I thought there were no more negative surprises for me in the field of TV advertising campaigns until I caught the promo for Hamed's arrival for the Kelley fight. A "Prophet of Doom"—no less—on the roof of a New York hotel, shouting at the skyline of Manhattan, "A Prince is coming . . . he will defeat you . . . you will fall at his feet. . . ."

This was in the Christmas season, and one wondered for a moment if this was not Big Advertising and HBO's paying homage to the Prince of Peace, the Son of God. But the next shot, showing the Prince somersaulting over a ship's railing into a waiting limo, brought us back to reality or what passes for reality in a world of billion-dollar communication where the word "hyperbole" is already an understatement. To describe the praise and attention heaped on Prince Hamed by HBO in the buildup to his first appearance in America as "hyperbole" is like calling Tiger Woods an "effective" golfer or Greta Garbo "pretty."

So you finally want to hear about the fight? That's right, after all the hoopla, there finally was a fight, even if they played it as a mass-media rock show. And after the eight minutes of pretentious foreplay, after the Prince made his slow dance on the silly ground down a special $20,000 Disneyish ramp to the ring as the disco music blared and thousands of converts swayed and clapped to the beat, screaming "Naz! Naz! Naz!" while loyal New Yorkers chanted "Kel-ley . . . Kel-ley. . . ." After all this, in just fifty-eight seconds of the first round the self-proclaimed inheritor of the mantle of Ali ("He could only fight one way. I can fight five ways") looked as if he were fighting a sixth way, a losing way. The black American veteran was backing him up with sharp right jabs that not only stung but actually seemed to wobble him a little bit. Ali pulled away from jabs too, in a style not entirely kosher, as trainers prefer their fighters slipping the jab and countering. Ali could get away with it because he was, well, Ali. The supposedly elusive Hamed was pulling back awkwardly, off balance, and not quite far enough to get his chin out of the way. Taking an eight count.

Round two was exciting, with the confident, forward-moving Kelley dropping Hamed again, though the surprisingly hitable little superstar did manage a knockdown of his own. But Kelley was still in control in the third, able to nail Hamed again with overhand rights that the lionized Prince did not know how to avoid.

By the fourth round Naseem was already down three times, in danger of being exposed as a fraud, a vehicle of overblown promos. That Prophet of Doom seemed to be calling down the skies not on willing and able Kevin Kelley but on the HBO mavens who had put all their golden eggs in their Little Prince's grocery basket. He pulled their twelve million bucks out of the fire with a dramatic knockout in the fourth round, a hard right hand that caught Kelley as he was coming in. He had been knocked down earlier in that round, but Hamed had been down again too, in a wild stanza that reminded some of the Hagler-Hearns classic rounds (though neither of these boys is of their caliber).

At the end, Kelley was glassy-eyed, and his legs refused the commands of his mind. He had let what looked like almost certain victory, and an historic upset, slip away from him. In the post-fight press conference the always articulate Kelley summed it up neatly. "I lost because I saw the end of the fight, not the present." Dwelling on the spectacular knockout he was about to score, he overlooked a minor detail: Hamed could punch too. Boxing is the art of hitting without getting hit.

Kelley's reflections on Hamed's abilities were also on target. "He's a good fighter, but he's not as good as he thinks he is. He's no Roy Jones."

So the stage is set for the second act of HBO's Prince Hamed extravaganza. Maybe the supporting player will be Kennedy McKinney, who also pulled out an uphill, fourth-round victory over Junior Jones, who was looking forward to his own Hamed paynight. Whoever the overrated Prince fights next should make for an interesting evening, because even if he did compare himself, to his advantage, he's no Willie Pep. He gets hit easy, and the chin is suspect. But he can punch, and he gets up, two qualities that never hurt fistic success.

My advice would be, for all the braggadocio, all the supercilious comparisons to Pep and Ali, he'd better try to hold on to those millions rolling in and get out while he's ahead, or he may find himself walking down Queer Street rather than Bond Street.

But maybe now I'm beginning to sound like the Prophet of Doom. You listen to these Mighty Mouths long enough (the lucky Prince was insufferable at the press conference), they take a bite out of your brain.

(Fax to Hamed: Next time, cut the pre-fight disco dance to, like five minutes. Please. Zero minutes would be nice too. Oh, and Prince, after the somersault, watch your chin.)

[1998]

P.S. My warning was well taken. In time Hamed would face one of those indomitable Mexican featherweights (junior lightweights), Marco Antonio Barrera, and be exposed for what he was, an oddity with a good punch but no real conception of defense, a victim of his own, insufferable hubris and an overhyped promotion. Millions of dollars were lavished on a pig's ear mislabeled and sold to us as a silk purse. So it's hail and farewell, Little Prince of the Kingdom of Hyperbole.

[2001]

16

The Night of the Undisputed

NOT SINCE JIM CORBETT went 61 three-minute rounds with Peter Jackson at the Olympic Club in San Francisco in 1891 have fight fans been asked to defy the arms of Morpheus as they were last Saturday night by Don King's unprecedented eight championship fights in Atlantic City's Boardwalk Hall—a fistic marathon that began at five o'clock in the evening and went on until one o'clock the following morning. It was an eight-hour immersion in pugilistica at its very best—underdog Cory Spinks' exhilarating defeat of Don King's latest cash cow, the Nicaraguan terror, Ricardo Mayorga—and at its very worst, the 12-round and seemingly interminable wrestling match with boxing gloves between two heavyweight sloths, John Ruiz and Hasim Rahman. Hailed by the WBA and Don King as the "Interim Heavyweight Championship," the spectacle involved two Goliaths who sweated and strained, pulled and pushed through twelve of the dreariest rounds in heavyweight history. Fortunately the evening was saved by the underrated young Spinks and the Old Man River of the middleweights, the cantankerous thirty-nine-year-old Bernard Hopkins, winning his record seventeenth defense of his 160-pound title over the brave but outclassed WBA veteran William Joppy.

There was another notable contest involving our irrepressible promoter, Mr. King. Just two days before King's Saturday night mega-card, it was fought not in a ring but in a court of law in New York, where the world's most famous promoter squared off

The irrepressible Don King, in 1977. (© Bettmann/Corbis)

against "Terrible" Terry Norris, the nifty junior middleweight champion of the mid-nineties, now retired, somewhat brain-damaged and broke, not an unfamiliar condition for top fighters who stay too long and never learn how to protect themselves in the bigger ring of business management. Terry was suing for the $7.5 million he had earned but never saw. Known as Teflon Don for winning so many lawsuits his opponents thought were shoe-ins, King must have sensed he was in trouble when the jury sent out for a calculator and a magnifying glass. And a short time later came the decision: The unsinkable Mr. King had to write a check for half the seven-five-mil on the spot, the remainder to be paid in monthly installments.

"Only in America!" is Don's trademark slogan, and you could say that again as he ducked out of the courtroom, right into his limo and on to Atlantic City where he was back in polysyllabic form, lording it over the press conference. There the usual taunting and self-promoting predictions between the fighters began with Hopkins, unbeatable for a decade and even knocking out

Tito Trinidad, who still felt deprived of the respect and money he thought he deserved. Now he was dissing his opponent, WBA Champion William Joppy, promising to knock him cold. When Joppy tried to fight back, verbally, Hopkins offered to fatten Joppy's purse by fifty thousand dollars if he was still on his feet at the final bell.

That was mild compared to the trash-talking Mayorga, the hottest name on the card, who had come out of nowhere to knock out two marquee welterweights, "Six-Head" Lewis and Vernon Forrest. The new champion was a wild man in and out of the ring. He flaunted outrageous behavior, not only brazenly drinking beer on the eve of a fight but showing up on the dance floor with a pretty girl on his arm at three o'clock in the morning. And in the ring after his hand was raised, nonchalantly lighting a cigarette. Nothing like this has been seen since the legendary bad boy of boxing, Harry Greb, the middleweight champ of the 1920s, who also trained on beer and broads but licked the best middleweights and light heavies of his day. At the press conference Mayorga, the street kid from the slums of Managua, insulted Corey Spinks's dead mother, questioned his manhood, and told him he was not only going to knock him out but probably kill him. For those who knew Spanish, Mayorga's gutter talk was unprintable. Son of the unruly Leon of Ali fame, young Spinks—the IBF title holder but still virtually unknown—seemed unfazed by the verbal onslaught. Speaking very quietly, he said, "All that craziness and silliness won't bother me. This isn't a toughman contest. It's the art of boxing, the ability to hit and not get hit in return. That's the skill I have worked hard on."

True to his word, the Spinks kid came out of his corner "gaily," as my notes described it, borrowing the word from the eighteenth century's Pierce Egan, the daddy of boxing writers. As cool and fearless as he had seemed at the press conference, Spinks met the caveman lunges of the surly Mayorga with textbook slipping of punches, confusing him with lateral movement and sharp counterpunching. By the end of round one we knew we were in for one of those classic contests between a scientific boxer and a primitive but hard-punching brute. The suspense built dramatically as Mayorga hit out with vicious, awkward punches from all angles. Spinks would slip them or gracefully slide away with great aplomb. All the pre-fight fanfare had focused on the ferocious Mayorga, with Spinks cast as just one more sacrificial Christian to be thrown to King's lion. Apparently Cory hadn't read the script, which had Mayorga's moving on to meet Sugar Shane Mosley in King's next major promotion. Spinks was to be just one very small bump on the road to the next Vegas super-fight on March 13.

Frustrated by more boxing science than he had bargained for, Mayorga tried every dirty tactic he knew. Not since Fritzie Zivic half a century ago have I seen so many rabbit punches, holding and hitting, hitting on the break and after the bell at the end of a round.

At the end of the second round, the alert referee, Tony Orlando, warned Mayorga, but down and dirty seemed to be the only way he knew. He was teeing off with huge roundhouse blows, but nine of ten hit nothing but air. Every time he missed, he was open to counters, and Spinks was scoring with straight lefts to Mayorga's solid chin. For students of the art, it was lovely to watch.

The fifth round gave Mayorga his first real chance when he finally caught his slippery opponent with a solid right hand to the jaw. Spinks lost his poise for a moment, and Mayorga tried to follow up with fast but mostly off-target punches. It was his round, but he blew it when he threw another whopper after the bell, losing a point on the scorecards.

Round after round it was Spinks boxing nicely, Mayorga punching wildly. Every so often King's new favorite would land a heavy right hand, but Spinks proved he had chin as well as skill. As the rounds dwindled down, Mayorga's frustration grew. Billed as the Matador, he was much more like the bull goaded into charging at the air.

In the eleventh Mayorga caught Spinks with another of those wild looping rights, and might have won the round but holding behind the neck while punching Spinks in the face cost him another penalty point. In the final round when Spinks went down, either from a wild punch or a wet spot on the canvas, the furious Mayorga thought he had a two-point round, but Orlando called it a slip, as he had two others in the early rounds.

There is a saying in boxing, "Always bet the house fighter," and when the fight goes to a decision, the cynical view is that judges will favor Mr. King, who can do them a lot of favors in return. But no such luck for him this time. Winner and now undisputed welterweight champion of the world, on the radar screen at last, the 5 to 1 underdog Cory Spinks!

A world title fight is a ritual involving the press conference, the weigh-in, the fight itself, and the epilogue, the press conference. An hour after Bernard Hopkins had left poor William Joppy with a face his own mother would not recognize, "The Executioner" was assuring the press that this was his last performance for Don King. "After this I'm a free man. I'm out on parole." From now on he would be his own promoter. After five years in the slammer and all those years being exploited by promoters, he was finally in control of his destiny. "I am the American dream."

As for Don King's darling, the ferocious Ricardo Mayorga was still snarling. "I know I won the fight. I had to fight him and the referee. I knocked him down three times. Next time I will stop his heart."

The quiet and unscathed Cory Spinks simply smiled. Would he accept a rematch? "Yes, but in all fairness I deserve to take Mayorga's place to meet Shane Mosley on March 13." Easier said than done. Let the shenanigans begin! In the absence of a true commissioner of boxing to keep the sport honest, Don King won't give up that easily on his crowd-pleasing Mayorga. Chances are, he'll feed him some soft ones and then push Spinks into the rematch.

The twenty-five-year-old Cory Spinks understands adversity. A few years ago his older brother Leon Jr. was shot in the mean streets of St. Louis where they were raised by a single mother. Then his best friend was lost to gang warfare in that tough town.

And soon after, his mother died of a stroke at age forty-eight. Maybe that's why he's so quiet and serious. I talked to him for a few minutes after the press conference. "If I have to fight Mayorga again, I will. I'll outbox him again. But I don't think it's right. Tonight I earned the right to fight Mosley." He gave a little sigh, as if thinking of all the little wheels within wheels spinning in Don King's head. "We'll just have to wait and see."

P.S. Hovering over the weekend like the Ghost of Christmas Past was the legendary, all-time great Roberto Duran, ex-lightweight, welterweight, and junior middleweight champion of the world, still with that wicked glint in his eye. But like nearly all ex-champions, dead broke. A sad reminder that our boxers are the only professional athletes in the world without a pension. Fifty years ago I received an award from the University of Notre Dame for promoting this idea. In the year of Our Lord, 2003, I'm still waiting.

[2003]

17

The "Heavyweight Championship of the World"— or, Four for the Price of One

YEARS AGO, as the first boxing editor of *Sports Illustrated*, I confessed it: I'm a sucker for the heavyweight championship of the world. No sports event in the world can compare with it, I contended. It's more than a fight between, ideally, the two best heavyweights in the world, competing in the most prestigious division of what used to be eight and has now metastasized to triple that traditional amount. At its best, it's a celebration, a ceremony, a profound rite. When the world champion meets his natural challenger, be it Dempsey-Tunney, Louis-Schmeling, Louis-Conn, Marciano-Charles, when the mercury-footed Ali faces the brave bull Joe Frazier or the thunder puncher George Foreman, these classic battles take on epic proportions. Indeed, one is reminded that the progenitor of our current boxing writers—be it Dave Anderson of the *New York Times* or Hugh McIlvanney of London's *Sunday Times*—is Homer himself, who described in poetic blow by blow, the stirring victory of Epeus over Euryalus in their ancient championship go.

There's magic in the moment when the lights go out in the great arena, with millions watching all over the world as the announcer reaches for the mike and pronounces those incantatory words, "Ladies and gentlemen, for the heavyweight championship of the woooorld!!!" How many times have I flown across the country, or the ocean, not to be absent from that spectacle! New York for Louis-Conn, Louis-Schmeling II, and Ali-Frazier I; Zaire for Ali-Foreman. For the *undisputed* heavyweight championship of the world? How could any self-respecting fan of the sweet science stay home?

Raised in that tradition, following our champions for three score years and ten, imagine my reaction to picking up the daily paper and seeing an ad not for one heavyweight championship fight but *two*! And the audacity, selling "Two for the price of one!" What's this? Our precious heavyweight championship being pitched like a bargain-basement sale? As if two heavyweight champions side by side were better than one! Forgive all these exclamation points. But this subject seems to invite them. It's as if two presidents were better than one, two chiefs of staff, two film directors, two writers of the same novel, two managers of a major sports team.

In this case the two-for-one deal on heavywieght title belts involved John Ruiz, the Puerto Rican octopus who (God help us!) wears the WBA version, and his challenger, Fres Oquendo, another oversized, undertalented Puerto Rican. The other part of the bargain involved light-hitting Chris Byrd, the IBF heavyweight champion of the world, facing Andrew Golota, better known as the South Pole for his propensity for saving his best punches for the area south of the belt line. Golota had earned his shot at Byrd's title by fouling out to Riddick Bowe back in the twentieth century, quitting to Lennox Lewis and Mike Tyson, and then scoring recent dubious victories over two sacrificial lambs. Only Don King could explain how this discredited Polish disaster waiting to happen could qualify for a title shot.

Don has revised Barnum's famous teaser, "There's a sucker born every minute." In our speeded up twenty-first century, the prison-library-intellectual Professor King would tell you there's a sucker born every thirty seconds, and prove it with every PPV triumph. Anybody who's got the brass to bring the octopusian John Ruiz back for still another soporific display of his "championship" prowess deserves our respect, at least for chutzpah above and beyond the call of promotional overreaching. Instead of being anointed with a belt, Mr. Ruiz should be arrested for impersonating a professional heavyweight fighter. Don's waving his little Puerto Rican flag for him reminds us that he also touted Peter McNeeley, another of Mike Tyson's one-round wonders, as "that great warrior from Boston."

The Ruiz-Oquendo fight in Madison Square Garden could be the worst heavyweight title fight ever fought anywhere. Ruiz grabbed, held, hugged, and mugged. As the boos of the fifteen thousand suffering fans crescendoed, one exasperated (and apparently embottled) fan rose from way up in the bleachers and bellowed, "This is the worst fight I ever seen!" He received a standing ovation. It was without doubt the most exciting moment of the long evening.

Finally, in the eleventh round, Ruiz actually threw a few punches that landed, and maybe Oquendo was so surprised he dropped his hands as if in distress. The referee promptly stepped in and stopped the fight, not to save Ruiz's dance partner from further punishment so much as to save the paying customers from further punishment. This could be the first heavyweight title fight ever stopped on account of boredom. The referee simply decided he couldn't stand another second of it and raised Ruiz's hand. The World Boxing Association (from which I confess I accepted its Living Legend of Boxing Award) should be ashamed of itself, if all the boxing commissions hadn't long ago surrendered any sense of shame.

At least the second half of Don King's two-for-one title bout bargain was an improvement. Chris Byrd, the slippery, small-heavyweight defending his IBF belt went the distance in a close fight with the renovated and supposedly reformed Polish bruiser Andrew Golota, who restricted himself to only a few low blows and a couple of punches after the bell, his way of observing the Marquess of Queensberry rules. Among the surprises in the bout was Byrd's allowing himself to be hit by the usually wild Golota, choosing to stand and trade punches with his bigger and stronger opponent rather than employ the evasive, defensive style that has brought him to the top while not pleasing many fans. "Look at me, I look like a fighter!" he exulted over his bruises, as if they had earned him a medal in his brutal trade. Whether he had fought a stupid fight or one calculated to win over doubting fans, only the highly intelligent and personable IBF champ knows. His 115 to 113 victory seemed a fair call, even if Golota galumphed out of the ring angry about a decision he thought he deserved. In any case, to everyone's surprise, Byrd's back in the heavyweight picture, such as it is.

Last Saturday the heavyweight express—or is it a slow freight?—moved on to Los Angeles, the adopted hometown of the fighting Klitschko brothers, Vitali and Wladimir, a pair of giant Ukrainian Ph.D.s. Wladimir was reduced to cornerman for his brother now, having been humiliated by the journeyman underdog Lamon "Relentless" Brewster by way of knockout a few weeks earlier, thereby surrendering his WBO heavyweight belt—one of those four belts now up for grabs. Any moment now, Don King will be offering four heavyweight title fights, all in one night. Four for the price of one, made to order for that sucker born every thirty seconds.

In the most recent heavyweight contest, Vitali, the harder puncher but less fluid of the Klitschkos, was in there with old Corrie Sanders, the South American game farmer who had starched his crystal-chinned brother a year ago. Corrie, at least ten pounds over his best fighting weight, looked as if he had been training at his favorite pub. "For me, either way, whatever happens, I can now say I've had a nice career," Sanders said, not after but before the fight, as if he were already preparing his own postmortem. In spite of that defeatist approach, he fought the first round as if he really thought he could win, catching his larger foe with big, roundhouse punches that actually staggered Klitschko and drove him across the ring.

Vitali regrouped in the second round, boxing from that stiff, stand-up British and Russian stance, reminding us of Bombardier Wells, the celebrated, horizontal British heavyweight of the 1920s. He was putting his jabs in Sanders's face and finding the range with right hands. Not that that was too difficult to do, with Sanders fighting flat-footed and with a barroom defense.

Still Sanders kept trying, with more guts than stamina. In a rousing exchange in the third, Klitschko was tagged—but his chin was proving more durable than Wlad's, and the South African's tank was running low. In the good old days he would have been just a tough four-round fighter, and that's what he looked like in the fifth, with the Ph.D. from Kiev backing him up with combinations.

It was really all over, and through the ensuing rounds what was most notable was Sanders's ability to absorb so many punches without going down. Also notable was Sanders every so often throwing a looping punch out of exhaustion and still driving Klitschko into the ropes.

By round eight the only question was how many straight right hands Sanders could take and still keep lurching forward. The referee answered that by stopping the fight with Corrie still on his feet, a proud but bloody mess, and Vitali winning the WBC title that Lennox Lewis gave up when he announced his retirement.

Lewis was in the audience, as he had been the week before in New York when he had walked out on Ruiz. "Let the next era begin," the old king had proclaimed. So where does that leave us? Gone at least for the moment is my old heavyweight mystique. Now it's more of a heavyweight mess. Vitali Klitschko looked like the best of a sorry bunch. He was durable but robotic, with a pretty good jab and a pretty good right hand. Everything just pretty good. Mechanical, and too easy to hit, he'd barely qualify for Joe Louis's celebrated Bum of the Month tour. And now he's decided he'd rather run for mayor of Kiev. Who else? Chris Byrd is clever, but he can't punch. Good field, no hit. Mike Tyson? After surrendering to journeyman Kevin McBride, it's the final nail in the coffin where rests Tyson's tragic career. Roy Jones, flattened twice by light heavyweight rivals, is ready to be retired to his chicken fighters. No wonder pure, used-up Evander hangs around. And another Old Man River, the ring-savvy but aging and overgrown James Toney, who may still be the best of this depleted lot.

Oh where have all the heavyweights gone? Where are Rocky Marciano, Muhammad Ali, Joe Frazier, and Larry Holmes now that we need them? Maybe George Foreman should tear himself away from his multi-million-dollar grill business, Meineke mufflers, and new clothing line and teach these bargain-basement "champions" a lesson in what it takes to be truly the heavyweight champion of the world.

[2006]

18

Ricky Hatton and Kostya Tszyu:
The British Are Coming!

WATCHING the longtime king of the 140-pounders, the Russian/Australian Kostya Tszyu, give up on his stool in exhausted defeat after 11 grueling rounds with the underdog local boy, Ricky Hatton, replacing him as IBF junior welterweight champion of the world, I realized once again why the dean of boxing writers, Hugh McIlvanney, calls boxing "the hardest game."

You are in there alone, bone-tired, your eye is swollen and your jaw is throbbing, and despite a last die-hard effort, you face nothing but more of the same on your way to inevitable defeat. Common sense tells you to quit. But tradition urges you to persevere, to walk through the wall of pain, to defy reason in pursuit of pride. It is a cruel tradition, but not without its standards of nobility. The venerable manager and fistic guru Cus D'Amato reminded us that the difference between true champions and contenders is "character." "Character is more important than boxing ability," he preached, "without character, the power of the mind, willpower, you'll never be a champion."

The history of the ring reflects Professor D'Amato's philosophy. All the way back to the primitive beginnings of the demanding sport, in 1750, when the old champion John Broughton faced the underdog challenger Jack Slack and found himself blinded by a terrible blow between the eyes. When taunted by his disappointed backer, the Duke of Cumberland, Broughton famously said, "I can't see my man, your Highness. I am blind but not beat. Only let me be placed before my antagonist and he shall not gain the day yet."

Watching Kostya's trainer ask his man if he wanted to continue, and then taking passivity for an answer, tell the referee, "No more, no more," I was reminded of all those abortive endings of famous fights when the loser quietly folded his tent and slunk away. Will we ever forget the infamous "No mas, no mas" of Roberto Duran when he raised the white (or was it yellow?) flag in his rematch with Sugar Ray Leonard? And there was Sonny Liston sitting sullenly in his corner and refusing to come out against his irreverent tormentor, Cassius Clay (soon to be Muhammad Ali). And in the rematch, reclining after the first punch, as if to say, "That's it. Who needs this embarrassment?"

On the other side of this hard equation is the raging bull, Jake LaMotta, who in their sixth meeting took an unbelievable battering from Sugar Ray Robinson. Stubbornly planting his feet, he absorbed punishment like a human sponge, with a Jack Broughton pride that Cus would have admired as willpower supreme, even though if it had been one of his boys, like Floyd Patterson, he would have erred on the side of compassion.

This is not to say that Kostya Tszyu is a fighter without character. His has been a distinguished career, beginning in 1992, with only one previous loss, to Vince Philips, eight years ago, and with dramatic knockouts of top contenders Sharma Mitchell and Zab Judah. He has been a gentlemen and a scholar of boxing, with a memorable right hand, a nifty left, and a pleasing boxer-puncher style. At his best he belongs with the top junior welters of all time. And if he chooses to retire after this unexpected defeat, he will be remembered with honor even if he didn't go down with all guns firing as usually demanded of our fading champions.

At this moment, when the tearjerker *Cinderella Man*, with Russell Crowe as Jim Braddock, is up for an Academy Award, it may be remembered that Braddock's finest hour wasn't really his underdog victory over an out-of-shape, clowning Max Baer, it was his gutsy stand in a lost cause in his ensuing battle with Joe Louis,

Ricky Hatton (right) in his grueling battle with Kostya Tszyu. (© Darren Staples/Reuters/Corbis)

when Braddock's manager, Joe Gould, told his fighter he was getting ready to stop the fight to save his fighter from further punishment, and the bloodied Braddock said, "If you do, I'll never speak to you again." Braddock had the Broughton spirit to the last gasp, and was counted out as the champion he never really had been before.

It's exciting when a new face and a new force takes center stage, as Joe Louis did in the thirties, as Rocky Marciano did in the fifties, Mike Tyson in the eighties, and now as Ricky Hatton moves onward and upward from being a local idol to take his place on the world stage. The Manchester lad won the fight with wild, take-no-prisoner aggression, and while Tszyu won more of the first six rounds with sharper punching, Hatton kept coming and coming, with a rough brawling style that comes naturally to him and was his game plan, tiring the aging champion in the clinches, which referee Dave Parris seemed reluctant to break, and showing a stouter chin against Tszyu's shorter, harder punches than we had foreseen.

In the sixth round a punch on Hatton's belt-line that was called low dropped the determined young man for a moment, and in the next round, hit by several low blows again, Ricky retaliated with a low blow of his own that looked intentional, as if to say, "You keep hitting me low, I won't depend on the ref, I'll take care of this myself." The blow was a telling one that seemed to drain the champion, who was wearing down in the late rounds anyway, as youth and a fierce resolve were being served at the expense of experience and science. By round ten, Kostya's thirty-five years were weighing on him, he was growing older by the moment, and Ricky Hatton pressed on with remarkable vigor, missing a lot but every so often nailing the old champ in a way I had never seen before—and I had seen him win notable fights over the years.

The 23,000 local fans were delirious, and this time it wasn't Frank Bruno or Prince Hamed, who weren't up to scratch with Mike Tyson and Marco Antonio Barrera respectively. They had a legitimate hero at last, in what strikes me as the most notable British victory since Randy Turpin upset the first (and best) Sugar Ray more than fifty years ago.

So where does the pride of Manchester go from here? He's ready for prime time now, Madison Square Garden, PPV, multi-million-dollar fights against the best. Floyd Mayweather, Jr., may be an overreach, but in Ricky Hatton at last England has a fighter with no quit in him. He's young, strong, determined, has his own rough-and-ready ring smarts, and this time, when that throng of drunken Brits comes over and fills the gallery to root their man on and sing their beery chants, they'll have something to root for. He could be a throwback to those doughty middle-sized battlers of the nineteenth century, Jack Randall the Nonpareil and Gallant Tom Sayers.

[2005]

▪ 19 ▪

Requiem for a Middleweight

BERNARD HOPKINS has done what no middleweight in the history of the toughest of all the boxing divisions has done, setting a record that will almost surely never be surpassed: holding the middleweight title for a full decade with a record twenty successful defenses against the top contenders from the middle 1990s to the present year. Knocking out both the super-rich superstar Oscar De La Hoya and the Puerto Rican legend Felix Trinidad, the fighter who calls himself the Executioner and enters the ring with a death-row black mask and hood, as if he were in the wrestling circus, was the overwhelming choice for No. 1 pound-for-pound honors until he took on young, brash, likable, flashy, Jermain Taylor last July. Hopkins lost a razor-thin and controversial split decision that night, setting the stage for last Saturday's encounter, which fight buffs were anticipating as the biggest fight of the year.

In their first encounter Hopkins, always a cautious starter using the early rounds to study his opponent, searching for weaknesses he will exploit in the later rounds, gave away the first six rounds, doing little or nothing, but turning the tables in the second half of the fight when the undefeated but inexperienced contender, who had failed to pace himself, was running out of gas. The forty-year-old Hopkins closed the show convincingly enough to earn at least a draw, which would have enabled him to keep the four belts that signify the undisputed championship. Hopkins was so sure he had won that he threatened to have the scoring investigated. In truth, one myopic judge had given the last round to

217

Taylor, a round in which Hopkins had staggered his young opponent and clearly dominated. But his overly cautious start had cost him dearly, a shortcoming the headstrong and always confrontational Hopkins refused to acknowledge. Next time, he promised, he would make the first round the thirteenth round of the last fight, when he was finally backing up the twenty-seven-year-old pretender to his throne, and pouring it on.

"I'm coming into this one with a Blue Horizon mentality," Hopkins warned. Translation: Hopkins is a Philadelphia fighter, in a town known for training sessions that are bloody wars, and where those die-hard brawls are associated with the Blue Horizon. When you think Philadelphia, you remember the tough ones all the way back to Philadephia Jack O'Brien, Marvelous Marvin Hagler, Benny Briscoe, Joe Frazier—call the roll and remember the toll.

Bernard's brave talk made him a slight favorite over the new champion, and at the opening bell he came out firing with both hands at the young man "who had stolen my title." An offensive that lasted all of twenty seconds. And then, as the expectant audience began to boo, Hopkins reverted to his passive posture of the previous fight. The two of them spent more time looking at each other than punching. I scored the first round 10-10, even. But it should have been scored 0-0, because nothing happened.

After that the two of them proceeded to give one of the dreariest performances in the history of this notable division. As they clinched repeatedly like two contending octopuses, with the referee working more strenuously than the fighters, I found myself thinking back to some of the memorable middleweight title fights I've been fortunate to see—Robinson and LaMotta in Chicago, Robinson and Basilio, and Griffith-Benvenuti in New York, Hagler and Hitman Tommy Hearns in Vegas—champions whose spirit matched their ability and who gave it everything they had to the last gasp. That's what makes the sport of boxing so demanding and so compelling, when it lives up to its promise and tradition.

In this disappointing excuse for a fight, the booing grew louder round by round as Hopkins went on studying his young

Bernard Hopkins after knocking out Oscar De La Hoya in 2004. (© Steve Marcus/Reuters/Corbis)

opponent, who was winning the rounds with his rapid jabs while missing with wild right hands. Occasionally Hopkins would land with his right and score a point for Philadelphia, but there was no follow-up, no combinations, no fire. Once again the former champion seemed content to concede the first six rounds to the kid from Arkansas, who wasn't doing much either, just enough to win.

Finally, like a carbon of Hopkins-Taylor I, the old man picked up the pace a bit in the seventh and won the round, and managed to win three of the last six, mostly catching his rival with those right hand leads that a more experienced fighter would know how to avoid. The big difference between this fight and the lackluster first encounter was round eleven, where Taylor used his fast jab to good advantage and at last was scoring combinations that gave him the round and a commanding lead. Now Hopkins would have to knock him out to win, but young Taylor's athleticism and Hopkins's creeping immobility made that so unlikely that the crowd seemed more bored than expecting any last-round fireworks.

The best punch Hopkins threw in round twelve was a right to the groin, but he did connect now and then in his now almost-forty-oneish desultory way. The final bell brought relief from the boredom, and of course when all three judges decided in Taylor's favor, Hopkins again signaled his disagreement. How the once undisputed king of the modern middleweights thought he won this one is hard to figure. But if you have ever talked to Hopkins eye to eye—and he has a way of really getting in your face—you would know that you have met the master of self-assertive positive thinking. As the promotional partner of the enterprising Oscar De La Hoya in their Golden Boy Productions, Hopkins will be a formidable promoter able to stand and deal with the likes of Don King and Bob Arum. To his credit, I remember a long-ago post-fight interview in which he expressed his indignation at the way boxing promoters exploited their fighters, and vowed to do something about it. Now, as he faces retirement, already wearing his promoter's hat with the bouts he's staged for his nephew Demetrious Hopkins, he's ready to take on the reigning impresarios. He's a stubborn dude, this veteran of five years' hard time in the slammer where he learned his hard trade, and we can't help wishing him well, at the same time also wishing he had gone out with all guns firing instead of the passive performance he brought to the rematch.

He'll be forty-one a few weeks hence, and that's when the reflexes begin to betray the best of intentions. How many Archie

Moores are there who can challenge Rocky Marciano for his heavyweight title at age forty-three, and then knock him down so hard in the second round that it took all of the Rock's depthless bottom to get back into the fray?

The drama in Hopkins's last fight was all in the back story, as they call it in the movie business. Taylor's promoter, Lou DiBella, a breath of light in a dark world, had been Hopkins's promoter for many years. They not only fell out, but the characteristically suspicious and somewhat paranoid Hopkins had accused DiBella of taking a $50,000 bribe from HBO. DiBella, who just may be the one completely clean practitioner in the game, sued and won a judgment of $600,000. And then, in fairy-tale fashion, he developed the young Olympian who became the only serious challenger for Hopkins's undisputed reign.

It couldn't happen to a nicer man or a nicer kid who now goes home to Arkansas with all the belts. A heartwarming story. Except for one thing. It says something about what's wrong with the present-day boxing scene. In the good old days, back in the 1950s, '60s, '70s, Jermain Taylor would still be a promising young boxer a long way from the top. His jab is nice, and he's quick and athletic. But still too easy to hit, with his left jab his only trusty weapon, he still has an awful lot to learn. The trouble is, given the dearth of talent, Taylor may never get a chance to hone his skills. Can you see him in there with Robinson or LaMotta or Cerdan or, for that matter, with Emile Griffith or Hagler, or the middleweight Archie Moore? Tough nonchampions like Charley Burley, Georgie Abrams, Solly Krieger, and a dozen more buzzing in my head would give this promising young man major trouble.

But it's not the twentieth century. Alas, it's the twenty-first, and all we can do is go on to the next and hope for the best.

[2005]

20

Felix Trinidad

I. Trinidad vs. Mayorga: Brain vs. Brawn

A LONG TIME AGO I tried to describe boxing as a sport far more complicated and mental than casual observers or critics of the manly art may believe. Jose Torres, the great articulate light heavyweight champion of the sixties, a disciple of the trainer-philosopher-guru Cus D'Amato, was applying this rule to the explosive Felix Trinidad–Ricardo Mayorga brawl at Madison Square Garden a week ago Saturday night.

"A champion's fight doesn't start in the ring. It begins here," Torres said, tapping his head. Meanwhile Trinidad was pounding the bombast out of Mayorga, knocking him down for the first time in the Nicaraguan wild man's tempestuous career, and then again and again, until a fight that lived up to Don King's most exuberant predictions was stopped at last, with the victorious Felix Trinidad on his way to new glories and the brutally battered Mayorga on his way to the hospital.

While Mayorga was throwing wild punches, landing occasionally, the mentally far superior Trinidad was fighting a thinking man's fight, boxing with a clear plan in mind and executing it with precision. The punishment Mayorga absorbed was painful to behold. Near the end of the fifth round Trinidad was using Mayorga's tough head for a punching bag, and empathetic ringsiders were getting a headache from the rat-a-tat-tat of Trinidad's punches to Ricardo's battered noggin.

In the pre-fight hype, the hard-talking, hard-drinking, hard-smoking, hard-punching wild man had been billed as Ricardo "El Matador" Mayorga. But once the bell rang, and he charged furiously from his corner, almost at once he was transformed into El Toro. Indeed this fight reminded me of the many *corridas* I had seen in Mexico City, in the rare times when the bull was up to the challenge and would charge and charge again, under the relentless punishment of the sharp points of the banderillas and the steel of the picadors, before accepting the sword of the matador.

That's exactly what the hopelessly brave Mayorga did, weakening for a moment and beginning to look discouraged, and then, when it seemed as if he must drop, suddenly reaching down for some hidden strength and charging again.

The hype for this fight had involved the memory of Hagler-Hearns, that unforgettable middleweight drama 20 years ago, and this was one time when hype and reality actually began to overlap. For the first round did remind me of the opening round of Marvin Hagler's battle with "Hitman" Tommy Hearns, when Hearns put enormous pressure on the champion in the opening two minutes, cut him and hurt him, only to see the resilient Hagler turn the table so dramatically in the final 60 seconds that Tommy went back to his corner having faced a terrible reality against which he struggled until he finally caved in to Marvelous Marvin two rounds later. The first 180 seconds of Trinidad-Mayorga was almost a replay of the earlier three-minute war, with Mayorga swarming as if to make Trinidad's comeback from two and a half years of retirement a two-minute affair, and then Trinidad finally coming into the fight, finding his rhythm and beginning to administer a boxing lesson. The only difference is that Tommy Hearns was far superior to Mayorga, who was long on heart but short on skills. For all his swaggering braggadocio of the days leading up to the fight, Mayorga was revealed as nothing more than a supper-club fighter with a cement chin, a resolute fighting heart, and the manly art of no defense.

The final coup de grace came in the eighth round, when Trinidad dug a left hook to Mayorga's liver—we used to call this

Trinidad (left) vs. Mayorga: the bull was up to the challenge until the eighth-round liver punch. (© Shannon Stapleton/Reuters/Corbis)

"the Mexican liver punch"—and the brave bull was finally ready for the meat house. In the old days body punching was often the clincher, but in the twenty-first century it has seemed a lost art. But with Bernard Hopkins knocking the air out of De La Hoya in the ninth a few weeks ago in Las Vegas, and now Trinidad digging to the body to stop the supposedly unstoppable Mayorga, we may be seeing the renaissance of the punch that brought immortality to the likes of Jake LaMotta and Marvin Hagler.

It was just that kind of a punch that brought the light heavyweight belt to Jose Torres when he took out the master boxer and champion Willie Pastrano in the Eighth Avenue Garden almost forty years ago. "When you get hit with that punch," Torres said to me after that fight, "you feel as if you're dying. You can't breathe." (Precisely what De La Hoya said right after his defeat.) "I could hear Pastrano make an awful sound—*ugh*! I felt sorry for him. But then I told myself, be objective. Be objective. That punch made you champion of the world."

Felix Trinidad isn't champion of the world again. That honor still belongs to Bernard Hopkins, now looking for his all-time record twentieth defense of the title he won a dozen years ago. But now the drums start beating for a Hopkins-Trinidad rematch of the fight in which our reigning middleweight punched Trinidad into premature retirement.

But for Hopkins-Trinidad II we may have to hold our breath: Trinidad is in the clutches of the octopusian Don King. And the outspoken, hardheaded, and independent Bernard Hopkins has sworn he will never bow to a Don King promotion. Let the machinations begin. It may be the only big-money fight for Hopkins, now that the arrogant old No. 1 pound-for-pound Roy Jones has been taken down a peg or three. Let's hope it takes place before the undisputed middleweight king enters his fistic dotage. But in the aftermath of Hopkins's destruction of the Golden Boy, I did find myself wondering (and hoping) that in the thirty-nine-year-old Hopkins we have the second coming of the aging legend Archie Moore who successfully defended his light heavyweight title when he was forty-eight and fought a draw with Willie Pastrano when he was pushing fifty.

Live on, fight on, Bernard. And I'll do my best to do the same. So I can cover Hopkins-Trinidad II. *"La regrese! La regrese!"* (I'm back! I'm back!), Trinidad was shouting in his final sparring session before sending Mayorga to the hospital and then back to his rape trial in Nicaragua—and if convicted, permanent retirement.

What makes boxing the most dramatic of all sports is that it so often brings us to that one night in which one fighter achieves immortality and the loser retreats into the shadows of oblivion.

That was Trinidad-Mayorga. Adios, Ricardo. Viva, Felix! And may the devious Lords of Boxing bring us Trinidad-Hopkins. With our heavyweights in total disarray, as *vide* the miserable bunch of heavyweight "champions" being thrust on us in the Garden a month from now, let us count our blessings with the middleweights, the 160-pound division that best combines power and speed. Think Jack Dempsey ("The Nonpareil"), Stanley

Ketchel, Harry Greb, Mickey Walker, Jake LaMotta, Sugar Ray
Robinson . . .
Onward!

[2004]

II. Winky Wright vs. Felix Trinidad: The King Is Dead! Long Live the King!

AS I WATCHED Winky Wright embarrass and dismantle the
pride of Puerto Rico, Felix Trinidad, I found myself thinking of
Daniel Mendoza, Mendoza the Jew, who came out of the ghetto
of London's White Chapel to become champion of England in
1791. At 160 pounds and only 5 foot 7, Mendoza was a natural
middleweight, but he met and defeated twenty bigger men on his
way to the heavyweight crown.

His surprising success against this array of big 'uns was due to
a unique approach to the brutal sport of fights to a finish. Before
Mendoza, the brawlers were accustomed to stand right in front of
each other and bash away until one of them fell for good. Sometimes they even locked their feet together and traded punches until one of them failed to make it back to the scratch line in the allotted thirty seconds. Hence our slang expression, "He's not up to
scratch."

How Mendoza compensated for his lack of size was to use his
feet—the first use of footwork—and to develop a sophisticated
defense that defused the power shots of the maulers who towered
over him. There were cries from the Fancy and the toffs that the
Jew was cheating, that he was refusing to stand and fight, that this
type of subtle avoidance of punishment wasn't exactly what the
British prize ring had in mind. But the articulate Mendoza challenged the sporting bloods to find anything in the Broughton
Rules that forbade the defensive tactics he was introducing.

Some two centuries later the sweet science of Mendoza has
passed on to Winky Wright, the 2 to 1 underdog to Felix "Tito"
Trinidad, who was facing the hardest puncher he—or anyone

else on the contemporary scene—had ever fought. In his forty-two victories over fifteen years, Tito had knocked out thirty-five, and the seven who survived included master boxers like Pernell Whitaker, Oscar De La Hoya, and Bernard Hopkins. "I expect Wright to outbox Trinidad and win most of the early rounds, but as soon as Trinidad figures him out, he will be able to stop him," said one of our "experts." "Wright has never faced someone with the power that Trinidad possesses. . . . I'm picking Trinidad to stop Wright in ten."

That was the conventional wisdom of a majority of the press section as the puncher and the boxer came to the ring. Steve Springer of the *Los Angeles Times* had it like this: "Winky has a great defensive style. But there is no defense against Trinidad unless your name is Bernard Hopkins. Body shots . . . will lower Wright's arms and leave him defenseless. Trinidad by TKO. . . ." And Richard Hoffer of *Sports Illustrated*: "Tito over Winky, hard puncher will penetrate defensive maestro's peekaboo mitts with surprising ease."

As for this ringsider, yes, I had seen the Puerto Rican banger use Ricardo Mayorga for a punching bag in his first fight out of retirement, but Mayorga's style was another example of the Manly Art of No Defense. Winky Wright was at the opposite end of the fistic spectrum. He was by far the smartest and trickiest of modern-day boxers. To make matters worse for Trinidad, Winky was a southpaw, which meant he was at you with a *right* jab, and it was the best in the business, accurate and punishing.

My dear friend Jose Torres, the light heavyweight champion of the sixties, a fierce puncher who fought out of the peekaboo style that boxing guru Cus D'Amato taught him, had an apt metaphor for the puzzlement of facing southpaws. "It's like, if you're a good typist and you know all the keys without having to look, and all of a sudden you're typing on a machine where all the letters have been switched around. What you used to do right is now all wrong. A sense of confusion is the worst thing a fighter can have in a fight. His confidence is drained. His game plan is out the window."

That was my call too. I had seen Winky winning those fights with Bronco McKart and the clever Sugar Shane Mosley. It was the best jab I had seen since Larry Holmes's. And if the left cross did not have knockout power, still it was crisp and effective. So let me make a confession. While I know it's not quite kosher for boxing writers to bet on fights, lest that color their judgment, I couldn't resist a flyer on Winky. Those 2 to 1 odds were a siren call. Winky had the defense of a turtle, his head pulled in, the gloves kept protectively close and strategically placed, his reflexes at age thirty-four showing no signs of deterioration. He was in superb shape, and he was hungry. While the Trinidads and De La Hoyas were making their millions, he was getting old watching them from the outside in. Nobody wanted to fight a slick no-name southpaw who figured to beat them. Relegated to fighting in Europe for meager purses, when he finally got a shot at top-rated Fernando Vargas, he knocked down the favorite son of Oxnard. Most writers thought he won the fight, but—what else is new?—the decision went where the money was.

After all those years in the ring, Winky was still the outsider, with a defensive style that didn't sell tickets. He might have faded away, but when Sugar Shane Mosley gave him a second chance he seized the moment to take the 154-pound title. In the big time at last, after barnstorming in Europe for five years, he was in there with Trinidad: with 15 years and 50 fights behind him, his first big money, four million smackers. Even though Don King's boy was making more than twice that much, it was by far the biggest fight in Winky's long, Sisyphean career.

I called it the fight between the Prince and the Pauper, and in the Mandalay Bay Arena there seemed to be some fourteen thousand fanatics from the Carribbean Island Commonwealth flashing their Puerto Rican flags and already beginning to chant their TITO . . . TITO . . . TITOs half an hour before their hero was to enter the ring.

When his young majesty finally appeared with the names of his four daughters on his resplendent robe, the roar shook the hall like thunder. The appearance of Winky, looking very fit at 160, elicited a prolonged chorus of boos. Las Vegas had become the capital of Puerto Rico, and Tito's cheerleaders were already looking forward to his rematch with the perennial middleweight champion, Bernard Hopkins.

But from the opening bell, Winky's snakelike jab was in Tito's face. It seemed positively attached to the Puerto Rican icon's noggin. It tormented him, kept him off balance, hurt and discouraged him. My ringside notes became a round-by-round repetition. "Winky jabs, jabs, jabs . . . and every so often sharp left hands. Tito fails to land a single punch as round ends. Tito goes back to his corner very discouraged." And his Island rooting section, fourteen thousand strong? After a few rounds of All Winky All the Time, they fell painfully silent, as if they were attending a funeral, which in a historically boxing sense this was. With an exhibition of scientific boxing that called back the great practitioners of the past, Winky Wright was writing "Adios" to Trinidad's illustrious career. After the third round, you would not have known there was a Puerto Rican in the house. Only the extended Winky Wright family, who happened to be sitting alongside me with their friends, were cheering, "That's the way, Winky! You got 'im, Winky! Keep poppin' 'im, Winky."

And that's the way it went, right to the end of round twelve. One judge gave Winky every round. Two others, a tad more charitable, gave Tito a single round. Winky had pitched a virtual shutout. The Compubox printout passed to the press at the end of the one-sided contest told the story. Winky had landed 185 jabs to Trinidad's 15. Only one of every 20 Trinidad jabs had connected, for a miserable 5 percent. And as for total punches thrown, Winky connected with 262, Tito with only 58, fewer than five in every three minutes, and most of those deflected.

All those experts predicting how Trinidad's vaunted power would break through Wright's vaunted defense were left not just with egg but a whole big omelet on their faces.

At the press conference, impressario Don King waxed eloquent, which is like saying that birds fly. Hiding his disappointment that his box office star had been badly dented if not destroyed, like a true Pagliacci he went on to extol the victor: "What you have seen tonight is the epitome of the sweet science. A virtuoso performance played on a Stradivarius violin. For twelve rounds a frustrated Tito was unable to penetrate Winky's masterful defense. A masterpiece! Real boxing at its best. Tito was discombobulated. Winky Wright is the greatest fighter I have seen in years."

"So is this the end of Trinidad?" one intrepid reporter asked. "Not at all," Don was back to pitching again. "Tito has a rematch clause in his contract, and I am sure Winky will honor it. Encore! Encore! Encore!"

An encore for what turned out to be a mismatch? Only Mr. King—Mr. Barnum and Mr. Bailey combined—could try to sell that one. Even Winky got into the act, with dreams of sugar plums, like doubling his four million, dancing in his head: "I had a game plan and I executed it perfectly. I've had to keep proving myself over and over again, and I did it again tonight. He underestimated me. He has a great hook and I watched it through the fight [it was hitting Winky's smartly placed gloves 99 percent of the time]. I hit him some great shots. But next time I expect he'll do better. He'll know how to prepare for me."

But a few days later Trinidad dashed Don King's and Winky's dreams of rematch millions. Winky's demolition of him had sent him into permanent retirement. The pauper would be the new prince. Now, instead of Hopkins-Trinidad again, the stage is set for Hopkins-Winky Wright for the undisputed middleweight title. After Hopkins's record twenty successful defenses, Winky could prove the most troublesome opponent the champion ever faced. He's almost as slick as the old Willie Pep. It could be one of those fascinatingly boring bouts where they outthink each other. Boring to fight fans looking for action, but not for insiders aware of the intricacies of our misunderstood sport. Take those sophisticated contests between the two heady veterans who succeeded Joe Louis, Ezzard Charles and Jersey Joe Walcott. Their contrasting styles of defense simply neutralized each other, like two chess masters able to block every move of the other. Oh what those bogus, overweight "champions" later in the century might have learned if they had been students rather than spongers of the game.

[2005]

21

No. 1 Pound-for-Pound:
Pretty Boy Floyd Mayweather, Jr.

ALL WEEK LONG the Atlantic City spectacle—pitting the crowd-pleasing puncher Arturo Gatti against the slick and undefeated "Pretty Boy" Floyd Mayweather, Jr.—had been hyped as "Thunder vs. Lightning." Gatti, the poster boy of the Manly Art of No Defense, has won fame and fortune for his "gluttony," an eighteenth-century word describing his ability to absorb severe punishment, on the verge of a knockout, and then somehow digging down for one desperate effort that turns the tables and gives him the final victory. Over the years this punch-absorbing, gladiatorial approach has won him an army of loyal fans, and they were lining up as early as 4:30 a.m. on the first morning tickets went on sale for his challenge to the nifty but unpopular Floyd Mayweather, Jr. The people's favorite bringing it to the betting favorite, the peerless but unloved and self-styled "Pretty Boy" Mayweather.

In the week building to the fight, the trash talk went on. Gatti bragged that his new trainer, a former champion himself, Buddy McGirt, had added a new finesse to his brawling style that would surprise the egomaniacal Mayweather and destroy his perfect record. But no one has ever outtalked the brash "Pretty Boy," who scorned Gatti all week as "a paper champion who doesn't deserve to be in the same ring with me. What you are going to see is a superb, young champion out there, executing what he was taught as a young boy."

Floyd wasn't born with a silver spoon in his mouth, but maybe a mouthpiece, as his father was a top contender and his uncle, Roger, his erstwhile trainer, a former champion. Having seen both the elder Mayweathers in action, I knew that the twenty-first century version is an improvement on both of them put together. He has, by far, the fastest hands in the division, and his offensive skills are equal to his defensive skills, which is why he has been rated as one of the top two or three pound-for-pound fighters in the world—although "Pretty Boy" would question that statement, telling everyone within hearing distance that he is clearly No. 1. With his thirty-three victims, including Diego Corrales and Jose Luis Castillo (whose recent battle will never be forgotten by ring historians), Floyd must be given credit for backing up his nonstop arrogance with performances that convince his audience that he's almost as great as he thinks he is. "You call it arrogance, I call it self-confidence," Floyd defined it before the fight, and he has a point. Where is that fine line between a healthy self-confidence and chest-thumping arrogance?

Maybe the best answer is the Mayweather-Gatti fight itself. When the cheers for their hero—twelve thousand strong, chanting "GATTI! GATTI! GATTI!"—and the prolonged boos for Mayweather were finally punctuated by the opening bell, Floyd went right to work, flashing the lightning. But, alas, for the local hero, there was no thunder. Nothing but lightning and a hard rain of punches to Gatti's face and body that came so fast, from so many angles, that once again I was reminded of my oft-repeated description of this masochistic warrior: the manly art of no defense. Near the end of the round, with Gatti turning to the referee to protest what he thought was an infraction of the rules, and with his head turned away from his opponent, Floyd showed no mercy by smacking him resoundingly on the jaw. "Protect yourself at all times" is the unforgiving maxim that Gatti forgot and Mayweather opportunistically remembered. As Gatti started down, the referee gave him an eight count.

It was an omen of what was to come. My second round notes read: "FM's handspeed. Outclassing AG. Landing at will." That

Floyd Mayweather, Jr., after beating Phillip Nadu in 2003. (Pat Orr)

could describe every round thereafter, into the sixth. By now Mayweather was scoring with five- and six-punch combinations that poor Arturo was absorbing with a Jake LaMotta determination to endure punishment that made you feel sorry for him while admiring his futile courage. When trainer McGirt decided his battered warrior had had enough, even Gatti's legendary fighting spirit was failing him. His protest was muted, and his battered face told the story. After eighteen painful minutes, he knew he had met his master. All the great nights were behind him now. He was exposed for what he had always been, a glorifed club fighter, on his way to the laughing academy if he doesn't hang 'em up.

As for the winner, the showboating and braggadocio that has not endeared him to the public was noticably absent when he talked with us after the fight. Clearly aware of the negative image he had created, not only with the nasty trash talk but for marital disturbances, assaults in nightclubs, and his ugly fights with his father, whom he had fired as trainer and thrown out of his house, Junior was now saying, "Don't judge me by my past. I'm not perfect. Nobody's perfect. Anyone can change. I don't go to clubs anymore. I'm a family man now. They need to judge me on how I seem now, not on what I did. All I wanna do is be the first. Like Sugar Ray was the first. Ali was the first."

I traveled all over the world with Ali, from Miami to Dublin to Zaire, and there was something about the way he proclaimed, "I'm the prettiest! I'm the greatest!" that didn't irritate us as have Junior's "Hooray for me!" There was a touch of insouciance and humor in Ali's advertisements for himself that have been noticeably lacking in Floyd's self-hyping persona. As for his readiness and ability to reform, I have my doubts. Too many times he has seemed to be auditioning to play the lead in a remake of *Champion*, the old movie with its nasty, anti-hero champ, as created by the gifted, sardonic Ring Lardner and acidly acted by Kirk Douglas. But maybe this is a generational thing. My son Benn, the psychology graduate student and boxing writer for www.thesweetscience.com, who is more of an age with young Mayweather, came away from an exclusive one-on-one talk with the champion with this observation:

> Mayweather admitted that boxing's not a gentleman's sport, like golf or tennis. And that he trash talks because it goes with the territory. Yet, after the fight, we saw a different man, humble, respectful and genuine, and he admitted to making mistakes in life. He even showed compassion for his fallen opponent after telling the world he wanted to punish and embarrass him. "He's tough, I respect him. Gatti's a good guy. I even said a prayer for him before the fight that he could come back another day."
>
> Maybe we should scratch the "Pretty Boy" nickname and call him "Gentleman Floyd" as this Mayweather has seemingly turned his lifestyle around and matured into a champion we can all be

proud of. So don't be fooled by his flashy antics inside the ring. The mink hoods, the talking to the commentators while fighting, the outlandish entrances, including Saturday night in which he was carried to the ring on an emperor's throne by Roman soldiers, are all part of his plan to make an everlasting mark in this sport. "I gotta be flashy in the ring 'cuz I gotta be the first," he explained, "all I wanna do is be the first."

But a humble "first"? All I can say, in Spanish, is *Vamos a ver.* We will see what we will see. I wish I knew how to say it in Scottish. Or, maybe we'll settle with the old bromide, "The proof is in the pudding."

So what's next for our undefeated junior lightweight king? Ricky Hatton was at ringside, and he would be an obvious choice in a mega-fight to unify the belts. Floyd has already started the trash talk, in describing his own "God-given talent. I showed them this sport is called boxing, not wrestling [referring to Hatton's defeat of Kosta Tzsyu]."

If I were Ricky, now with American fans as well as British at my feet, I wouldn't want to rush into a fight with Floyd. I imagine Frank Warren would agree not to burst the bubble by exposing his boy to those super-fast hands and accurate punching power. An aggressive brawler, Hatton seems made to order for Mayweather. If I were he, I would think about cashing in on my instant American fame with some name fighters in the division who could bring me some money without yet exposing myself to a buzzsaw who could chop me up.

As for Mayweather, the fight these old eyes are looking forward to is his imminent challenge to Zab "Super" Judah, the undisputed welterweight championship of the world. Both of them can outfight everybody else around. Not to mention outtalk them. But when they get ready to rumble, if you're a betting man, go with "Pretty Boy." Alas, the fight game ain't what it used to be, but the pride of the Mayweather dynasty may be the only boxer on the scene today who could hold his own with the great ones of old.

[2005]

22

Weightgate, and on to World War III: Diego Corrales vs. Jose Luis Castillo II

IT WAS ONLY five months ago that the WBO lightweight champion of the world, Diego "Chico" Corrales, met the WBC lightweight champion Jose Luis Castillo in what turned out to be one of the greatest fights of all time, if not *the* greatest. Knocked down twice and nearly out in the tenth round, somehow Corrales reached down for a last-gasp effort. Seconds later it was Castillo who was barely conscious, with his eyes rolling frighteningly in his head. Never stopped in his illustrious nine-year career, except on cuts in his early fights, the solid-chinned Mexican idol was out on his feet when the referee jumped in to prevent the miraculously rejuvenated Corrales from throwing that next right hand that could have been fatal.

Veteran boxing writers, including this one—by far the oldest of them all—were calling Corrales-Castillo I the most theatrically climactic of all time. And these eyes have seen Louis-Conn, Marciano-Walcott, Pryor-Arguello, and Hagler-Hearns.

Corrales-Castillo I not only had a "Hollywood" ending but produced enough controversy to set the stage for Corrales-Castillo II. After going down the first time, Diego had spit out his mouthpiece, and after the second knockdown spit it out again. A point was deducted from the WBO champion for this infraction, and Castillo

Diego Corrales after winning the lightweight title from Alcelino Freitas in 2004. (Pat Orr)

accused him of using a deliberate ruse to steal more time for Corrales to recover, a charge Diego indignantly denied. He was a clean fighter who had always abided by the rules, he insisted, he loved boxing as a sport and had too much respect for it to bend or break its rules. He had removed the mouthpiece only to be able to breathe more easily, and it had slipped from his gloves to the canvas.

In their explosive first fight, the two best lightweights in the world had fought like human pit bulls. There was none of the usual feeling out, no fancy Dan boxing, just nonstop, take-no-prisoners, *mano-a-mano* warfare. Onlookers marveled at the rivals' stamina and ability to absorb punishment while refusing to take a backward step. It was almost frightening. In Corrales-Castillo I we were watching as classic a test of wills as we have ever seen, or maybe ever will.

For their first fight the arena in Las Vegas was only half-filled, and in Corrales' dressing room were only the fighter himself, his dedicated trainer, the articulate Joe Goossen, his assistants, and this writer and his son Benn, intimate friends of the champion. But nothing succeeds like success, and now Diego's stunning victory had attracted a roomful of opportunistic celebrities—the living American baseball legend Cal Ripken, Jr.; the movie mogul who cranks out those hundred-million-dollar action movie mega hits, Jerry Brookheimer; the top honchos of CBS and Showtime; and the local politicians, movers, and shakers. Also on hand were Jeff Lacey, the current super middleweight champ, and Sugar Shane Mosley, conqueror of Oscar De La Hoya, the classy former champion and now welterweight contender. This time the dressing room was so crowded there was hardly enough space for Diego to do his necessary warm-up shadow boxing.

Beyond the sweet smell of success that's always honey to the celebrity bees, interest in the impending match had been intensified by what we might call *weightgate*. The contract called for both fighters weighing in at the lightweight division limit of 135 pounds the day before the fight. Corrales made sure he met it *un punto*. With a walking-around weight of 150, he had punished his outsized 5 foot 11 frame with dieting to extreme and sacrificed drinking water to meet the required title weight. But Castillo weighed in two pounds over the weight at 137. Castillo's physician, Dr. Armando Barak, had tried to give his fighter a helping hand, or foot, by sneaking that foot under the scale to hold it to the weight agreed to, but alert Nevada State Boxing Commissioner Marc Ratner had caught him, suspending the Mexican medico and fining him $1,000. Castillo was given two hours to see if he could sweat off the offending pounds.

The old "foot under the scale" trick used to be standard procedure back in the bad old days of the thirties, forties, and fifties when the Mafia's notorious Frankie Carbo, "Mister Grey," was boxing commissioner without portfolio. Now a replay of the "funny business" days was taking place outdoors in the scorching

Vegas sun near the old Caesars Palace Roman Plaza where Larry Holmes had inflicted that humiliating knockout of the sadly over-the-hill Muhammad Ali, and where Hitman Tommy Hearns fought his classic, if losing, battles with Sugar Ray Leonard and Marvelous Marvin Hagler. This afternoon the battles were purely verbal but just as heated. Corrales' promoter, Gary Shaw, was chewing out Castillo's promoter, the veteran honcho Bob Arum, who was turning interesting shades of green. The weigh-in was out of control, with Corrales' people and Castillo's people engaged in a vocal free-for-all. There was wild talk of canceling the fight. But with millions of dollars for the fighters, the sold-out arena, and all those PPV sales at stake, Castillo was given the extra time to see if he could work off the troubling excess. To everyone's surprise, he came back to the scale in less than an hour. This time he weighed 138-1/2! Instead of shedding the offending weight, he had actually gained a pound and a half.

Now the hard truth was dawning on the Corrales camp. They had been had. For it was obvious that Castillo had never intended to make the contract weight. More screaming followed. "They tried to cheat," Gary Shaw said. "They didn't even try to make the weight. And that dirty business of the foot under the scale. They were going to cheat Diego out of his championship belts." Was Castillo involved in the scam? From his days as a Golden Glove champion, Diego Corrales has always brought an amateur's pure love of the sport to his distinguished professional career. It was painful for him to admit that Castillo must have known all along he wasn't going to make the weight. "This is really what gives boxing bad blows. I love my game. I love my sport. I love my job. As I said before, I don't break the rules. I don't bend the rules or manipulate the rules." "When a guy's nearly six feet tall and he has to make 135, that's debilitating," trainer Joe Goossen added. "I wish I knew he was coming in at 138-1/2. We'd've come in at 138-1/2 too."

Weightgate carried over into Saturday, fight day, with Castillo ordered to make 146 for what was now a nontitle fight, and having to pay Corrales $75,000 for every pound over that weight.

Castillo had already been fined $120,000, with half going to Corrales and the other half to the Nevada Commission. Back in Corrales' luxurious suite in a Caesars Palace penthouse, Corrales relaxed with his family, this writer and his son Benn, and two massive seven-foot bodyguards. "Chico," as his friends call him, joked that he'd take that extra $60,000 of Castillo money and buy himself a motorcycle. "No, Chico," his personable and pregnant wife Michelle objected, "I'm taking it to buy jewelry."

Since Corrales had fulfilled his weight obligation, he had the option of calling off the fight and still receiving his $2 million. But he wasn't about to cancel the rematch with Castillo. "I'm not doing this for money," he told us in his suite twenty-four hours before fight time. "I'm doing it because I love my job and I owe it to my fans to deliver. The sport of boxing needs this fight. This is about pride and my legacy."

By fight time Saturday night, both fighters were up around 149, but with a big advantage to Castillo, who had maintained the higher weight all along while the conscientious Diego had roller-coastered from 149 to 135 and back to 149 again. So much for *Weightgate*.

Now on to Corrales-Castillo II. This time the arena was packed to the rafters, seventeen thousand overheated fans, with a throng of vocal Mexicans waving their eagle-and-snake emblazoned national flags and chanting the name of their idol at the top of their lungs. If they needed any further incitement, it was the commanding ringside presence of the greatest Mexican fighter of all time, Julio Cesar Chavez, whose young son, Julio Cesar Chavez, Jr., was fighting the semi-windup. Castillo had served his apprentice years as a sparring partner for the legendary Chavez, and he had learned his brutal trade from a master. Chavez had prevailed over the years with his relentless combinations of short left hooks to the liver (the famous or infamous "Mexican liver punch"), nasty little uppercuts, and straight crushing rights to the jaw.

That's exactly the way Castillo fights too, and in the controversial rematch he lost no time demonstrating his bad intentions.

This fight had been hyped as "Round Eleven"—in other words, picking up where the last one had left off in that explosive tenth round five months earlier. The human pit bulls were at it again, ignoring boxing niceties, just toe-to-toe, hit-and-get-hit, with both fighters refusing to back off, going at each other with the same ferocious intensity once again. Only this time, by the end of round one Castillo's dominance was painfully clear. Corrales was scoring with some two-fisted flurries, but it was Castillo who was doing the sharper punching. There were all the old classic Chavez combos, those short left hooks to the body Diego couldn't seem to avoid and the straight right hands to the champion's unprotected jaw. In the third round Castillo answered an effective Corrales attack with a straight right cross that had his rival in trouble at the bell.

Castillo had won all three rounds now, and he came out for the fourth with mounting confidence. He had been catching Corrales with his trademark left hook again and again, and that was his weapon now, a classic left hook to the jaw that put Corrales down as hard as he had in the first fight. No, even harder. Because now, for the first time in his life—his other two losses in his forty-two fights due to stoppages on cuts—he was unable to beat the count. After all the buildup and all those months of training, it was all over in less than a minute of round four.

Back in the dressing room, Gary Shaw was fuming. It was *Weightgate* that did Diego in. He was blaming himself for not having called off the fight after Castillo's shenanigans. To top off Shaw's misery, he had lost a $100,000 side bet he had made with Castillo at the tempestuous weigh-in. This was no publicity hype. Your correspondent was there when they made the bet. In the aftermath, everyone was blaming the outcome on the cold-blooded cheating of the Castillo camp. Everyone, that is, except the always classy Corrales. At the post-fight press conference, which the Castillo camp had disrespectfully walked out on after having their say, under a cap jauntily pulled down to cover a blood clot on his right eye, Corrales said, "I'm not going to muck up his win by entertaining the thought that he had an advantage. He landed a good shot. Congratulations to Castillo. Good job. I made a silly mistake. I should have remembered from our first fight. I dropped my right hand and I paid for it."

Does Corrales want a rematch? "Absolutely!" He was even saying that in the ring right after the knockout, before he had fully recovered his senses. There's a rematch clause in their contract, and after a hard-earned rest, he's eager to go back into training for Corrales-Castillo III. Only this time, he, Gary Shaw, and Joe Goossen insist on 135, so both championship belts will be in play. And so Castillo will not come in with the unfair advantage that tainted his victory.

So the stage is set for one of those classic three-fight rivalries. Think Graziano-Zale fifty years ago and still vivid in the memories of old fight fans. Stay tuned, my fellow aficionados. This is what fist fighting is all about. A battle of wills. Character in action. Get ready for the War to Settle the Score.

[2006]

P.S. Instead of the eagerly awaited Corrales-Castillo III, we had *Weightgate II*. All week long the working press was beating the drums for the last act of the trilogy. All the great trilogies of old were invoked in bated-breath anticipation for the showdown between lightweight champion Corrales and the hard-nosed Mexican challenger Castillo, who knocked out his rival in their second fight, but didn't earn the belt because of his miserable failure to make the demanding lightweight limit.

As intimate friends of the straight-arrow Corrales (our journalistic objectivity in threads), my son and fellow boxing writer Benn and I had flown out to Vegas five days before the fight to be with "Chico" as he faced the ordeal of getting down to that wicked 135. Hour after hour and day after day the tall, lean, lightweight champ punished himself in a rubber suit, plus several layers on top of that, skipping rope, shadow boxing, hitting the heavy and light bags in a gym with the heat turned up to 140 degrees. I think I lost five pounds just watching him.

As he stepped on the scale for the moment of truth, the official weigh-in the day before the fight, the press and a host of fans held their breath for the official announcement: "Diego Corrales . . . 135." The champion raised his arms in triumph. Then it was Castillo's turn. On and off the scale he stepped, four times. In his last attempt, he stood up on his toes, as high as he could go, as if that would somehow reduce the offending weight. But he couldn't cheat this time, as he had done so blatantly for their second fight eight months before. "Castillo . . . 139-1/2" came the fateful call.

Pandemonium. Crisis. Castillo's promoter Bob Arum turning green again. "I'm embarrassed, humiliated, disgusted. They lied to me. Week after week. Last night they said 137." A multi-million-dollar promotion was going up in smoke. Last time a weakened Corrales decided he didn't want to let the public down, and went through with the fight and paid the price. This time he was there with his wife Michelle and his two-month-old daughter Daylia, and put them ahead of the fans. He had tortured himself to make the weight and all for nothing. He was in no mood to forgive Castillo. "If he had called me last week and let me know, we could have fought at catchweights. I could've come in at 140, 145. This way I made the sacrifice and he didn't. It's as simple as that."

So after three months of intense training, three months of ballyhoo, three months of comparing Corrales-Castillo III to Zale-Graziano III, Ross-McLarnin III, Ali-Frazier III, Gatti-Ward III, the War to Settle the Score Ain't Gonna Be No More.

Back in his Caesars Palace suite later that night, the righteous, self-deprived "Chico" Corrales was knocking back a beer, dreaming of banana splits, frustrated that he was forgoing a purse of $1.2 million, but with his wife and baby by his side, sure he had made the right decision. "I love my wife and my new baby and all my kids and I want to see them grow up, get an education, get married, have a good life. If it was an equal playing field I'd love to fight him, but this way. . . ." He picked up and cuddled the baby, Daylia.

So Castillo goes home in disgrace, fined $250,000, with promoter Bob Arum and the WBC (which should have been minding the store) saying, "No mas," and Corrales goes home without the million bucks he worked so hard for, but with his honor and his health intact. So where do we go from here, Chico? I smell money with Ricky Hatton, the banger from Manchester, who was there at ringside, comes to fight, and won't pull *Weightgate* like the *schnorer* from Sonora.

23

Boxing Movies 101

THE RELEASE of the recent Ali bio-film, starring Will Smith as our iconic Muhammad, prompts the question: Why so many boxing films? Along with the clinkers and stinkers that mindlessly Hollywoodize the fight game, at least a diamond dozen hold their own against the great films of all time. What magnet draws such a cluster of top directors: John Huston, Martin Scorcese, Robert Wise, King Vidor . . . or stars such as Errol Flynn, Kirk Douglas, Robert DeNiro, Paul Newman . . . ? Or the invisible authors without whom there'd be no characters to play, no script to direct, the writers—Vincent Lawrence, Ernest Lehman, Paul Schrader, Rod Serling, and this one. Boxing historian Mike Silver tells me almost twice as many boxing films have been made as all the other sports combined.

The answer may be found in novelist / boxing maven Joyce Carol Oates's observation that the prizefight is so full of *agon* that you don't *play* it as you play basketball or baseball or soccer. You do boxing. You endure boxing. You survive boxing. No other physical contest, not tennis or fencing, puts such awesome pressure on the individual. If Andy Roddick loses a grueling five-set match in the Open, there'll be another Grand Slam. If a top jockey is nosed out in the Derby, he'll be back for the Preakness. But for the boxer there are one-stop nights of do or die. Go out a winner or loser for the rest of your life. The high-wire drama is made for the screen.

Calling to mind my favorites, I realized how many focus on the agonies, the dark side of the ring, rather than on the sweet smell of fistic success. The prizefighter is the most unprotected and the most exploited of all professional athletes. Out of that gritty reality came classics like *The Set-Up*, based on a unique book-length poem by Joseph Moncure March, a gifted alcoholic, with like-it-is direction from Robert Wise and a truth-oozing performance by Robert Ryan as the washed-up pug fighting that one-last-fight in a seedy arena called Dreamland in a seedy tank town called Paradise.

Another classic, *Body and Soul*, has John Garfield getting it right as a young Jewish boxer who fights his way to the top and then finds in his gang-ridden sport that that was the easy part. Everything about this work is Oscar-time: the performances, including ex-fighter Canada Lee as a grievously damaged contender, Robert Rossen's direction, a strong screenplay from Abe Polonsky, and superb photography by James Wong Howe. A little genius, who actually boxed himself at the Hollywood Legion, Jimmy used roller skates to move his camera around the ring in a way boxing had never been photographed before. My late friend Bob Parrish, a jewel of a man, was the film editor. My dark-film list includes *Champion*, Ring Lardner's acidic portrait of a champ in the ring but a bum in his heart, with a searing performance by Kirk Douglas. Who can forget his punching out his crippled brother? Carl Foreman's on-target screenplay is targetly directed by Mark Robson.

If ever there's a Festival of Boxing Films, Mark Robson would be remembered for also directing *The Harder They Fall*, based on my novel, often described as the strongest attack on boxing corruption ever made. It's Bogie's last picture, and as a cynical press agent who helps the crooked manager (Rod Steiger) build a hapless giant to a title fight with a parade of fixed fights, his ambivalence and growing guilt are perfectly calibrated.

Like a sequel to *Harder*, Rod Serling's *Requiem for a Heavyweight* replaces my battered and bilked "Toro Molina" with "Mountain Rivera," who leaves the ring broke and brain-damaged to face even grimmer humiliation as a pro wrestler. Anthony Quinn breaks your heart as the ruined fighter. I was so moved by the film that I had to forgive Rod for encroaching on my terrain.

Another winner about losers, *Fat City*, the dead-on Leonard Gardner novel with a Gardner screenplay, is faithfully brought to the screen by John Huston. I saw this film in Dublin when John invited Ali and his team to a screening while the self-anointed "Greatest" was training to fight Blue Lewis there. It rang so true that Ali cried out, "That's it! That's for real!" If you want to know what it is like to ride a bus into a strange town alone, get beat up for fifty bucks, piss blood, and hitchhike home to a wife who may or may not be talking to you, Gardner's and Huston's *Fat City* is your meat.

Space limits fuller program notes on my virtual Fight Film Festival: Martin Scorcese's and Paul Schrader's mean, nasty, but brilliant film-bio of old champ Jake LaMotta, *Raging Bull*; another film-bio, of knockabout champ Rocky Graziano, *Somebody Up There Likes Me*, rates four stars for *The Set-Up*'s director, Robert Wise, and four more for its star, Paul Newman, in an unlikely role as the mobbed-up, likable Rocky. My title for this one is "Somebody Down Here Likes Me Too."

Then there's *Rocky*, of course, the Sylvester Stallone operetta, wherein the underdog cult hero, Rocky Balboa, fights a winning-in-losing battle against the Ali-clone, "Apollo Creed." The fight scenes are ridiculously over the top, and if you train as Rocky does, by punching sides of frozen beef, you'll break your hands—but fistic truths don't apply to this one. The sometimes silly Sylvester touches a nerve. He's every nebbish's dream of glory. No wonder it copped an Oscar and box office gold.

I liked *The Boxer*, the Irish entry connecting boxing with the political tensions of the IRA. Irish director Jim Sheridan and the British actor Daniel Day-Lewis deserve a bow for this one. A feminist first, unknown Karyn Kosama's *Girlfight*, starring unknown Michelle Rodriquez, finds a new way to tell an old story: how the violence of personal anger finds a positive release in boxing discipline.

There's some nice lighter stuff, too, of course, the ageless fantasy *Here Comes Mr. Jordan*, the witty send-up of boxing's ubiquitous rogues, *The Great White Hype*. . . .

The beat goes on. *Ali*, the heralded $100 million Michael Mann production, was hardly an improvement on the old, low-budget *The Greatest*. Sandra Schulberg has just produced *Undisputed*, starring Wesley Snipes in a role described as Mike Tyson-ish. Up there with the best I've seen is the lean, mean *Million Dollar Baby*. Every good film, we writers know, starts with the writing, and here we have the taut, knowledgeable prose of F. X. Toole (*Rope Burns*) adapted for film by an Emmy-winning but first-time screenplay writer, Peter Haggis, and then placed in the versatile hands of Clint Eastwood, who shows a respect for Haggis's and Toole's words that every writer dreams about but never really expects to find. "I always believe in keeping the writer involved," Eastwood said. "Writing is always the foundation. It's best when one writer writes it. My instinct is to trust the writer as the source of what I build on." Thanks to Eastwood's creative instincts, we have a film we can now rank with the other tough ones, like *The Set Up* and *Fat City*. Still in the works is *Save Me, Joe Louis* (working title) on the impact of Louis on civil rights, his seesaw relationship with Max Schmeling, and his tragic downward spiral, from this corner and Spike Lee, with input from boxing historian and "character" Bert Randolph Sugar.

Why are boxing movies so deeply embedded in our culture? Bill Heinz, author of the impeccable novel *The Professional*, says, "Boxing is the one totally honest art form. It's the most fundamental form of competition and the most completely expressive of the arts." Or as irrepressible Mr. Sugar sums it, "Filmmakers will always be attracted to the fight game . . . the silver screen and the sweet science is a matchup made in entertainment heaven."

[2001]

24

Fighters and Writers:
At the Boxing Hall of Fame

AT MY INDUCTION into the Boxing Hall of Fame I didn't mean to frighten my audience, but I drew an audible gasp when I mentioned the first title match I ever saw—"It was sixty-eight, no *seventy*-eight years ago. . . ." And there I was, the wide-eyed eleven-year-old at ringside with his devoted fight fan of a father when our Olympic gold medalist, Fidel La Barba, won the flyweight championship from Frankie Genaro. All those nifty little flys and bantams of my childhood, Newsboy Brown and Corporal Izzy Schwartz with those six-pointed stars on their trunks, and all the Filipino battlers: at night instead of counting sheep I'd be murmuring their magical names—Speedy Dado . . . Young Nationalista . . . Clever Sencio. . . . Since boxing was a shamelessly ethnic sport, we rooted for our local Jewish champions Mushy Callahan (Morris Scheer), Jackie Fields (Jacob Finkelstein), and the Newsboy (David Montrose), but as loyal Californians we cheered the Eastern campaigns of La Barba, who was holding his own with future Hall of Famers Kid Chocolate, Battling Battalino. We marveled as our little nonpareil Henry Armstrong took New York by storm in winning the featherweight crown from Petey Sarron, then the welterweight title from Barney Ross, finally the lightweight belt from Lou Ambers, all within ten months, a fistic hat trick never accomplished before, and that never will be again.

Since my old man was running Paramount Studios and since Eastern champs always wanted to meet the movie stars and visit the studios while local fighters were looking for jobs after retirement—James Wong Howe, a club fighter at the Hollywood Legion, wound up one of the great cinematographers (*Body and Soul, Hud*, etc.)—it was S.O.P. for me to meet and get to know our boxing heroes from my early teens. After his retirement, Fidel La Barba brought me articles he was hoping to publish in *Esquire* in the mid-1930s and was later a best man at my wedding to Geraldine Brooks, along with the endearing battler Art Aragon, the original Golden Boy.

Hang out with boxers long enough and you'll often find yourself involved in some offstage drama. Flying out to Los Angeles with my friends Billy Soose, the middleweight champion, and his manager, Paul Moss, for Billy's title defense against Ceferino Garcia, back in '41, I decided to visit my old stamping ground, the Main Street Gym, where Garcia was training. Paul saw this as an easy paynight outdoors in the ballpark because he assumed Ceferino was over the hill after losing his title to Ken Overlin, whom Billy had just defeated. But Garcia looked in surprisingly good shape to me. When his manager, George Parnassus, took me for a drink at Abe Attell's bar nearby, he hinted that his fighter was getting ready to retire after averaging one fight a month for a dozen years. I connected the dots and told Paul they were looking to throw the fight. Paul shrugged it off. "We don't need to get involved with Parnassus. Billy will box Garcia's ears off."

That's how it looked for almost seven rounds. Billy was a picture-book boxer. But just before the end of the round, suddenly blood was streaming from a deep cut in Billy's eyelid. The Latinos in the bleachers were screaming, sensing an upset win. Crouched in the corner, I could hear Billy saying, "Paul, I'm not going out. Nothing's worth losing my eye." When the bell rang and Billy remained on his stool, the bleachers exploded. "Viva Ceferino!" Then came referee Abe Roth's decision: Due to a head butt, he had stopped the fight, calling it a technical draw. So Billy would retain his title. Now the Latinos exploded in a different way. They busted up the seats and set them on fire. Gringos were in trouble. Pushing my way to Billy's dressing room, I was stopped by my father, whom I didn't recognize for a moment in the frenzy that engulfed us.

So many of these boxers were not just fighters I followed as a fan, but close friends. As I recently confessed in *Fight Game*, back in the fifties I found myself co-managing a promising young heavyweight when Archie McBride came to the regulation ring I had set up in my barn in Bucks County, Pennsylvania. He needed money for his family and asked me to get him some fights as a pro. After we wiped out all the local boys, I got Archie a semi-windup in Madison Square Garden. Winning that one we were on our way to the big time.

After holding his own with the top contenders, when the Garden wanted Archie for coming-champion Floyd Patterson, I've already described my anxiety attack, and my offer to spar with my guy—anything to help get him ready for the ordeal of facing those pinwheel-fast hands of Floyd's. Half a century later I still touch the dent in my nose with pride. Like the old scar of a *torero* that becomes his badge of valor. And blessedly still in good shape fifty years later, and having bought his own home and put his sons through college with his ring earnings, Archie joined me last fall at the New Jersey Boxing Hall of Fame where we were both inducted.

For the last fights of Rocky Marciano's storybook career, I stayed with him in the modest farmhouse at Grossinger's where he was training for the graceful Ezzard Charles, the plodding Don Cockell, and the crafty Archie Moore. A week before facing "the old Mongoose" he confided in me that he was planning to retire. He could no longer stand the tension between his wife and family and his well-connected manager, Al Weill, who kept him up at Grossinger's for months at a time, barring him from family visits and even severely limiting his telephone calls. The feud went all the way back to his wedding banquet where old-fashioned Italian family members made effusive toasts to the happy couple while the single-minded Al Weill spoke just eight offensive words: "To the next heavyweight champion of the world!"

Rocky survived a second-round knockdown to take old Archie out in the ninth, and then shocked his apoplectic manager and the entire fight world by announcing his retirement as the only heavyweight champion to go undefeated, 49-0. Five years later, after Sonny Liston's two-minute destruction of lost child Floyd Patterson, I was with Rocky in the Playboy mansion in Chicago along with a gaggle of literary camp followers—Norman Mailer, James Baldwin, Ben Hecht, William Saroyan. Rocky beckoned me into a bedroom and shut the door. "Budd, you always level with me. I got a hunch I c'n lick Sonny. I won't be afraid of him like Floyd. I won't go down from a punch like Floyd. And I think I c'n get under the jab an' hurt 'im to the body." At age thirty-nine, Rocky was dreaming of all the money he could make in the more lucrative sixties. I'm sure I wasn't the only one who urged him to stay retired. Hang on to the legend. Forty-nine straight victories. Mr. Invincibility. Rocky went on pursuing his money dreams outside the ring, but a small plane he was hopping to a business meeting in the Midwest did to him what the toughest opponents had been unable to do in all those hard fights, took him out for good at age forty-six.

I wish another friend of mine, Muhammad Ali, had followed Rocky's example and hung 'em up after the Thrilla that was really the killa in Manila. It was all downhill after that. Of all the painful losses I've seen my friends endure, my all-time worst was having to watch (and describe for the *New York Post*) the sadly diminished Ali in his ill-advised comeback against his worthy successor, Larry Holmes. After taking a frightful beating for eleven rounds, and after having survived all those terrible punches from Sonny Liston, Oscar Bonavena, Joe Frazier, Ernie Shavers, Ron Lyle, Ken Norton, and George Foreman (my head hurts at the roll call), Ali suffered the only knockout of his Ali-in-Wonderland career.

I had followed him from Miami to Dublin to Zaire, and had written a book about him, *Loser and Still Champion*, in which I tried to find words for the Pied-Piper spell he cast over the faithful of five continents.

**A fellow inductee at the International Boxing
Hall of Fame, George Foreman. (Pat Orr)**

Of all my dear friends in the game, the model for wise retirement is still Jose Torres, who married power to intelligence in
knocking out the elusive Willie Pastrano to win the light heavyweight title. Losing two razor-thin decisions to the estimable Dick
Tiger, triggering riots in the Garden by his loyal Puerto Ricans each
time, he retired to launch what would have seemed an unlikely career. With English as his second language, he became a columnist
for the *New York Post* and the biographer of both Ali and Mike
Tyson, whom he knew as the protégé of his own inspirational man-
ager/trainer, Cus D'Amato. As a neophyte writer, the kid from
Ponce took his early literary efforts to Norman Mailer, Pete Hamill,
and me. Today he takes great delight in telling how he hid from
each author the fact that he was also showing his efforts to the

other two. So all three noted the improvements and each thought that he alone was responsible for Jose's literary progress.

As a fighter for social justice, a better life for the Puerto Rican people at home and in Spanish Harlem, and for democratic causes, currently counseling a long-needed union for boxers, Jose Torres is a best-case scenario for professional fighters. The worst-case scenarios we know all too well. Of all professional athletes, boxers are the most endangered and the least protected. No pension, no medical plan, defenseless against the machinations of promoters and managers who too often treat their charges like chattel to be tossed aside when no longer useful. As my old chum Art Aragon says with typical self-deprecating humor, "You know, after being the hottest attraction they ever had out here, the original Golden Boy, when I retired I was only two thousand dollars in debt, and I only had a little brain damage. Now how can you knock a sport like that?"

Sitting between George Foreman and Marvelous Marvin Hagler and near Ken Buchanan (as in a fight fan's dream) at our induction into the International Boxing Hall of Fame last week, I was reminded of a talk I had had with the late Nelson Algren (*The Man with the Golden Arm, A Walk on the Wild Side*). Why this affinity of writers and fighters? Where one has a promoter, the other has a publisher. One has a manager, the other has an agent. One has a trainer, the other has an editor. But when the bell rings, it's sort of interchangeable. You're out there under the bright lights feeling naked and alone. And what you do or fail to do out there can make or break your reputation for life. That's what makes fighters and writers bond so easily, as Lord Byron bonded with London prize-ring champion Gentleman Jackson, as George Bernard Shaw bonded with Gene Tunney, and as it's been my good fortune to bond with so many great champions, from little Fidel La Barba to big George Foreman and most recently with the articulate and prideful lightweight champion Diego "Chico" Corrales.

In the days counting down to Marciano's fistic farewell, he sounded out with me the notion of a novel organization: Fighters and Writers. We never got it off the drawing board. But it lives on in spirit. And it involves more than writing and boxing. It invokes nothing less than mankind's ability to cope, to struggle, and, finally, our determination to overcome all obstacles, and to endure.

[2003–2006]

▪ 25 ▪

Machiavelli on Eighth Avenue

IT WAS THE EVENING of Mike Jacobs's bow-out from the Garden, the last promotion with which he was to be directly associated—the Kid's last fight.

But the world's champion fight promoter, the man who had set the stage for Joe Louis, Ray Robinson, Henry Armstrong, Barney Ross, and a dozen other ring immortals, who had been associated with or personally promoted every million-dollar gate in the history of the game, whom the sport had made a multi-millionaire, was winding up with a match that stood in pitiable contrast to the big-name shows and fat paynights of Jacobs's prime.

It was just Pete Mead and Robert Villemain, a couple of middleweights of no particular distinction other than being able to bleed with considerable stoicism. The fight fans who had made a rich man of Uncle Mike were staying away from this one in such numbers as to mark Mike's passing from the scene with one of the poorest gates in big-time boxing history.

With Mike's stroke the year before, boxing had suffered its own collapse. For Mike Jacobs—Monopoly Mike as the sports writers liked to call him when they were being polite—had been to the boxing game what FDR had been to the game of politics. A standout. A natural. The Man. For all those constituents who went along with FDR, let us hasten to add that the only connection between the four-time winner and Squire Jacobs of Rumson is their preeminence in their respective fields. Notable differences are that Uncle Mike never tolerated an opposition party, never

256

confided in any Brain Trust other than the one he carried around in his own bald pate, and never cast anything upon the waters until he had made damn sure it would be returned at least four- or five-fold.

The evening of the Mead-Villemain box office fiasco found Mike Jacobs in his big, rambling country manse in New Jersey, a restless old man of sixty-nine with a face not unlike that of a bald eagle, a comparison which one of his detractors (which seems to include the entire guest list of the Forrest Hotel and the whole schmear of Jacobs Beachcombers) ascribes to the fact that "having spent all of his life chasing a dollar, he just naturally began to look like one." A sick man who has been down twice with cerebral hemorrhage and a heart attack, and who had been warned to take it easy if he didn't want his license revoked for all time by the only Referee he couldn't approach, Uncle Mike was sitting around chewing on his toothless gums, squinting impatiently at television, pacing the oversized living room like a jungle beast not yet used to his cage. Suddenly, in the loud, harsh tone he uses for English, he ordered the ex-fighter chauffeur to drive the car around—he was going into town for his last fight.

"Drive all that way just to watch a coupla bums?" said Josie, his wife, a good-hearted, two-fisted, spade-calling, fifty-five-year-old bottle blonde and, like her husband, a graduate summa cum laude of the University of Hard Knocks.

By way of an answer, Uncle Mike chewed determinedly on his gums, a retort that has confounded some of the slickest and the toughest in a business where an honest man is automatically down in everybody's book as a suspicious character.

"Why doncha see it on the television?" Josie persisted.

"I'm goin' in," Mike shouted in the voice he developed when he was first hawking excursion tickets at the Battery some fifty-five years before.

"Seems like a helluva lot of trouble just to give the few bastards who'll be there a chance to boo ya," Josie said.

For years the mention of Uncle Mike's name from the Garden ring had been a cue for an expressive Bronx cheer from the fans.

We'll come every Friday and pay through the nose to see your shows, that prolonged razzberry seemed to say, but we don't have to like you. In fairness to Mike, it should be explained that this personal unpopularity with the general public bothered him about the same way a horsefly disturbs the cast iron horse under General Sherman in Central Park. Mike has never run for any office except the box office. As long as the people paid the price on the ticket— or, better yet, a little something over the price—the people could call him anything they wanted—which they usually did.

"Getcha coat, we're goin'!" said Mike, who was once described as a man of a few ill-chosen words.

Having been Mike's helpmate for some thirty-five years, Josie protested no further. For Mike Jacobs ran his household with the same iron hand and apparently iron lungs that have for nearly half a century terrorized his office help and business associates.

Even when Mike was being a charming and gracious host, he was inclined to couch his generosity in terms of harsh commands. "Go ahead, take more turkey," he'd bark at you, and should you mumble a polite "No thank you," he'd growl at the butler, "Put more turkey on d' plate—MORE!"

So Josie got her coat while Mike, an impatient man with a deep compulsion to be on the move, bad heart and all, was already in the car with the motor going. In a few minutes they were roaring toward New York. Sixty miles an hour is crawling to Mike. Before his illness he had always done his own driving, and it was a common sight to the Jersey cops to see him careening through highway traffic at eighty miles an hour. "Compared to him, Barney Oldfield was a bum," said the valet and masseur who lived with him for years. "Every time I rode with him, I said 'Good-bye, life.' He cracked up five beautiful cars that I know of, but somehow he never got hurt. I'd've said that God was watching over him, only why the hell should God watch over a S.O.B. like that?"

As they shot through one small New Jersey town, a highway patrolman took pursuit, but when he was close enough to see the familiar license number, he waved and turned away. Cops never bothered Mike. Early in life he had learned never to argue with the Shields. Not when there were easier ways to get around them.

They reached the Garden just in time for the usual gathering of celebrities in the ring before the main event. Commissioner Eddie Eagan, the gentleman boxer, Rhodes scholar, and favorite target for uncouth remarks from the boxing fraternity, was receiving a medal from the French consul general for services rendered France. The Honorable Mr. Eagan had earned this award by suspending the officials who had been so provincial as to have voted for Jake LaMotta, the Bronx capitalist, in a tug-of-war with Monsieur Villemain.

The blundering if well-meaning commissioner had dealt harshly and perhaps impetuously with a popular local sportsman by the name of Rocky Graziano, and the fans were in no mood to look kindly upon his being given anything except the gate. His appearance in the ring was a signal for the kind of inverted cheer that had for years been Uncle Mike's reception.

Perhaps to deflect these rude noises from himself to some other victim, Commissioner Eagan announced that Mike Jacobs was in the house for his farewell promotion and asked the fistic dean emeritus to stand and take a bow. To everyone's amazement, not the least Uncle Mike's, the fans rose as if this were Eisenhower and cheered and applauded for three minutes. For the first and last time in his thirty years of association with the game, Mike was in right with his cash customers.

"Now what's all the cheering about?" we asked the fight manager sitting next to us.

The manager shrugged. "Go figure out fight fans," he said. "One minute they're yelling for murder and the next minute they're so sentimental they're yelling for the fight to be stopped to save some bum a little punishment. One minute your guy's a hero, and just like that they turn on 'im and call 'im a yellow bum.

"Same with Mike just now. All of a sudden he got to 'em. They get thinking back to all the great fights he made for 'em, starting with Ross and Petrolle, then Armstrong-Ambers, Armstrong-Zivic, and the first Louis-Conn, and they remember how he tried to buck the gamblers and how he insisted his fights go on the square no matter what Dan Parker says. They think how much more he had on the ball than anybody else who ever set himself up as a fight promoter, how he was strictly a Big Dealer who came into the Garden when the joint was dying on its feet and built it up into the only major league club the boxing business has. Then they think of this guy living on a rain check, ready to cross over any minute, coming in on a slow night like this just to smell a little of that resin for the last time, and they think, well, let's give the old bastard a send-off he'll remember."

After the fight some of the boys were sitting around Lindy's, tearing into herring, chicken liver, and Mike's motives for having gone to all the trouble of coming in for this farewell appearance.

"For a man who's supposed to be guided strictly by what's-in-it-for-me, doesn't it seem he deserves a little credit?" I asked. "He's a guy who never cared anything about the limelight, so he didn't drive all the way in from the country just to get a hand. Don't you think it's possible there's a streak of sentiment in him? Now that he's stepping down, maybe he can afford himself the luxury of acting like a human being once in a while."

They looked at me as if I were from the country, which I was.

"I think the only reason Mike came in was to count the house for the last time," an old-time fight manager said. "When he heard it was only sixteen thousand dollars, he thought they were holding out on him."

"Either that or he just didn't know what to do with himself," a publicist said. "He doesn't know how to sit still. He's been hustling too long."

"If he ever gets to heaven," said the old-timer, "ten to one he finagles the choice tickets from St. Peter and makes a bundle scalping 'em outside the gate."

"He was a promoting son of a bitch," the old-timer went on. "Did you know he made eighty thousand dollars off Caruso one season before the First War? Another time he did all right with Emmeline Pankhurst, the suffragette. He could promote shit and make you buy it for sugar candy."

Mike Jacobs with Sugar Ray Robinson, 1943. (© Bettmann/Corbis)

"If it hadn't been for him, Rickard would've gone broke on that Dempsey-Carpentier," the publicist said.

"I'll tell you the secret of Mike's success, he never let his right hand know what his left was doing," the fight manager said.

"Hell, not even his forefinger would know what his second finger was doing," said the old-timer.

"Not to mention that middle finger," said the publicist, and everybody laughed.

"Isn't there anybody who likes him?" I asked, for after all, I had no axe to grind. I had never had to go up against Mike on a business deal. I had never hated his guts like some of the fighters, managers, and sportswriters who despised him for what they considered his ruthlessness and greed. And I had never gone to him with my hands out like certain politicians, law enforcement officers, and a compromised minority of boxing writers to whom Mike was a friend as long as they could be of any use.

The old-timer shook his head. "His mother used to like him, but she's passed on."

"He was sure good to his mother," the publicist said. "Only person he respected in his whole life, if you ask me. Gave her a car and a chauffeur and a swell apartment. Had a great big painting made of her. And he's always been a sucker for kids. This little girl Joan he's adopted, when he starts telling you how smart she is, he's a typical doting pa."

"Didn't he have any friends?" I persisted. "Wasn't there a special fondness for some of the fighters? Like Billy Conn?"

"Sure," the old-timer said, "he was crazy about Conn. Especially that night Billy helped him draw that two million."

That led to one of the classic stories of Mike's capacity for friendship. One evening as Mike was leaving for the country, a marginal character called Billy Stevens happened to be hanging around the office. Billy was what might be called these days a five-percenter, a small-time angler who specialized in making himself useful to as many people as possible. This happened to be at a time when Mike was having a little more trouble than usual pinning Eddie Mead down to a Garden date for Armstrong, and Mike must have figured that Stevens might be able to wise him up as to just how well this horseplaying manager was fixed at the moment. Maybe Mike, a man of sudden moods, was feeling a little lonely too. Anyway, he asked Stevens to drive down and spend the weekend with him.

Throughout the weekend Stevens was wined and dined with a lavish hand, the way Mike knows how to do it when he's out to please. Stevens talked freely, and Mike must have welcomed the information for when he put Stevens in his car to send him to the station late Sunday afternoon, he pressed his hand warmly and told him how much he had enjoyed the visit. "See you first thing in the morning, Mike," Stevens said, and Mike's benign smile and nod seemed to indicate that nothing would please him more.

When Stevens got back to town that night, he told all his pals how badly they had misjudged Mike. "I never met a friendlier or more considerate guy," he insisted. "We hit it off something wonderful. From now on it looks like I'm gonna be his right-hand man."

The next morning Stevens was in bright and early to begin his career as Mike's right-hand and confidante. "The Boss ain't in," growled Donnelly, the hulking ex-cop who guarded the door to Mike's inner office. But Stevens smiled confidently. He knew the Boss's habit of getting to his office every morning by eight o'clock. "Just tell him his pal Billy Stevens is here."

In a moment Donnelly returned. "The Boss says—I mean I says—he ain't in," said Donnelly, in a kind of ominous gargle, and started pushing Stevens away from the door.

At this moment Uncle Mike appeared. He could hardly avoid bumping into his erstwhile guest as he passed, but if he recognized him he gave no sign.

"Hi, Mike!" Stevens called. But though he was only a few feet away, Mike did not seem to hear.

"But I just spent the weekend with him! I'm one of his close friends!" Stevens screamed as he was being dragged along.

"Hey, Boss?" Donnelly called to Mike, now engaged in earnest conversation with his Girl Friday, Rose Cohen; the guard indicated Stevens and then, with an eloquent thumb gestured toward the main door. Mike merely nodded and, while his weekend guest was being propelled into the corridor, went on checking the number of tickets sent out for his next fight.

"That's our Uncle Mike," said the old-timer. "When you had something he wanted, he couldn't do enough for you. But once he squeezed you dry, you could be lying in the gutter and he'd step right over you and never look down.

"There never was a man in this town chased the dollar quite so hard as Uncle Mike. No pursuit of happiness for him; strictly pursuit of the buck. He'd tell you that himself. 'If I made a hunnert grand this morning, I'd be out hustlin' for a quarter this afternoon. I can't help it. I got to be on the go,' he admitted one time. It's kind of a disease. Mike came up out of the slums, one of eleven ragged kids in a couple of stinking rooms. He was out hustling a buck when most kids were still rolling hoops. By the time he was ten, he was a full-time business man."

I made a mental note of this for future reference. It's sort of a hobby, trying to figure out what makes a phenomenon like Mike Jacobs run. I had the feeling that night it wasn't quite as simple as calling him names. He seemed to have the complexities of a Machiavellian prince, twentieth-century Eighth Avenue style, and I'd need the objectivity of Machiavelli himself if I were going to understand him.

Meanwhile I was listening to another anecdote in this fabulous career. The supply seems endless, for Uncle Mike, like Jimmy Walker, Wilson Mizner, and a rare few, had become a legend in his own time. "One thing Mike had twice as much of as anybody else," said a sportswriter who had joined the table, "is chutzpah. I don't know exactly how you translate chutzpah," said the sportswriter who happened to be Irish but had been raised in Lindy's. "It's like when you go to a dinner party without being invited, insist on being served first, and then complain to the hostess the steak isn't the way you like it. That's mild chutzpah. But Uncle Mike was the all-time chutzpah champ. Like Joe Louis, he retired with the title undefeated.

"For instance, the story of him and Fritzie Zivic. One night Fritzie calls him at his suite at the Edison. It's pretty late and Mike is in bed. Fritzie says he could use five grand, against some future fight in the Garden. Mike blows his top. Who the hell does this bum Zivic think he is to wake Mike up in the middle of the night to put the bite on him? Why doesn't Zivic go back to Pittsburgh and leave him alone? Who wants to throw money away on a stinkin' has-been? He lets loose with a string of obscenities, including all the old standbys and a couple of new ones he invents for the occasion, and crashes the receiver back on the hook.

"A few minutes later Mike's matchmaker Nat Rogers calls with terrible news. Bob Montgomery was sick and the big lightweight match with Beau Jack was out the window. With only forty-eight hours to fight time, it seemed hopeless to find a suitable substitute match, and without one they'd lose a big paynight and have to return the sizable advance sale. 'I thought of moving Vinnie Vines up from the semi-final,' Rogers said. Vines had been impressive as a minor club main-eventer and was considered a promising rookie. 'But we'd need somebody with a name in there with him to draw any money.'

"When Mike is faced with a crisis like having to pay money back, nobody in America thinks quicker. 'Lissen,' he says, 'call Zivic right away. Right here in the hotel. Ask him what's the big idea hangin' up on me. Tell 'im I'm sore. Shut up. Do like I tell ya.'

"A few minutes later a bewildered Zivic called Mike again. 'Mike, what goes on? I thought you hung up on me.'

"Uncle Mike's tone became positively fatherly, for Uncle Mike. 'Fritzie, would I do that? We're old friends, ain't we? We made a lot of money together.'

"'s funny, I was sure you hung up on me,' said Fritzie, not altogether convinced. 'An' all them things you called me.'

'Aah the fuckin' operator cut us off,' Mike said. 'An' you know I'm only kiddlin' when I call ya names. If I didn' like ya I wouldn' call ya anything,' and Mike with rare cordiality went on to inquire as to the health of Zivic's wife and children and finally of the fighter himself.

'Feeling fine,' said Zivic, a cutie outside the ring as well as in. 'I'm always in shape.'

'Then you're fightin' Friday night.'"

The last-minute match between a rising young star and a famous veteran caught the imagination of the fans, what might have been a night in the red turned out to be solidly in the black, and everyone was happy except young Vines, who proved too green for the ex-champion and was banged out by old Fritzie in two minutes of the first round.

Everyone agreed this was a typical Operation Jacobs. The popular pastime of putting the knock on Uncle Mike, indulged in even by those who had profited by his ingenuity, showmanship, and readiness to pay off for services rendered, might have gone on into the small hours if Ray Arcel hadn't come along at that moment and helped get things back in perspective.

Ray was something of a rarity in boxing circles for besides being an outstanding trainer and a manager of impeccable honesty, he never went in for the backbiting and belittling that monopolized the monologues of some of his prominent colleagues.

"Mike may be a hard man to love," said Arcel. "Somehow I don't think he even wanted people to like him. He was a lone operator. He played all his cards close to his chest. I don't think he ever let anybody get very close to him. After all, he's been operating in this town all his life. He's worked with thousands and thousands of people and done favors for thousands more. Some of the biggest people in this city call him Mike, and yet he hasn't got a single close friend.

"But I'll say this for Mike, we've begun to miss him already. No one else could make us that kind of money. Sure, maybe it was a monopoly and all that, but Mike knew how to fill a house. And the more money he made for himself, the more he made for our fighters. And I'll say another thing for Mike. He drove the toughest bargain he could, but once he said you had a deal it was like money in the bank. You didn't need a contract. If Mike said 25 percent, he didn't pay off on twenty-four and a half. He stabilized this business. Before Mike it was always hit or miss. But with Mike, if you had something to offer, you could count on a good living. And anytime you got in a hole, Mike was there to stake you. There was nothing small about him that way. I don't know how many managers are into him for ten, fifteen thousand in advance for fights that never came off. And Mike's never put the squeeze on them. When he goes, he'll take at least a couple of hundred thousand with him in IOUs."

The sportswriter pointed out that these advances, in Joe Louis's case as much as a hundred thousand, had been Mike's way of cornering the market on big-name fighters. Once they were into Mike for ten or fifteen Gs they had to fight for him to get off the hook. It was more binding than an exclusive contract, for contracts, as Mike was the first to know (and as will be investigated later in some detail), could be bypassed. But once you owe a man fifteen or twenty or twenty-five thousand dollars, and he runs the only club in the world where you can consistently make that kind of money for one evening's work, you're going to think twice before you skip off to fight some bum in Wilkes-Barre without the Boss's okay.

"If Mike had a monopoly," Arcel persisted, "it was because he was so completely head and shoulders above anybody else in this business that he naturally came to dominate it. His judgment of what a match would draw was uncanny," Ray Arcel said. "There were a lot of people who knew more than he did about fighters' abilities, but nobody knew more about matching up the fighters who would draw the money. He could say Janiro and LaMotta—that's good for eighty-six thousand and Janiro and Pellone won't do better than forty-eight, and nine times out of ten he'd come within a thousand dollars of the final gross."

"You think he was good for boxing?" I asked.

"All things considered, I do," Arcel said. "After all it's just a business like any other. The man who can make the most money for you is the man to have around. You check the records you'll find the total income of main-event fighters doubled or maybe tripled while Mike was in the driver's seat. Mike's yearly business was two, three, four, sometimes five million dollars. You've got to figure the fighters were cutting in for 50 percent of that. Would you rather gross a couple of hundred thousand with a guy you love like a father or five million with a so-and-so like Mike?"

There isn't much question as to whether the fight game's been good for Mike. The tallest Horatio Alger tale is mild stuff alongside Mike's upward climb from the seamiest slums of Manhattan to the palatial home in New Jersey and only the Lord (and probably not even the Treasury Department) knows how many millions. Whether Mike's been good for the fight game is what might be called along Forty-ninth Street a "mute pernt." It's good for an argument any time a fight crowd gets together, and even the sports columnists who have kept close tabs on Mike for years can't seem to agree.

The *New York Mirror*'s Dan Parker, who preferred to call him Uncle Wolf, thought Mike the most arrogant and ruthless dictator the sports world ever had, and fired regular broadsides at him for allegedly favoring a fight manager's clique, countenancing the sale of boxing titles, buddying up to mobsters like Frankie Carbo (whose fighters were always on the cards and sometimes gave performances that did not look altogether kosher), raising ticket prices beyond the pocketbook of the average fan, scalping working press tickets for outlandish prices, preventing first-rank fighters from their legitimate crack at titles, and at least half a dozen other crimes against the public interest.

But Red Smith, an equally honest and able observer of Eighth Avenue doings, took a kindlier view: "Although it is certainly true that nobody ever exerted such absolute dictatorship as his over any sport and while it is probably true that no one else ever made such profits as he from boxing, it is emphatically true that no man ever ran boxing as well as he, anywhere. . . . If anyone in the world has run fights on the level, Mike has."

Jimmy Powers of the *Daily News* is on Parker's side, agreeing with his colleague from the *Mirror* that the second Louis-Conn fight was "a swindle," and out-Parkering Mike's severest critic when he urged Mike to retire from fight promotion because he was running the game into the ground—not only in New York, he wrote, "but in other great cities of America where Monopoly Mike's blighting hand has ruined the sport and left darkened arenas."

But Jimmy Cannon of the *Post*, whose indictment of the game as "a racket founded on deceit and treachery" is on record in any number of eloquent columns, who has called Mike "the stingiest man in the world," who tabbed the buildup for the second Louis-Conn fight "a phony" and nailed the Louis-Mauriello match as an insult to the fans' intelligence, still seems to agree with Smith that, by and large, Uncle Mike was on the square and promoted more memorable fights than any other single promoter.

The Broadway bard Damon Runyon, himself once a partner of Mike's in the Twentieth Century Sporting Club, in one of his last comments on fistic matters seemed to line up with the opposition. Critical of Jacob's monopoly, he wrote: "There is none of the old incentive to managers to hustle up new fighters. . . . Mike Jacobs, the boxing Boss, has a radio deal that nets him a profit whether the boxing performers are stars or hamdonnies, so he has no interest in that constant development of new headliners that was once the lifeblood of the fight game."

But it's one of those endless controversies, for such respected newspapermen as John Kieran, Bill Corum, and Frank Graham bylined that without being blind to the personal foibles of Uncle Mike, they considered him a beneficial influence. And, apparently, despite the violence of the opposition, the vote of boxing writers was in Mike's favor, for prominently displayed in Mike's richly, if somewhat eclectically, furnished living room was an impressive gold trophy inscribed to him from the Boxing Writers Association for "his lifetime exemplary service to the sport of boxing in America."

Fighters themselves were as far apart on the question of Uncle Mike as the sportswriters. Jack Dempsey had been blasting Mike for years for monopolistic tactics he claimed were milking the game dry, choking off incentive, and generally running it into the ground. But Joe Louis would tell you Uncle Mike always dealt fairly with him, that he gave greater opportunities to black boxers than anyone before him, and that more good fighters were developed under his management than at any previous time because Mike's shows raked in the kind of practical encouragement that talks loudest to hungry fighters. As of this writing, Gene Tunney had not been heard from. Perhaps it is not considered cricket for one millionaire and country squire to discuss another. Or perhaps Gene, as a student of Shakespeare and Bernard Shaw, went at it more subtlely and had Mike in mind when he made those general blasts against the low company of scurillous characters with whom one had to deal in the boxing business.

Despite the controversy over Uncle Mike's business methods, there is one subject on which all disagreement ceases—his phenomenal capacity for success. With no education, no knowledge of a trade, no one to help him, and no money in his hands that he didn't earn peddling papers, running errands, or slinging hash, he hustled himself a thousand-dollar stake before most kids are halfway through high school. "After sixteen I was never broke again," he said. In the next half-century he rang the bell (a cash register's, naturally) in at least three different fields—excursion boat concessions, ticket speculation, and the fight business—with successful side forays into the stock market and real estate. As a ticket seller, his ingenuity amounted to genius. "Put a ticket in his hand, he could squeeze three times as much money out of it as anybody else," says an old associate. "I swear it was more miraculous than squeezing blood out of stone."

The scope and cynical brilliance of Mike's ticket speculation is a chapter in itself, to be studied in detail as a way of life that was paying top dividends come boom or depression. On the second Dempsey-Tunney fight he is said to have made as much money as the official promoter Tex Rickard just from the sale of choice, reserved seats at twice, three times (or ten times if he could get it) their printed value of seventy-five dollars. On the night of that fight he had so much money in cash that he broke it up into twenty-thousand-dollar lots, concealed it in the clothing of his various relatives, and put them on a train back to New York with it. He was careful not to buy them Pullman berths though. "If I let 'em get comfortable," he told Bobby Dawson, the old boxer who served as a sort of rough and ready Knight of the Bath to Mike, "the sons-o'-bitches might fall asleep."

When Rickard died in 1929, Mike made no effort to fill Tex's shoes himself. Let the other fellow have the headaches, all I want is the choice seats to hustle, seemed to be his philosophy then. It was more or less by accident, as we shall see, that he found himself in the role of promoter bucking Jimmy Johnston and the Garden from 1934 until he came in as top man in 1937. But in the next decade he hung up box office records outside the ring that promise to stand as long as Joe Louis's inside the ring. He staged sixty-one championship bouts, promoted three thousand boxing shows, signed five thousand boxers, grossed over $10 million with Joe Louis alone, staged approximately 70 percent of all the bouts below the heavyweight division that grossed over $100,000 (totaling $3 million, with a mass attendance of half a million), attracted in a single year, to thirty-four Garden shows, nearly half a million people, grossed in that same year $5.5 million, and sold tickets over a fifteen-year period to more than five million people who pushed at least $20 million through Mike's ticket windows.

And yet, to anyone who knows the strange and devious ways of Uncle Mike, even this record of official financial success doesn't begin to tell the story. For whereas Mike's Twentieth Century Sporting Club might show a net annual profit of $200,000 or $300,000, Mike could make himself a hundred thousand or so in hidden profits from the "ice" in selling ringside seats through the Jacobs Ticket Agency or through under-the-counter sale of seats in a highly privileged in-front-of-ringside section that Mike called euphemistically "the working press."

At any championship fight this "working press" was always an interesting gathering of big-shot politicians, Hollywood and Broadway stars, judges, and the Who's Who of New York and New Jersey millionaire hoodlums, who might have paid anywhere from a hundred to three hundred for their "complimentary ticket." A "working press" section of five or six hundred, at these prices, adds up to a nice little bonus, especially when it's all in cash and not subject to luxury or income taxation.

But despite the commanding position he maintained in New York for three decades, surprisingly little was known about the personal life and actual career of Uncle Mike. As late as 1929 the ex-sportswriter Westbrook Pegler referred to him merely as "the box-office man for Tex Rickard." Except for occasional reference to excursion boats, the columnists seemed more interested in Mike's exasperating presence than in his somewhat incredible origin, his grotesque childhood, and the compulsive money-hunger of his young manhood.

Undoubtedly this reticence stemmed from Mike himself, whose habitual secretiveness found a natural ally in his inarticulateness when talking anything other than the fight business. People who worked and lived with him for years fell strangely silent when his early days were mentioned. His own family approached the subject with a strange caution, as if under a heavy load of pressure or fear. The one man most often mentioned as a personal friend, Captain George Foster, formerly of the New York Fire Department and now a baseball executive with the New York Giants, testified to Mike's secretiveness even about matters which seemed relatively innocuous.

"He wasn't much of a talker unless there was some definite point to be gained," said Foster, the only one of at least thirty interviewees who confessed to a genuine liking for Mike. "Sometimes on the drive out to Rumson, he wouldn't say a word all the way. Only once in a long while he'd let down and reminisce a bit. Mike knew how to keep things to himself. That was a large part of his success.

"He knew who to take care of and he always paid off, and nothing small about it either. He was a great judge of human nature—knew just how far he could go with everybody he dealt with. That's how he had everybody in his pocket, from the police to the boxing commission. Not always with money you understand. With tickets. With favors. He was a great fella for knowing the other fella's weakness. Liquor. Girls. A mortgage falling due. A political jam. Some rap he could square. He was always getting you obligated. Not a bribe, understand. Just insurance against some time when you could do him a favor. And the fella could always depend on the fact that Mike would never talk. Operating in this town like he had all these years, he knew a thousand things that could hurt a fella. But he never opened his mouth. You've got to give him credit."

That no one knows just how much money Mike had was an example of just how close he played 'em to his chest. Captain Foster is authority for the statement that Mike had more cash money than anybody else in America: "it runs into millions—hard cash." General John Reed Kilpatrick, president of Madison Square Garden, estimates Jacobs's fortune as "several million anyway." A sampling of opinions at Forty-ninth Street and Eighth Avenue, Lindy's, Toots Shor's, and other strategic points ran from "at least a million" to "maybe ten."

But apparently not even Josie Jacobs, after living under one roof with him for thirty-five years, was completely taken into Mike's confidence. At dinner one Sunday Josie was protesting what she considered the exaggerated accounts of Mike's wealth. "Mike was a great promoter, but he never made as much money as people think," she insisted. "We're, well, comfortable but that's about all. Living like this, with his big family to support, an' all my nephews and nieces to put through schools, in ten years we'd both have to go back to work. If we've got a million dollars, I've never seen it."

When we first sat down to dinner the expression on Uncle Mike's face had been positively benevolent. He had been beaming proudly when their adopted daughter, five-year-old Joan, sang all the lyrics to "Rolling Down the River" in a clear, confident voice. But as Josie went on about their poverty, an expression began to cross his face that looked to me suspiciously like embarrassment. He began to growl and then to mutter to himself, and finally blurted, "Okay, okay, talk about somethin' else."

Sitting on the impressive veranda under a bright canopy looking out across his well-kept lawns and broad fields and meadows rolling down to the Shrewsbury River, I tried to resolve the various contradictions in the tyrannical and somewhat sinister personality of Uncle Mike.

Secretive, friendless, inarticulate, he would suddenly drop in on his chiropractor or some other casual acquaintance for a few minutes of isolated garrulousness.

Greedy almost to psychopathic extremes, "the stingiest man in the world"; yet his longtime rival and enemy, Jimmy Johnston, was said to be into him for thirteen thousand dollars when he checked out.

So ruthless and inhumane that at the time of his heart attack, a popular gag along Jacobs Beach was: Since when can a man without a heart have a heart attack? Still, at the age of sixty-five he could take to his heart, in a way that could not be feigned, an adopted little girl.

So silent and poker-faced in his business dealings that even when his mind had been made up as to a certain match a year in advance, the principals would not know it until the last moment, yet whose very hardness seems to conceal an emotional instability that can give way suddenly to the most violent outbursts. His temper had sent more than one employee to the hospital with a nervous breakdown; its violence had been felt in a most direct way by Josie herself, and even the children were not immune when Mike flew into one of his tantrums.

"He gets like this every time it rains," said one of his youthful relations as Mike, in a kind of Jekyll-and-Hyde, was changing from a doting father, an amiable husband, and a gracious host into the rampageous personification of abusiveness and pugnacity. "Uncle Mike has to have action all the time."

A few moments after such an outburst, Mike would be as calm as if it had never happened. He might even grin at you sheepishly. But he would never apologize. "Mike never knew how to say I'm sorry," a close associate said. "He might call you some horrible names or even throw you out of the office and then start to feel bad about it, but the next time he saw you he'd never mention it, he'd just say 'Hello, Joe, let's get some lunch,' and pick up as if the fight had happened to two other guys. I wouldn't say Mike had bad manners. I'd just say he never had no manners at all."

Sitting with Mike on the comfortable veranda of the great twenty-five room house, I looked out into the driving rain and pondered these intriguing complexities of his character. More than ever, I wanted to get the whole story. But it was not one that any single person could tell me, not even Uncle Mike. In due time it led me literally from the Polo Grounds, where I talked to Mike's "one friend," Captain Foster, to the Battery, where I talked to seventy-year-old Leonard De Conza, who remembered "hustling excursion tickets shoulder to shoulder with Mike some fifty years ago." I walked through the wretched slum building where Mike was born. I strolled through the neighborhood where little Mike hustled his first nickels and dimes, and I talked to a few old-timers who remembered his family. I talked to relatives, early associates, servants, managers, boxers, sportswriters, doctors, employees, to the distinguished General Kilpatrick and highly respected Ray Arcel as well as to jailbirds, gamblers, and racket-eers. I talked to whatever friends I could find; enemies were eas-ier to locate. As soon as they heard I was on the trail of the true story of Uncle Mike, with no axes to grind but no punches to pull, they called to volunteer. I listened to as many as I could while re-serving my right to evaluate, remembering that every man who comes to power in America gathers a fat list of *Ins* and *Outs*, and the *Outs* are bound to come up with some hair-raising tales. From George Washington down. Even if you're an eagle scout and in step with the Lord.

But what stuck in my craw was that old-time fight manager's crack about Mike's childhood. "What got this man started on this golden treadmill?" I asked myself. What pressures, what hungers, what influences?

And so I went back, all the way, to a birth certificate that said Michael Strauss Jacobs, born March 10, 1880, son of Isaac and Rebecca Jacobs, 651 Washington Street.

That's just off Christopher Street, below Tenth, near the Bat-tery, a block from the waterfront. A tough district even today. A tougher district when baby Mike came bawling into this world.

II.

When Uncle Mike first saw the light of day—or what passed for light in the grimy atmosphere of a waterfront slum—his parents Isaac and Rebecca were living with six children in two small rooms partitioned off behind their tailor shop, in the heart of what was then a predominantly lower-class Irish neighborhood.

Except for a privileged few, these were not the Irish of Tam-many Hall and the Force, who had caught on quickly to big-city ways and had their pick of soft jobs and the graft that ran to countless milions every year. The Irish of Jacobs's neighborhood were more bare-window than lace-curtain, refugees from the ter-rible famines that racked their island from the mid-1840s on and drove a million and a half people toward the greener fields of America in a single decade.

But instead of green fields they settled for the steaming cobblestones of the lower West Side and wages of a dollar a day or less as sailors, brewery workers, stevedores, and teamsters.

They were a hardworking, hard-drinking, quick-tempered, pugnacious, God-fearing lot, rarely more than a step ahead of starvation. Sanitation was a stranger. The closest thing to a bathroom was the dingy outhouse that had to serve all the families crowded into a two story tenement. For heat the slum dwellers broke up boxes or salvaged driftwood from the river to feed into their stoves. In 1880 the Board of Health described the conditions into which Mike was born: ". . . the living have very little more ground space than is appropriated for the dead—a distribution which is not less fatal than it is impartial."

Squalid but challenging, harsh yet teeming with vitality—such was the world in which this third son of Isaac and Rebecca first learned to crawl, to talk, to stand upright, and—most important in that waterfront world of want and grab—to stand up to his fellow men.

To understand why a man called Isaac Jacobs should have chosen to set his family up as a tiny Jewish island in a swarming sea of Irish Catholicism instead of gravitating toward the ghetto on the opposite side of Manhattan, one has to go back to 1850 when Isaac's parents emigrated from Poland to Dublin, Ireland. Driven across Europe by the pogroms, Isaac's family was attracted to the sizable Jewish population in Dublin, where a popular synagogue was guided by a bearded rabbi, traditional in every way except that he spoke Gaelic as well as Hebrew; and his English contained as unmistakable a brogue as ever was heard in County Cork or Hell's Kitchen.

Isaac was an infant when he was brought to Dublin. Growing to young manhood in that city, his brogue was a natural. He took pride in his perfect Gaelic as well, and as the years passed he seemed even to become convinced that he looked more like a true son of St. Patrick than of Abraham. This may have been mere wishful thinking, a chameleonlike urge of a persecuted people to lose themselves in assimilation. But early photographs do reveal a round and ruddy face that might pass more readlily for a phiz of St. Patrick than of Saul.

Tintypes of the Child Mike seem to repeat this Mendelian accident for they show us a moonfaced, strong-featured boy who must not have stood out too strongly from his Irish playmates—or should we say in that hungry world of shortened childhood, competitors. Whether justified or due to the pressure of environment, Mike and his brothers grew up believing they looked more Irish than Semitic. But it would probably be more accurate to say that Mike has one of those faces that give the lie to racial stereotypes.

It seems to be the kind of face on which no racial group has a corner—a strong, unhandsome face with a forceful, bulbous nose, eyes that narrow easily in a way that seems shrewd and appraising, a mouth that can change quickly from a hard, narrow line to an open, roaring furnace. The jaw—even when unsupported by dentures—is powerful without being oversized. Many a manager or unwanted boxer knows how this face can close up so that not a flick of eye or muscle gives the slightest indication of recognition; yet it has some of the qualities of those little rubber faces we used to squeeze into various expressions, for when it is genuinely pleased or ingenuously pleasing it can relax into a warm, infectious grin.

When they came to America, Isaac and Rebecca always gravitated to neighborhoods that were Irish and close to the docks. Isaac was a tailor specializing in sailors uniforms, emergency repairs, and pressing for crews arriving in port. When ships were being moored, he would be on the docks trying to coax a little business from the hard-boiled sailors, more interested in refreshing their thirst than their wardrobe. A little Jewish tailor trying desperately to make a way in America for his growing family, he would startle an Irish tar with a "Shure and ye'll be wantin' a fresh pair o' duds fer to please the ladies, me boy."

To which the growling answer would usually be: "The ladies I'll be visitin' 'll take me as I am."

Though Isaac worked from dawn until far into the night, the wolf was a permanent resident at the Jacobses' door. There were nine children now, and Isaac had to supplement his meager earnings by doubling as a "runner"—a professional greeter and guide to immigrants arriving by steerage. These displaced persons of an earlier day, bewildered and unable to speak the language of this promised land, would rely on the runners to get them through customs, obtain the necessary entry papers, and even find them a place to live.

It was a job that left a great deal to conscience, for it was a simple matter for the unscrupulous to find out how well-heeled the new arrival was and then extract from him all sorts of exorbitant fees on the pretext that he would have to return to the Old Country unless these were paid. Many an immigrant was separated from his life's savings between the gangplank and the entrance to the street. Honest runners extracted small fees for their services and, judging from the poverty of the Jacobses' menage, it seems more probable that Isaac was one of these.

Throughout the childhood of Mike and his eight brothers and sisters, it took all the resourcefulness of a strong woman like Rebecca to keep this overpopulated household alive.

The painting of Rebecca that hangs in the luxurious living room of Mike's Rumson estate shows a matriarch of impressive physical strength and determination rather than a woman of beauty, delicacy, or sensitivity. But these qualities would hardly have sustained her through the ordeal of raising nine children on Washington Street. The boys remember that it was their mother who taught them to fight back against the conditions that might have crushed them. One day when Mike was seven or eight years old, he came home crying that an older boy, a well-known Irish bully on the block, had called him "sheeny" and pushed him off the landing into the river, at that time a favorite sport for kids whose only playground was the docks. As the youngest son, Mike was the family favorite, and his elder brothers were eager to avenge his injuries. But Rebecca had a different idea. "Let him learn to fight his own battles," she said. "Nobody ever helps anybody else in this world. Whatever he does, he'll have to do himself. The earlier he learns that, the less he'll be hurt."

It was the only workable philosophy of survival. Mike went out and took his lickings. He learned to fight back. "Mike could handle himself as good as the next kid," his family remembers. "But he wasn't the kind who went looking for fights. He was, well, like he's been all the rest of his life. He was a good businessman, hardworking and smart even when he was selling papers. He knew how to keep his mouth shut and go about his business. But if someone tried to grab his papers away or push him off the corner, then he'd fight like a wild cat. He was a good strong kid. He's always had an iron constitution. It wasn't too easy being the only Jews in an Irish neighborhood—even if our old man did talk their language. But the Irish gang on the block learned to respect Mike. He was just as tough as they were. Once they saw they couldn't scare him, they stopped bothering him."

Somehow, like the wretchedly poor Irish families around them, the Jacobses survived. The daughters helped with the cooking, washing, and mending. For the boys, school soon became a distraction from the main job of bringing in those few extra dollars each week that meant the difference between frightful want and just getting by. At ten, Mike was a newsboy, proud of bringing home fifty cents a day. A scrapper's ability is a traditional part of a newsboy's equipment, but in those days it was a good 90 percent.

An old man who remembers hustling papers in Mike's neighborhood around 1890 tells us, "If you had a bunch of papers under your arm, you were fair game in those days. You could never relax and you could never trust nobody. You'd be standin' on a corner mindin' yer own business and peddlin' yer papers an' first thing you'd know a fella'd come along and say, 'Hey Johnny, or Mike, lookit the apples on dat dame leanin' out the winder.' You'd look up and *wham*, it would be goodbye papers. Not just the boys either. The girls on that street and alla way down to the Battery were just as tough. They'd sneak up behind you, give you a push, and be off on the run with a dollar's worth of your papers. There was one girl I remember, we used t' call her Dirty Mary. Dirty Mary by the time she was ten could swear like a sailor. She'd grab our papers an' if we'd catch her she'd fight back just like a boy—only worse'n any boy because she'd scratch and bite and before you knew what happened you'd look like something that ran into Terrible Terry McGovern instead of a little girl."

Many a time young Mike would come home scratched and bruised, but never without his day's earnings. It was about this time that he included himself out as far as formal education was concerned. "What was the good of learnin' all the crap," he reasoned, "when I c'n be out makin' myself a buck?" From that day to this, Mike has behaved with extraordinary consistency. Whatever you need to know, know it better than anybody else, has been his motto, but if you can't make a dollar on it, don't waste your time.

It is this that has made some outside acquaintances wonder how a man so singularly ignorant as Mike could be so successful. But the opposite side of this coin is single-mindedness, a trait Mike cultivated from the age of ten. On Washington Street every dollar Mike brought in went toward survival. A few years later money would be a ladder to lift him out of the slums. Then a cushion against a deep-rooted dread of insecurity. Then independence, power, compensation for all the things he never had, nor could ever learn to appreciate. Begun as necessity, moneymaking became not just a way of life but the whole reason for living, until at last the ragged ten-year-old newsboy clinging desperately to his newspapers would cross the finish line as one of that handful of American millionaires who did it the hard way, by making every one of those ten hundred thousand dollars himself.

But, to go back some sixty years and at least $999,999: Mike was peddling his papers on Fourteenth Street one day when a man who looked like a sharper came up and said, "Hey, kid, wanna make an easy buck?" Mike hadn't been on the streets for nothing. He wasn't anybody's sucker. "Whatta I have to do?"

"Just stand in line at the Garden an' buy me a couple o' tickets."

Half an hour later Mike had his dollar. He and the sharp-looking fellow in the derby did business regularly for a while after that. By the time he was twelve, Mike was earning three or four dollars a week as a "digger"—a purchaser of tickets for scalpers who otherwise might become too familiar at the box office. At first Mike was a little puzzled. This fellow must certainly be a real sport to keep buying all these tickets. But his elder brother Jake soon put him wise. The fellow who was paying Mike a dollar to front for him in line couldn't afford to use one of his own seats—not when he could sell them for twice their official price. After years of selling papers for pennies, Mike was impressed.

"How much you think that guy makes a week?"

"Oh, twenny thirty dollars easy," Jake guessed.

"An' that's all he does, buys tickets and sells 'em on the street?"

"Yeah."

Mike didn't say anything, but next afternoon when the scalper for whom he had been working gave him the money to buy some tickets at the Opera House, he bought them but didn't return immediately with the money as he had done so many times before. Instead he loitered near the lobby on Fourteenth Street. He saw a couple go to the box office and turn away disappointed. The house was sold out. "Hey, mister, wanna buy two good tickets?"

He quickly disposed of his two-dollar tickets for four dollars each. Then he went back to the scalper who had broken him in. "Here's yer two bucks back," he said. "I'm through workin' fer ya."

"What, you don't want to make a dollar for doing practically nothing?" the scalper demanded.

"Nope," Mike said, "Take ya dough." Even at twelve, he had learned never to do any more talking than you had to.

With his two-dollar profit, Mike was in business. Next day he bought his own tickets. He held them until show time and sold them for a nice profit. But this time the sharp who had first put Mike to work as a digger saw that his young stooge was brazenly muscling in on his territory. He followed the twelve-year-old speculator around the corner and jumped him. "Yer a smart punk. Lemme catch ya doin' that once more and they'll find ya in the river."

It was the newsboy battles all over again, in an even rougher league. But Mike knew a simple law, and he lived by it. Next day he was back at the same spot scalping his tickets. The older scalper tried to bully him off the curb. Seeing a cop on the corner, Mike yelled "Help! Help!" The officer came running. "What's the trouble, me boy?"

"This crook tried t' gyp me on a ticket, an' when I squawked he started chokin' me," Mike said.

The cop turned on the scalper suspiciously. "I've had me eye on you," he said, and started going through the man's pockets. He found a dozen choice seats for performances all through the week. "I ought to run ye in for a dirty scalper," he said, "but this time I'll be easy on ye. If ye know what's good fer ye, stay away from this theater."

Righteously the cop pocketed the confiscated seats, for in those freebooting days (and has it ever changed?) the boys in blue were a law unto themselves, and it was common practice for a patrolman to advise a well-known thief that he would be run out of the district unless he agreed to a fifty-fifty split. Mike watched the cop pocket the wad of tickets with a plaintive eye. "Gee, I sure wish I could have a couple. It's me old lady's birthday an' I wanna surprise her." The appeal to mother love pierced the formidable blue uniform and went straight to its wearer's Celtic heart. "Here they are, me boy, and God bless ye mother."

It wasn't more than five minutes later that the cop caught Mike across the street from the theater in the act of selling his tickets.

"Why you dairty little liar!" he boomed. "And you tellin' me they were to surprise your own mother!"

"Who's a liar?" young Mike demanded, in an early display of that *chutzpah* that was to carry him boldly through crises all his life. "How c'n I buy me old lady a surprise if I don' sell them tickets?"

If the amiable symbol of law and order on Fourteenth Street had any answer for this, it is lost to history. Mike's benefactor, it seems, just stared at this resourceful young man in stupefied amazement, perhaps even in awe. "He had more get-up-and-go than anybody around," a relative recalls. "You'd have to get up awful early in the morning to try'n get the jump on Mike—and then you'd find he'd been up an hour before that."

Mike's beginnings as a ticket scalper hardly lend themselves to precise reporting for a lot of tickets have moved through the box office window (or out the back door) since then, and fact, legend, and faulty chronology seem to become almost hopelessly entangled after sixty years. A contemporary of Mike's insists on a different version. According to him, Mike, as a newsboy outside Tammany Hall on Fourteenth Street, had scraped up an acquaintance with Joe Bannon, then a young politico, later the Hearst executive and longtime friend of Mike's. They had joshed back and forth about the respective merits of two of the greatest featherweights of all time, George Dixon and Terrible Terry McGovern. When the two were finally matched at the Broadway A.C. in the bout hailed by turn-of-the-century sportswriters as the "Battle of Little Giants," Joe Bannon gave Mike a pair of complimentary tickets and told him to take his brother. But when Bannon looked for the Jacobs boys at ringside, he saw a couple of strangers sitting in the seats he had given Mike. The Dixon-McGovern battle had New York fight fans at fever pitch, and tickets were at a premium. "No matter how bad Mike wanted to see the fight," this story goes, "he couldn't miss a chance like this. He sold those tickets for five dollars apiece."

It's a good story and at least half true, for Mike was a newsboy outside Tammany Hall, he did wheedle complimentary tickets to the Coney Island and Broadway A.C. fights and sell them whenever he could, and he did meet Joe Bannon early in his career. But the Dixon-McGovern fight took place in 1900 when Mike was twenty years old, and according to all the evidence we can muster, Mike had long since graduated from the newsboy ranks. In fact some of those who regard themselves as experts in Jacobsology insist that Mike was a successful full-time ticket broker at the age of thirteen. But Mike's elder brother Jake was also scalping tickets from the curb in the nineties, and since their careers run parallel for a time, our aging witnesses may be confusing the two.

At any rate, there can be little doubt that at an age when most of us are struggling over multiplication tables in our copy books, Mike was learning his arithmetic in the hardheaded Fourteenth Street School of Economics where the problems were far from hypothetical: If you work eight hours to make fifty cents peddling papers, Q.E.D. you're a sucker. If you can buy a ticket for a dollar and sell it for two, you're getting smarter. If you can finagle a couple of comps to a big fight and find a sport to buy 'em for a sawbuck, you're wising up to how the game is played in Little Ol' New York.

In this school of economics, you went to the head of the class by looking sharp, acting sharp, and being sharp years before you ever needed a shave. Young Mike never had to read Adam Smith to master individual enterprise. All he had to do was keep his eyes open and his mind on the main chance. When he was thirteen or fourteen, for instance, he happened to be in a candy store when he overheard an advance man for May Irwin offering the proprietor two tickets to her coming comedy if he would insert a poster in his window. Mike lingered until the legman had left, then asked the owner if he was going to use the tickets. When the shopkeeper protested that he had no time for such dalliance, Mike said, "I'll give ya four bits for the two of 'em."

It was found money for the proprietor, and he gladly parted with the tickets. Mike followed the advance man for twelve blocks. Every time he saw the May Irwin poster in a store window, he went in and offered to buy the complimentary seats for a quarter apiece. In an hour's time he had bought up twenty of them. He held on to them until the day of May Irwin's appearance. She was one of the great favorites of the day, and by loitering around the ticket window Mike had no trouble selling his tickets at what averaged out to a dollar apiece. Five dollars had brought him twenty. More than his poor old man made in a week of sixteen-hour days of backache and eyestrain. Poor Isaac could only shake his weary head in wonder when his youngest son would come home with such a fortune made in a single afternoon—"an fer doin' nuthin," he'd mutter to himself.

A new century was dawning, with new values, new opportunities, new shortcuts that Isaac, with his needle and thread and stoop-shouldered resignation to poverty, would never understand. When you ask Mike or Jake today to describe their father, they shrug in the familiar gesture of the inarticulate. "He was a schneider, a tailor, he worked hard all his life, just work work work morning, noon, and night—what do you want from him, a poor tailor with no time for anything but work?" A schneider, a nonentity, a human machine for cutting and sewing materials, a shadowy symbol of drudgery who rose before it was light and did not grope his way to bed until the night was half gone and still made less money than his youngest son could make in half an hour of what the lad called "smart hustling."

On Mike's block only the dull-witted of the new generation went in for backbreaking manual labor. If you had any brains or ambition or starch you collected from Tammany on Dough Day, voted a dozen times on Election Day, and planned a lucrative career in politics. Or you joined one of the gangs and muscled in on the thriving industry of crime in lower Manhattan. You gambled or managed boxers, or if you stood in right with your district leader you opened a saloon, a sporting house, or a cock-fighting pit. In those days when it would have been about as possible for a DeSapio to head Tammany Hall as for Paul Robeson to be elected Imperial Wizard of the KKK, you didn't get these soft touches merely by being born under the Shamrock, but it helped. If, like Mike, you didn't happen to wear the green but still found yourself allergic to poverty and unremunerative sweat, you clowned like Eddie Cantor if you had talent, you bullied your way up like Monk Eastman if you had the muscle, or you played the angles every way from the middle like our Young Man With a Ticket, little Mike.

But those who tell those gaudy stories of Mike's taking over New York's ticket business at the age of twelve not only anticipated Mike's actual development by some thirty years but distract unnecessarily from one of the more vivid periods of Mike's sixty-year pursuit of the buck that little animal Manhattanites have hunted with such vigor from the time when Peter Minuet swung his big real estate deal with the Indians that gave him the island for twenty-four bucks.

In the mid-1890s, if you were poor but ambitious and lived below Fourteenth Street, you either gravitated toward Tammany Hall and the old Madison Square Garden to the north or to the Battery at the southernmost tip of the island. From there the big excursion boats carried holiday crowds to Dreamland Park or Atlantic Highlands. On a warm summer's day Battery Park was a favorite place for promenading couples and curious tourists waiting to board the *Rosedale*, the *Dreamland*, or the *John Sylvester*. Nearly all of Mike's sisters and brothers worked these excursion boats as ticket sellers, candy butchers, and later as concessionaires. Mike was hawking candy and popcorn on the boats at about the same time he was breaking into the ticket business as probably the youngest scalper on the sidewalks of New York.

But, just as he resigned as a "digger" as soon as he had learned enough to go into business for himself, he considered it a sucker's play to spend time making money for someone else. The prevalent slogan of "A Fair Day's Work for a Fair Day's Wage" was much too slow for this particular teenager. Soon he was selling tickets to the boat on a commission basis.

Old Lenny De Conza, still going strong at the Battery in the Coney Island Booth in the early 1950s, remembers well when he and Mike were rival ticket butchers. "Yessir, he was quite a fella," Lennie recalled. "He was sellin' tickets to the old wooden boats and I was sellin' 'em for the new iron boats which were a whole lot better. But that didn' stop Mike none. In them days we'd just stand out here at the dock with the tickets in our pockets and yell 'Getcha tickets for Dreamland Park.' No booths or nothin,' understand. Well Mike, he's always tryin' to outhustle you, he gets the idea of buildin' a portable booth, and he carries it around with him through the park, wherever the crowd happens to be."

De Conza, a vigorous old man with a seagoing complexion though he had been standing there at the water's edge for half a century, interrupted his narrative to call to a passing couple,

"Tickets to Coney Island—only ten cents." Then he reached back through fifty years to pick up his memories of Mike in the days when the fight promoter was better known as Steamboat Mike. "Once he set up them booths, we all had to have booths to keep in competition."

"Then you were all even again?" we suggested.

He grinned, and we noticed that in spite of his Italian name he looked like a florid-faced Irishman too; he even talked like one. They say married folks grow to look alike, and maybe this begins to happen to a fellow living all those years among the Irish. "Wasn't too easy to keep up with Mike. By that time he was out of ticket sellin' and had his own concession. On the old *Dreamland* I think it was."

It isn't easy to lower a bucket through more than half a century and come up with the exact year, but Mike himself remembered that one way or another he had managed to save a thousand dollars by the time he was sixteen, for it was always his nature to save money as well as make it. With his savings he bought his first food-and-drink concession. One of his sisters had the *Rosedale*, but Mike wasn't interested in working for anybody, not even a member of his own family. He was generous in his contribution to the family household but, as Tex Sullivan was to describe him later, "He was always a single-O guy. He liked to handle everything himself, and even if you were his own brother he wouldn't tell you his business."

An excursion-boat concession at the turn of the century was— in the current Broadway cant—a nice thing to have going for you. But young Mike introduced any number of refinements that not only gilded the lily but enabled him to cash it in for gold. When you fed your best girl peanuts and pop through the courtesy of Steamboat Mike, you were apt to pay not only through the nose but through the eyes, ears, throat and any other vents you happened to have on you.

Mike, for instance, was obligated to provide a free lunch for each excursion ticket. But by working out the logistics of Coney Island appetites, he found he could cut the cuffo meal in half by having his butchers ply the passengers with salted peanuts for the longest possible period before the free lunch had to be served. Salted peanuts naturally led to mass thirst, and Mike always made sure there was no water available so his parched customers would turn more eagerly to his soft drinks.

"If you was an excursionist on one of those boats," another old-time Battery character chuckled, "it was just like having Mike's hand in your pocket all the time. F'instance, once in a while a broad 'd be afraid of gettin' seasick, so Mike was right there with his own seasick remedy—only ten cents—for what was actually cold weak tea with a squirt of castoria in it to make it taste like medicine. One day on board, Mike noticed a fella's straw hat blow off. Next day he had a little rubber band gadget that fastened from your lapel to inside your hat and sold for a nickel. He was always schemin' up new ways to hustle a couple of extra dollars that no-body else'd ever dream of."

By the time Mike was in his early twenties he had extended his operation to a small fleet of excursion boats. But it doesn't seem to be true, as often reported when Mike's life is reviewed, that he was out twelve thousand dollars when the *General Slocum* went down with the loss of a thousand lives in the spectacular river fire of 1904. Mike is often charged with having owned the ill-fated boat whose skipper was prosecuted for negligence, and his enemies will even tell you it was his niggardliness with safety equipment that led to the fantastic loss of life. It is altogether possible that Mike will have to outdo One-Eyed Connolly to crash the gates of heaven, but—if contemporary news accounts and ownership papers are to be believed—the *Slocum* affair doesn't seem to be one of his sins. His only connection with the tragedy appears to be that his brother Jake managed the concession on the doomed ship and was one of the few who managed to swim to safety. But good stories never die, no matter how many times corrected, and this one goes on to relate how Mike, to recoup his twelve grand, capitalized on his own hard luck by running sightseeing boats to the scene of the catastrophe.

As with many stories of Uncle Mike, and a good many anecdotes in general, this one smacks of a hindsight characterization truer to Mike's *modus operandi* than to any specific event. Like the story of the Dixon-McGovern complimentary tickets, it seems true enough in essence, for it so closely resembles another account of Mike's well-known ability to roll with a punch that we pass it on as authentic. In addition to his excursion boat and ticket activities, Mike invested in an amusement pier at Coney Island. A fire destroyed most of the pier, and one day when Mike came out to itemize the damage he found a couple of fishermen sitting on his pilings. That was all he had to see. Next day when the fishermen came back they found the wreckage of the pier had been roped off, and a sign tacked up: "Private fishing grounds— 10 cents an hour, 50 cents all day." The reports that have come down to us claim that Mike did all right that summer, maybe even a little better than he would have done with his amusement pier because there was no overhead.

That Mike should size up the situation, hurry off to make his own sign, and then tack it up himself indicated a pattern of behavior he was never to outgrow. Even as a millionaire fight promoter, his associates remember his helping to set up the seats for a championship bout at the Polo Grounds or impatiently grabbing a hammer from the hands of a workman not moving fast enough for him and nailing up a sign himself. Almost always, this was a sign of impatience, of restlessness, of dissatisfaction with slower-moving, slower-thinking men. Once at his New Jersey estate I even saw him grab a tray of steaks from his butler's hand and serve them himself because his guests' plates weren't being filled quickly enough.

Whether he was a pauper or a millionaire, his habits remained remarkably unchanged. Years after it was no longer necessary, he still rose at dawn, just as eager as ever to be on the move. No matter how extensive his office or his household staff, he was always driven to do everything himself, down to the most menial details. If some men succeed by the ingenuity of their schemes and some by sheer hard work, it would seem as if Mike wanted to make doubly sure, for no schemer ever worked harder and no worker ever schemed so incessantly.

Of course excursion boats were a seasonal trade, but since Mike had been a newsboy outside Tammany Hall, he solved that problem by moving into the Hall as a busboy and in time a waiter. These were the days of Boss Croker, Police Chief Devery, Silver Dollar Smith, Al Adams the policy king, Jim Maloney the pool room king, Frank Farrell the gambler, and Senator "Big Tim" Sullivan, who had a hand in almost everything and who held the boxing clubs of his day in the same single-handed control that Mike was to exert forty years later.

Those were the days of uninhibited corruption, when a Tammany leader could even write a book defending what he liked to call "honest graft," when Senator Sullivan and Chief Devery could be Farrell's partners in the powerful gambling syndicate and when *How He Did It the Books Don't Show* was not only a popular song but a good-natured slur at the Boss who had started out as a poor man and within five years had $350,000 in race horses, a Fifth Avenue mansion, a private railroad car, a great estate in England, and no one knew how many millions in cash. Croker himself had stated that he had never bothered with banks and preferred to keep all his money where he could get his hands on it.

To all these men of power, young Mike turned an obsequious smiling face. They liked him as a "good, smart, willing lad," tipped him well, and in time he became a head waiter. More valuable than the material tips were the psychological ones as to how to deal with big-time politicians. From Big Tim and the others he learned that every man—except perhaps the hated Republican Reformers—had his price, a lesson Mike was to embellish with the years. The atmosphere of that Tammany dining room was composed of unabashed self-interest, limitless greed, diabolical intrigue, an intricate system of payoffs and under-the-table deals, a ready acceptance of the meanest sort of alliance as long as it was profitable, and of course the most cynical disregard for public service or social responsibility.

If the streets of the lower West Side were Mike's elementary school where he learned to hustle and gouge and scrounge, Tammany Hall might be considered the finishing school, where a young, heady, self-reliant opportunist, who naturally looks up to the big men of his day, learns the fine art of the finagle, the fix, the payoff, the business—how to win friends and influence people in a way Mr. Carnegie would never dream of. The immediate political connections were valuable. Through a benevolent despot like Big Tim, he might pick up tickets to one of the fifty local boxing clubs that could be more profitable than the change he found on the table. For an up-and-coming ticket broker there could be no more strategic spot than this hub around which all the entertainments of the city revolved. But this tough-fibered, alert young man with his eyes and ears open and his mouth discreetly shut, was also absorbing a course in Political Economy ever so much more pertinent than any he could have learned at the Harvard Business School.

From these men he learned only what he wanted, or what he needed, to learn. The carousing, the easy living, the wenching, the gluttony, the thirst he left to those who had more money or more time. Without being exactly an ascetic, he was a nondrinking, nonsmoking, nonmerrymaking young man who took his young ladies in his own way, careful not to let them deter him from the business at hand. This was another characteristic he carried throughout his career. He was rarely seen out after dark except at his own promotions. Some said he was too miserly. Some said his only real pleasure came from conniving. Some said he never cared enough about his fellow men and women to have any desire to go out among them congenially. If he wanted them, they came to him, at his time and place to suit his purposes.

It would seem in the nature of things that so concentrated a young man should shy away from entangling alliances with the opposite sex. And even when Mike was in his early thirties, he seemed content to remain a single-0 guy in his private as well as his public life. But, as it must to nearly all men, love—or what passed for it on the Battery in 1910—finally caught up with Mike and dropped him for the count.

On a routine check of his concessions one summer afternoon, he couldn't help noticing the new cashier. She looked like the kind of strawberry blonde they were singing about, fresh of face, trim of figure, a sixteen-year-old eyeful. Next day Mike was back to check his concessions and this new cashier again. He took her to dinner, and she told him her story. Her name was Josie Pela, and she had run away from home in upstate New York because her father, an unemployed actor, wanted to marry her off to an old man who, in telling the story years later, Josie dismissed as "just some old jerk." For years she had helped her mother take care of her ten brothers and sisters, and she wanted to see a little of life before she settled down, so she decided to take her chances in the big city. But she wasn't going to desert her family. She had her looks and a healthy instinct for landing on her feet, and somehow she was going to lick this town and do her family more good than if she had remained a small-town girl.

Neither Mike nor Josie would tell me just how the romance blossomed. Broach the subject to Mike and you'd get one of his customary growls. Although Josie was a good deal more communicative—and under the proper stimulation as loquacious as Mike is taciturn—she was inclined to gloss over the actual courtship.

"But after all," I insisted in our conversation, "it isn't every romance that unites two people and keeps them together all their lives."

"Are you kidding?" said Josie, as much of a realist as Mike, which may help to explain the bond between them. "Whatta you talking about—romance! Lookit Mike. You think he looked any different then? Had a little more hair, tha's' all. I was a good-lookin' young kid tryin' to get ahead in the world. He was a smart fella who knew his way around. He made me a good proposition an' I took it."

While that may hardly be the sentiment of young lovers in the romances lady authors like to write, it seemed to have sustained Mike and Josie through forty years of intimate partnership which has withstood even the most intense pressure of family disapproval, for Mike's mother, the powerful matriarch of the House of Jacobs who died a few years ago, never hid the fact that she considered Josie a designing shiksa adventuress.

If she was—and no one would tell you more honestly than Josie just how practical were her girlhood hopes and dreams—she had found an ideal running mate in Mike.

"Mike and I, we never kidded each other," Josie reminisced in a way that isn't exactly satisfying to sentimentalists. "Each of us knew what the other one wanted. I got a living out of it and money to send home. But don't let anybody tell you I didn't work for it. We both worked like dogs. Mike 'n I earned every dollar we got. We made a helluva good team."

Pressed for some memorable detail of the early days of their union, Josie recalled, "In them days, before the war, the other war, Mike got a nice price for the boat concessions and went into the ticket business full time. He didn't have no office yet; he'd sell 'em right off the curb outside the Garden—the old Garden. He'd be on his feet so long hustlin' tickets he'd come home with his feet bleedin'. I'd soak his feet in warm water and tell 'im he oughta take it a little easier. But you know the Boss. He'd say 'Aah, it's nothin', and next mornin' he'd be up at the same God-awful hour figurin' how t' get the jump on the other scalpers. The Boss isn't the easiest fella t' live with, but you gotta give him this: he didn' have no inside track to the box office like he had later on. Six days a week he hadda pound the pavement outside the Garden or the Opera House or the fight clubs. Believe me, hustlin' tickets wasn't all cumshaw in them days. No big office where the buyers came to you. It was stric'ly heel 'n toe."

Then, maybe she caught a look in my eyes, maybe it was all in her own mind, for she added, "All right, maybe you think he was mostly heel. But he hadda keep on his toes t' clear twenny dollars a day. I oughta know. I'm the guy who pulled off his socks when he came home. As I'm sittin' here, it was sweat 'n blood. You c'n forget about the tears. Win or lose, up or down, I never saw the Boss cry in his whole fuckin' life."

III.

Contrary to popular belief, it wasn't through the old Garden box office and choice fight tickets that Mike Jacobs cornered his first market in the ticket business. It was through Grand Opera. The incongruity of the Marx Brothers at the opera had nothing on Mike, the precocious teenager who was hustling opera buffs outside the Metropolitan Opera House. In the beginning he doubled as ticket speculator and seller of librettos and the guttural come-on of Mike's "Get yuh Traviatuh librettos here," seems to have been a familiar sound to operagoers of that day.

Why Mike should have been hawking for small change after his profitable venture in excursion boats wasn't clear until an old student of Jacobsiana explained, "You gotta get Mike's philosophy. No matter how much hay you make while the sun shines, never turn down the nickels, dimes, and quarters in the rain."

That Mike should latch on to the Metropolitan Opera House rather than the Garden, where he might have felt more at home, is further evidence, if we need it, of his instinct for moving to the right place at the right time. Those were the days before radio or the movie boom, when the opera was in its glory and Caruso, Dame Melba, Galli-Curci, Geraldine Farrar, Tito-Schipa, and the other great names at the Met were not only hailed as great voices but as the Gables and Garbos of the hour. The Met didn't need Billy Rose to advise them. Caruso and Melba singing *La Bohème* or any of the other reliables gave ticket brokers an early taste of the *South Pacific* squeeze. There was no limit as to what a scalper could charge for those precious ducats. It was more or less a matter for his own conscience. Old ticket brokers who still carry the scars recall this as giving Uncle Mike considerable latitude.

The big trick in the ticket business is how to corner the choice seats for hit shows. Ticket brokers had always been willing to do business with box office men. But Mike, as he was to do so many times, made the big move that soon made him the man you had to see if you wanted to hear Caruso or Tito-Schipa. In his own inimitable way he got to the impresario of the Metropolitan Opera House, Gatti-Cazazza. In his stylish Vandyke and his cut-away, "Gaz" was a resplendent figure in pre-war society, moving in so completely different a circle from that of Uncle Mike that it hardly seems possible they should touch at all. But the touch is something young Mike knew all about, and, if old-time ticket men are to be believed, his early lesson as to every man's price gave him the inside track to the Met in a way his rivals never would have thought possible.

"What sort of fellow was he to do business with in those days," I asked a veteran ticket man on the Rialto. "Lemme give you this example," the old speculator said. "The President of Cuba came up with a big party for the opening of the season and wanted a box. I told him I was sure I could get them and rightaway called Mike at the old Normandie Hotel. I knew he was going to hit me over the head with a hammer, but this Cuban bigshot came up every season and was too good a customer to turn away. Mike says five hundred dollars for the box, which is like holding me up in broad daylight—that's almost a hundred dollars a seat—but he had me by the short hairs so I say okay I'll send my man right over to be sure and hold them. When my guy gets there Mike has sold the tickets out from under me for six hundred dollars. But at the last minute he calls me. He's got a last-minute cancellation on a box for my presidente. Only by now the tariff is seven hundred dollars. In this business most of us learn to scratch each other's backs. But not Mike. Turn your back to Mike and ouch! Right between the shoulder blades." The old ticket man shook his head. "Seven hundred berries for a fifty-dollar box. It's thirty-five years ago, and it still hurts."

When the opera company went out on tour after its New York season, Mike went along to continue the good work. It may have startled the leading citizens of the hinterland to hear this hard-faced man in the black derby assuring them that he had "t'ree good ones left for La Boheemey," but his relationship with the opera, like the occasional happy marriage of opposites, was mutually beneficial. Asked one time to name his favorite opera, Mike came up with "Carmen—always give us the biggest play." Josie Jacobs remembers this tour with the opera company as the closest thing to a honeymoon she and Mike ever had. "Them opera people was good sports," she remembered fondly. "But behind all that fancy talk they're just as cute as the jokers in the fight business."

Of course Mike couldn't differentiate between the styles of Caruso and Tito-Schipa any more than, in later days, he could between Louis and Conn. But nobody alive had a more accurate idea of just how much these opera boys would draw. "It was kind of a sixth sense, hard to explain," the old ticket broker had to acknowledge. "He'd have it about a show or he would have it about a certain personality. He could go out of town and see a show and he wouldn't even be able to tell you what it was about, but he'd say "No sale" and by God the thing would come in and go right on its face. Same with Caruso. Rightaway he knew this was something special. He could smell a hit from here to Hoboken."

At the close of one opera tour, Mike guaranteed Caruso a thousand dollars a night for ten one-night stands. Mike is said to have made more than Caruso on the deal. An inveterate, if not insensate, radio listener of the louder-the-better school, Mike happened to tune in one evening on an old recording of Caruso's *Martha*. Mike isn't known for his appreciation of classical music, but this time he stared dreamy-eyed into the loud speaker, to all appearances completely under the spell of the golden tenor. When the final high note of the solo died away and Mike failed to come out of his trance, the wife of a Garden official who happened to be sitting near him couldn't help observing, "Mr. Jacobs, I've never seen anyone so carried away. I had no idea you were so fond of operatic singing."

Abruptly Mike snapped out of his reverie, clacked his false teeth together, and growled, "Aaaah, I was just thinkin' of eighty thousand bucks."

Opera stars, famous beauties, Mansfields and Barrymores, six-day bike racers, or a boy with two heads were all grist to Mike's opportunistic mill. When Emmeline Pankhurst, the British suffragette leader, arrived for an American tour, she was detained at Ellis Island as a subversive agent. American suffragettes paraded, picketed, and demanded her entry, the chief result of which was that Miss Pankhurst received a million dollars' worth of free publicity.

When Mike noted the size of the crowds Miss Pankhurst attracted, he decided to enlist, temporarily, in the cause of women's suffrage. That such a drawing card should waste her services for free was a challenge to everything he held dear. The way we heard it from our old box office man, Mike took it upon himself to convince Miss Pankhurst that she should cash in on her popularity. "But, my good man, I'm not in this crusade for profit," the feminist reminded him.

"But ya dames need dough," Mike persisted. "Lookit ya fines, the bail, and a little ice for the politicians won't hurt you none either."

"I didn't realize you were interested in the cause of woman's emancipation," Miss Pankhurst said.

"Lady," Mike is supposed to have answered, "if dat means what I t'ink it means, it'll be a shot in d' arm for d' matineee business."

Though a rather unique approach to woman's suffrage, this apparently had its appeal. Emmeline Pankhurst did consent to a commercial tour which contributed substantially to the lady militants' war chest, with something left over for Uncle Mike.

"Them broads had a pretty good racket," said Mike years later in a rare moment of nostalgia.

When America went to war in 1917, the army had neither the time nor facilities to set up elaborate PX centers and snack bars to keep the GIs in candy, cigarettes, and short orders, as they would later in World War II. This phase of army life was left to private enterprise. Enterprise, officially defined as "boldness or readiness in undertaking, adventurous spirit or energy," was where Mike came in. With his excursion-boat training Mike was a natural concessionaire, and as a member of the top brash who knew how to get to the top brass, he soon tied up every kind of concession the camp at Spartansburg, North Carolina, was handing out, not to mention a few the CO hadn't even thought of.

When you went home for a furlough, you bought one of Mike's cardboard imitation leather suitcases. Then you went down to Mike's bus line, the only one in town. Mike's laundry kept you in clean linens. Josie ran the coffee-and-doughnut stand that did such a rush business; she remembers her arms going numb after standing over that hot counter all day. To keep the boys in haircuts, Mike imported fifty barbers from New York City; the profits from this branch of his scalping activities were said to be in the neighborhood of five thousand dollars a month—a pretty nice little neighborhood in anybody's town.

After operating Jacobs PX Inc. (but apparently unlimited) for a year, Mike reputedly sold out for $100,000. That instinct for divining just how long a show would run and how deep to buy in seemed to extend even to international fields, for Mike sold out at the time when the Germans were on the move and the concession seemed to be worth several times what the buyers had paid for it. But a few months later the Hindenburg Line was broken, and not only the kaiser was out of business. By this time Mike was back in New York ready to cash in on the entertainment boom that came with the Amistice.

But the hundred grand he and Josie cleared in addition to their weekly profits wasn't all take-home pay, Mike told us at his home one afternoon in a particularly affable mood (the advance sale on the Louis-Nova fight having already passed the quarter-million mark). Written off as overhead were the nine Packard limousines delivered as a little Christmas remembrance from Michael S. (for Santa) Jacobs. Not to mention another couple of thousand for Class B cumshaw to field-grade officers.

The Roaring Twenties got off to a flying head start in 1919 when Alcock and Browne beat Lindbergh to the first nonstop transatlantic flight by eight years. Ina Claire starred in *The Gold Diggers*, women's suffrage got the green light in the Senate, the Ziegfeld Follies featured Irving Berlin's *A Pretty Girl Is Like a Melody*, and a young man who seemed bent on committing manslaughter became the most famous fighter in the world by breaking the jaw and a couple of ribs of the ponderous, thirty-six-year-old giant who happened to be champion of the world.

Tex Rickard's Dempsey-Willard promotion at Toledo drew nearly half-a-million dollars, doubling the all-time box office record set by Tex himself with Johnson and Jeffries in 1910. The twenty thousand spectators who saw Dempsey batter big Jess into helplessness in nine minutes paid an average of more than twenty dollars apiece for this privilege. Despite a blazing temperature of 103, ringside seats were going for as much as a hundred dollars a throw by fight time. A triumphant young nation in a holiday spirit was getting ready for the biggest mass binge since the days of the Caesars.

The country had had its fill of solemn, long-faced politicians. They were ready to turn their ears and their pockets inside out for Babe Ruth, Benny Leonard, the Four Horsemen, Red Grange, Bobby Jones, and the young man from Manassa who could bust you open with a left hook. Post-war America was looking for laughs, for thrills, providing a new kind of gold rush for the movies, the Follies, the big games in the college stadiums, the fights. Tex Rickard, the flamboyant, mercurial figure who had worked his way east from the saloons and gambling rooms of Alaskan mining towns to cabarets in Seattle, big-time gambling, and fight promotion in the Nevada gold fields, knew the times were ripe for lavish spectacle.

It was Rickard's gambling philosophy that when you had a hunch, back it with everything you've got. Now he was ready to let all the chips ride on Dempsey in 1921 and a public going sports mad. In his suite at the Hotel Commodore he frightened his associates with the size of his thinking. He was going to stage a heavyweight title fight that would make his Dempsey-Willard look like nickels and dimes. A man with a rare gift for selling his dreams, he reached outside the sports world into the highest theatrical circles for his backing—William A. Brady and C. B. Cochran.

With the exception of three or four black heavyweight threats who might have given Dempsey an interesting evening but were not to be invited to the party, there wasn't anyone around who figured to give Dempsey any trouble. But this was the least of Tex's worries, for he was the master of the dream-up and the steam-up, and with his native understanding of mass psychology he cast around for a challenger who lent himself to high-pressure salesmanship.

Georges Carpentier was a happy choice. He was a Frenchman, which gave the match an international aspect, a war hero, which contrasted him dramatically with Dempsey's slacker reputation, and seductive to ladies in a blonde, debonair way which gave the match the modern touch of sex appeal. That Carpentier was merely a light heavyweight who had won his title from the aging Battling Levinsky, and that he was actually on the decline after almost a hundred fights over fifteen years was to be conveniently overlooked. But Carpentier and manager François Deschamps had few illusions when they went in to make their deal with Rickard. After the destructive fury Dempsey had unleashed on Willard, it seemed as if Carpentier was being asked to take greater chances than when he had gone into combat against the Hun. The only thing that could lure them into such a match was the promise of more money than any pugilist had ever received, $200,000.

The champion, said Dempsey's mouthpiece Doc Kearns, sharp as a razor blade and just as double-edged, was entitled to at least one hundred grand more than the challenger. Not even 40 percent of the gate would satisfy the astute doctor. Rickard, the plunger, was really over his head this time. With two such unprecedented guarantees before a ticket was sold, there wasn't a house big enough for the kind of business he needed to get off this half-million dollar hook. So the enormous bubble grew and grew. He would build an arena specially for the occasion, with the largest seating capacity in the world, 100,000 seats.

When Rickard broke ground for this at Boyle's Thirty Acres outside of Jersey City, Brady and Cochran were convinced they had involved themselves with a madman. No match in boxing history had drawn over half a million dollars, but Rickard was sleepwalking into one that would need nearly a million to break even.

His backers were sensible showmen, not wide-eyed gamblers. They picked up their marbles and went home.

Meanwhile the lumber mill was calling for its money. The contractor threatened to pull his men off unless Tex put the cash on the line. Tex Rickard, in New York to establish himself as the greatest fight promoter of the day, was on the verge of going bust, just another country boy who finds himself outweighed and overmatched in the big city.

At this dark moment in walked Uncle Mike, angling for the sort of inside track he had had at the Met. In a rare moment of discouragement, Tex said, "Don't bother me, there's not gonna be no fight."

"No fight!" Mike said. "There's gotta be a fight. This is the biggest fuckin' thing that ever hit the fight business. It's a million easy."

"Yeah," said the despondent Rickard. "I know. But I wish you could convince my backers."

Mike picked his nose thoughtfully. "What we need those suckers for?"

"Who else c'n keep this thing going?" Tex said. "If I don't get twenty thousand to the contractor by four o'clock this afternoon, I've got no arena. And that's just fer openers."

Mike reached into his pocket and pulled out twenty thousand-dollar bills. "Go pay the son of a bitch. An advance on the first five rows of ringside."

Tex began to look more like his usually ebullient self. "I'll need two hundred grand to open the show. The rest c'n come out of the receipts."

"Tex," Mike said, "ya fight is in."

"Mike, you're saving my life," Rickard said. "I'll never forget you for this."

"Aaaah, nuts," Mike said. "Just be sure ya don't forget me when them seats come off the press."

Then Mike went out to do a selling job among his fellow speculators. For years they had been suspicious of him as a predatory lone wolf who never ran with the pack, but this time Mike was all for intraprofessional solidarity. He convinced eight brokers to put up $25,000 apiece in return for choice sections of the house (after Mike got his, of course), and Rickard was saved.

Rickard's million-dollar daydream, which had frightened off the two outstanding showmen of the day, and which Uncle Mike had reached into his own sock to rescue, exceeded Tex's wildest hunch and Mike's shrewdest calculations. Official receipts were $1.8 million. Even Doc Kearns messed up on this one, for his $300,000 guarantee didn't look quite so large when compared with the $720,000 Dempsey might have earned for 40 percent of the gate.

Although Mike was actually a silent partner of Tex's in this extravaganza at Boyle's Thirty Acres, advising him on the price range, the fine art of stretching a ringside, and squeezing the maximum out of general admissions, Mike didn't ask to be cut in on the profits. His pick of reserved seats was adequate compensation, even for Mike. What his take-home amounted to that hysterical July evening no one can say exactly, but a former associate of Mike's, who prefers not to be identified, put it this way: "Suppose Mike had five thousand choice seats. The last two or three days New Yorkers were ready to hock their wives' jewelry or maybe even their wives themselves for a ringside seat. It was nothing for a guy to grab ten at two hundred bucks apiece. Let's say Mike's profits averaged fifty bucks a throw. That adds up to a quarter of a million—more 'n they paid Carpentier."

In 1923, Tex Rickard—now universally acclaimed as the greatest fight promoter of all time—served up two more spectacles, each drawing eighty thousand fans, first when poor old Jess Willard, now a blubbery forty-year-old has-been, was resurrected to build up Luis Firpo, and then when Firpo fought his knockdown-drag-out with Dempsey in Rickard's second million-dollar gate. The sports pages of that day failed to give Mike a single call. As far as the general public knew, Mike was just another ticket broker. But you couldn't insult Mike by keeping his name out of the paper. Although Rickard might have found himself back in the Southwest bending over a wheel if it hadn't been for his timely assist, Mike always refused to discuss his landing-of-the-Marines act. "Tex don't need no help," he'd growl when the question came up of Rickard's debt to him. Until Mike needed the spotlight to puff up his own promotions, he seemed perfectly satisfied to work behind the scenes. As long as he got the spot cash, the other boys could have all the light they wanted.

In a game noted for its feuds, Tex and Mike worked in unusual harmony from 1921 until Tex's death in 1929. But their friendship wasn't the kind to warm the hearts of fustian poets like Robert W. Service and Nick Kenny. If there are any vitamins in the human soul that create the capacity for friendship, Mike had a total deficiency of them. He and Tex had this in common, that each was to dominate the boxing world, and to some extent the entire sports world, as no one ever had before them. But there the resemblance stops. Tex was a good-humored, gregarious, witty, yarn-spinning man who liked to lift one with the sports crowd at La Hiffs where Heywood Broun, Damon Runyon, Grantland Rice, Tad Dorgan, Hype Igoe, and other good men of the day had a circle as congenial and amusing, if only slightly less cerebral, than the celebrated one at the Algonquin.

Even though this was the world in which Mike made his living, he seemed always a stranger to it. If he came to La Hiffs it was either to grab a bite and get out or to pick up the tab for someone with whom he was ready to deal. In general the sports crowd at La Hiffs that followed Toots Shor to his congenial spa on Fifty-first Street were a relaxed, companionable, friendly-drinking lot, good listeners and good storytellers who could sit from dinner until closing time over coffee or highballs, a goodly company. But Mike, even when he became the professional center of this world, had a pathological inability to offer or accept companionship. Just as fish in underground pools have been found with no eyes at all through generations of disuse, Mike offered an interesting field for research as a man under such compulsion to look after No. 1 that he becomes totally, physically blind to the pleasures of sociability.

Although Mike always worked closely with Tex, he wasn't one for keeping all his eggs, or rather his tickets, in one basket. At

304 · RINGSIDE

heart the same little hustler he had been on Fourteenth Street thirty years earlier, he had learned to play no favorites and to regard personal loyalty as a business liability. His relation to Rickard and to Jimmy Johnston, the fast-talking little manager who occasionally turned promoter, was unique in the business world. For Mike, by advance purchase of the best part of the house, actually bought himself a voice in the promotion (and what an overpowering foghorn it was!). When Jimmy Johnston matched Gene Tunney with Carpentier in 1924, Mike guaranteed to take enough seats to assure Jimmy of a promotional success. A few weeks later Mike heard that the fading Frenchman was going west for a fight with Tommy Gibbons shortly before the Tunney fight. Gibbons, the best defensive heavyweight boxer of the day and the only man to stay fifteen rounds with Dempsey in nearly ten years, had beaten everybody in sight with the exception of the incomparable Harry Greb. Despite his knockout by Dempsey, Carpentier was still a popular figure, and his coming fight with the new light heavyweight champion, Gene Tunney, promised another nice paynight for Mike. To jeopardize this by letting the aging Carpentier meet a cutie like Gibbons in a Western ring for pin money seemed to Mike not just a bonehead play but a backstab at his own investment. "What if this Carpentier busts a hand or stinks up the joint so bad he kills our gate? Christ he's been fightin' eighteen years," he screamed.

Jimmy Johnston, who usually knew more angles than a geometry teacher but had somehow slipped up on this one, shook his head. "I know, Mike, it's got me worried. We'll just have to pray to God that Carpentier comes through."

Mike looked at him sourly. "God ain't gonna be stuck with the stinkin' tickets."

When Sid Terris, the Jewish pride of the East Side, met Jimmy Johnston's perennial favorite, Johnny Dundee, in the last show at the old Garden on Twenty-fifth Street, famous figures from the past as well as an impressive turnout of New York celebrities were on hand to ceremonialize its passing. Joe Humphries, the little man with the big voice—whose never-use-a-one-syllable-word-when-five-will-do delivery has come down to us in the eloquent verbiage of Harry Balough and Johnny Addie—was not a man to underplay a good scene. The fight could not go on until he had delivered an elaborate funeral oration.

"Before presenting the stellar attraction in this, the final contest in our beloved home, I wish to say this marks the 'crossing of the bar' for this venerable old arena that has stood the acid test these many memorable years." Humphries was actually weeping as he recalled the great deeds accomplished there by John L. Sullivan, Jim Corbett, Bob Fitzsimmons, Dempsey, Leonard, Dundee himself. "And let us pay tribute to Tex Rickard and the other great gentlemen and sportsmen who have assembled within these hallowed portals," Humphries went on. Then, raising his arms to the rafters, he sobbed, "Goodby, old temple, farewell to thee, oh Goddess Diana standing on your tower. Good night all . . . until we meet again."

Some ringside spectators were visibly moved. Their lives had revolved around this sports center for a third of a century. The passing of the old Garden was a turning point in the life of New York. The arena was built to service a city of less than two million, and people had wondered how a twelve-thousand seat hall could ever be filled. Now the huge enclosure wasn't large enough for a sports-mad city that had tripled in size. Among those listening to Humphries's requiem, none should have felt more involved than Mike Jacobs. When he was still in short pants, he had stood outside this place as a "digger" for small-time scalpers. Now he had the Garden ticket office in his pocket and was growing quietly richer with every show. As Humphries reached his tearful peroration, Mike was seen to lower his head and hide his face in his hands.

"Lookit Mike—by God, I think he's bawling," said George McKitrick, a crony of Johnston's and Jimmy Walker's.

Johnston took a quick, skeptical look and said, "Nah, he's figuring how much better he'll do at the new Garden with twice the seating capacity."

Officially the Jacobs ticket office moved north with the Garden to the Forrest Hotel, but Mike's real office was a secret room on the fourth floor of the Garden, not much bigger than a good-sized closet. From here he had a direct inside line to the Garden box office. According to a well-known boxing press agent who went back a quarter of a century with Mike, "He had the inside track on all tickets for all Garden events because he staked the box office men. He was ready to stake everybody from top to bottom. He staked the switchboard girls who kept him informed as to what was going with Garden plans. He staked everybody and anybody who could help him run this business from the secret cubby hole on the fourth floor. The main thing I remember about Mike, he was always there with the ready. With Uncle Mike, the scratch was always up. And his mouth was always shut."

The most incredible part of this operation, according to our informant, was that Mike year after year was able to keep his actual presence in the Garden a secret. The office he used was a spare belonging to one of the Garden concessions. There was no listing for it in the Garden directory, nor any identification on the door. He'd enter the Garden by a side entrance, go up a back elevator, and slip in and out of this secret door. Command posts in combat zones maintained no tighter security. "I swear, not even Garden officials knew Mike was up there," one of his former employees said.

To Garden officials, even though they realized he helped them fill the house, Mike Jacobs was never entirely persona grata. While acknowledging his uncanny box office sense, they didn't exactly want to lie down in the same bed, or the same building, with him. But Mike, as usual, got his way by moving in first and worrying about the legalities later. This was another lesson he learned early and practiced to the end.

As a result of Mike's talent for obscurity during Rickard's regime, his name was practically unknown to readers of the city's press throughout the twenties. The only reference in the files of the old *New York World* deals with a now-forgotten suit against Rickard in which Mike was a witness. Richard Fuchs, former secretary to circus head John Ringling North, claimed Rickard and the Garden Corporation owed him $189,000, 10 percent of the first Dempsey-Tunney gross, for arranging the deal by which the fight was brought to Philadelphia in 1926. Jacobs was called in because Fuchs claimed Mike, as a partner of Tex, was in on the deal and was actually supposed to split the fee fifty-fifty with him. Fuchs described Mike as "the man who had exclusive access to the Garden box office. He's the official distributor of Garden tickets. Every agent who gets tickets for Garden events must get them from him."

Mike denied this as well as the suggestion that he was Tex's silent partner and guiding hand. He also testified against Fuchs that neither of them had gone to Philadelphia to help arrange the title fight. The plaintiff was finally awarded three thousand dollars, and it was largely due to Mike's testimony that the court decided against the full sum Fuchs was claiming. When she heard the verdict, Mrs. Fuchs sobbed, "I just can't understand how Mr. Jacobs can do this to us. We always thought of him as one of our best friends. Why, he gave us the baby carriage for our first baby." She was led from the courtroom in tears.

One of the minor sensations of the trial was the revelation of Mike's relationship to the Garden that no one had known before, not even his closest relatives.

"What are your connections with Rickard?" Fuch's attorney, B. F. Norris, had asked.

"I'm a stockholder in the Garden," Mike said.

"What?" Norris asked in amazement. "Since when?"

"Since 1926," Mike admitted, and even he couldn't suppress a tendency to smile.

It wasn't until 1935 that Sid Mercer, one of the few sportswriters for whom Mike never seemed to develop any genuine liking, described in the *New York American* the pivotal role that Mike played in engineering the Dempsey-Tunney return fight in Chicago.

According to Mercer, though Billy Gibson, Tunney's manager, had promised Dempsey a return match, Rickard had been unable to persuade the new champion to sign for the bout. The main hitch seemed to be that Tunney and Gibson had had a falling out, and the champion was using this as his reason for not going along with his manager's agreement. With a crew of sportswriters who could bring public pressure to bear, Rickard and Mike went to St. Louis where Tunney was appearing in vaudeville. There, said Mercer, Uncle Mike, who apparently had arranged the trip and took personal charge of the writers, served as mediator between Tunney and Gibson and was able finally to bring them together. Although Mike, characteristically, denied he had anything to do with it, Mercer claimed that Rickard gave Silent Mike full credit for working out the bugs in this latest "Battle of the Century" that drew an all-time record gate of $2,658,660.

IV.

When Tex Rickard died in 1929 and Madison Square Garden was left without a first-string promoter, the eminent gentlemen who ran that high-grade sweatatorium never thought of looking for Tex's successor on the fourth floor of their own building, where Mike Jacobs ruled the Garden's ticket business from his clandestine office.

Instead they turned to Mike's old—oops, we almost said friend—Jimmy Johnston, whom his pals liked to call the Boy Bandit, though it is widely doubted that Jimmy ever stole anything more valuable than a decision or another manager's fighter. And even these he always had the grace to return to their rightful owners when he was through with them.

At the party in the old Madison Square Garden Club given to celebrate Johnston's ascension to power, no one was more prominent than Uncle Mike, who wound up handing out the beer. "Leave it to Mike to ace his way into the job that gets everybody coming to him," the sharp-tongued Jimmy said to his chum Mayor Walker that night.

Uncle Mike was never much of a drinking man, but this night he raised his mug with the others when Johnston was toasted as the man who would pick up in the thirties where Tex Rickard had left off in the twenties. The cream of the sports world—from Extra Heavy to Watered-down—were gathered there that night: Jim

Farley, Damon Runyon, General Phelan, Jack Kearns, Dan Parker, Francis Albertanti, Bill Farnsworth, Francis Wallace, Joe Humphries, Fire Captain George Foster, Colonel John Hammond, Joe Gould, Jim Coffroth, Bill Duffy, Bill Corum, Wilbur Wood—people who knew boxing from every possible angle. Yet not one of them could have guessed that fewer than three years later this ticket shark who never actually had promoted a fight would dare to challenge the mighty Garden itself, and before many years had passed he would not only have Johnston's job but Rickard's title as the champion fight promoter of all time.

Uncle Mike's debut as a fight promoter came about more or less accidentally. Damon Runyon, Ed Frayne, and Bill Farnsworth, the three key men in the Hearst sports department, heard from Colonel John Reed Kilpatrick that the Garden, in the course of its new "no benefits" policy, was washing its hands of Mrs. Hearst's annual Milk Fund show. Deciding to stage their own promotion, Runyon and his associates turned to Mike Jacobs as the logical man to handle their ticket sale.

Thus the Twentieth Century Sporting Club was founded, with Jacobs, Runyon, and the two Hearst sports editors said to hold 25 percent of the stock. Of these only Frayne had a covering letter from Jacobs to establish his legal claim. The others, perhaps fearing to be nominally involved in the event the Garden should find cause for legal action, were content to be invisible as well as silent partners. With his talent for holding on to what is his, and sometimes even what isn't, Mike locked the stock in his safe in the old Hippodrome, where the young fight club took offices and planned its first promotion.

Back in the bread-line days when a fight between ranking heavyweight contenders could draw only ten thousand dollars, their first venture—the Barney Ross-Billy Petrolle Milk Fund Show—did all right. Not a man to separate himself from a good thing, Mike, with the backing of the Hearst group, decided to go on and buck the Garden as a rival fight club.

It was hardly a secret to the sports world that Runyon, Frayne, and Farnsworth were carrying water on both shoulders by putting in with Jacobs while retaining their positions on the *Journal* and the *American*. When the Garden heads pressed their claim that it wasn't exactly sporting for them to head sports departments reporting Garden events while sharing in the promotion of a rival outfit, Frayne and Farnsworth left their papers. Runyon's unique position as a nationally known columnist saved him from the fate of his colleagues, who suddenly found themselves working exclusively for the Sporting Club, which soon came to mean, as we shall see, working for Uncle Mike.

It struck Jimmy Johnston as highly amusing that a mere scalper and a couple of sports editors working out of the creaky old Hippodrome should give the mighty Garden any competition. Jimmy called the rival operation amateur night and said the only way to fill the Hippodrome was to bring back Houdini to raise his elephant to the ceiling. Jimmy and Mike would ride each other in a good-natured, spiteful way about their promotional contest. "Mike, why don't you stop all this nonsense and come back to the thing you're suited for, the ticket business?" Jimmy, a gifted needler, would say. "We'll work together the way we used to."

"Aaaah, go fuck yourself," Mike would answer with a good-natured scowl. "Your stinkin' shows don't do enough business t' give us a play on the tickets."

Mike was hardly exaggerating. In the trough of a depression, the free-spending sports fans of bygone years were home making out their monthly budgets. For all Jimmy's ingenuity, popularity, and connections, even the Garden regulars seemed to consider the place off limits. In addition, Jimmy had a lot of old friends among the managers, and he might have been more inclined to use their boys than to reach out for better fighters. As a result, Garden talent reached a low-water mark that hasn't been equaled since the doldrum years of World War II, when most of the good fighters were in uniform. In due time fight fans got the Garden habit again and would pack the joint to see Johnny Awkward meet Joe Tank. As a promoter, Jimmy Johnston was a good fight manager.

Meanwhile Mike was going on about his business, stoically ignoring the depression and fighting a two-front war, against his partners and the Garden. For the boys who had put him in business, Mike devised a somewhat unusual treatment. He not only failed to take them into his confidence, he refused to talk to them at all. He reached the office at eight o'clock every morning and cheerlessly did the work of ten men, including everything from helping to nail the seats down to convincing ("put this two Gs in ya pocket an' fergit it") the best Garden draws to switch to Uncle Mike.

A one-man man who would go to almost any lengths to be loyal to himself, Mike was soon convinced that his partners had signed on with him under false pretenses and that he was the victim of their plot to share equally with him while he did all the work. He began to feel that he should have it all. This was a feeling that was always to come over Mike as naturally as dizziness to a victim of vertigo. Since Frayne and Farnsworth no longer had their influential newspaper jobs, there was some basis for his contention that they had lost their initial value to him and that the original agreement should therefore be null and void.

Probably more painful to them than the financial wrangling that everyone went through with Mike was the fact that he seemed to take a sadistic pleasure in humiliating them in front of newspapermen who had respected them. Mike would hold press conferences without them, let them cool their heels outside his office, cuss them out like office boys, and if a reporter should ask a question he preferred not to answer, he'd say "Ask Farnsworth," gloating in the failure of this popular, former big-time sports editor to know the plans of the club of which he was nominally vice president.

The Sporting Club prospered moderately through its first year, but it was still more of a thorn than a lance in the Garden's side. Things might have gone on this way if it hadn't been for a young black heavyweight fighting out of Chicago in 1935. Mike was down in Miami staging a show with Barney Ross when one of Barney's managers, Sam Pian, a Chicagoan, told Mike a kid named Louis with fourteen straight wins was Murder Incorporated.

Ever since the Jack Johnson days, good black heavyweights had either settled for Europe or served themselves up as human sacrifices, fattening the records of the white mediocrities who passed for contenders. In the dog days between Tunney and Louis, Tom Heeney, Young Stribling, Phil Scott, Primo Carnera, and other alleged fighters met each other in a round-robin of waltzes, foul claims, and Italian fandangos that injured no one but the public.

If the game were to survive, much less revive, it stood in urgent need of such a fighter as Joe Louis, who was apparently both able and willing to fight, two qualities conspicuously lacking in his predecessors. Though the pigment of his skin was not quite as lily white as that of Fainting Phil Scott or Tearful Jack Sharkey, it occurred to Mike Jacobs and Jimmy Johnston at about the same time that more of an asset than the proper pigmentation was a right hand that could knock you dead.

The Boy Bandit, always a fast man with a telelphone, got the name of Louis's manager and put through a call to him in Chicago. The duel between Johnston and Jacobs was reaching its climax.

"Mr. Roxborough," said Johnston, "I hear you've got a pretty good thing out there in the way of a heavyweight. I'd like to give him a chance in one of the Garden shows this winter."

Roxborough told Johnston how much he thought Louis was worth for his first Garden appearance.

Johnston hit the ceiling, which was very nearly zero in this particular instance. "Listen," he snapped, "I don't care how many guys you've knocked silly out there, don't forget he's still just another nigger heavyweight."

There was a click at the other end of the line. Mr. Roxborough had hung up. Someone had neglected to tell Jimmy Johnston that Mr. John Roxborough had two things in common with his fighter: the color of his skin and the strength of his pride.

It isn't often that one pays so dearly, or so promptly, for his bigotry.

While Johnston was being caught with his racial slip showing, Mike Jacobs was heading for Chicago to size up Louis and talk matters over with the astute black businessmen who were managing him. Of course the first thing he did ("the scratch was always up") was to lay on the line a sum of money said by insiders to be at least twenty thousand dollars. That was for openers, to prove his intentions were strictly honorable (like an old-country bridegroom getting up some of the dowry money before he kisses the girl). Then he told Roxborough and Julian Black, in his own blunt way, that he was going to expect young Louis to go out and win every fight as fast as possible. Mike knew this is what they were hoping to hear.

It's one of the nicer ironies that Uncle Mike Jacobs, so often associated with all that is greedy, underhanded, and corrupt in the boxing game, and whose interest in civil rights had never been conspicuous, rates the credit for giving a black man the first chance at the heavyweight crown in America (Jack Johnson having had to chase his champion to Australia). Not that Uncle Mike deserves a Spingarn medal or a place among the great American humanitarians. He was simply shrewd enough to appreciate how times had changed. Depression and the dreary succession of pale-faced hammola champions had broadened the outlook of fans who no longer pleaded for "white hopes." Now they didn't care whether their "hope" was white, black, green, or pink-striped as long as he could hook off the jab, take you out with a right hand, and bring some excitement to the heavyweight division that had slumbered since the Dempsey days.

When Mike came back to New York he had an exclusive contract with Joe Louis. That little piece of paper tucked away in his safe at the Hippodrome was as good as legal tender for $15 million, payable in gate receipts to come.

One of Uncle Mike's curious contradictions is his schizoid attitude toward money. Said a well-known manager after years of trying to match wits with him, "Mike loves his little larcenies. I used to let him think he was nicking me for a grand here and there just to keep him happy."

But this same manager pointed out, "This is a big-league town, and if you want to cop the pennant you can't do it with bunts and squeeze plays. Mike could squeeze against the little guys, but every time he went against the big stuff he swung with everything he had." For example, he cited not only the tidy sum Mike was out before Louis faced a single major opponent but the excursion to Detroit Mike set up for all the New York sportswriters to unveil Louis against the highly rated Natie Brown.

"That little outing must've set Mike back at least twenty Gs," the manager said. "See what I mean? Nothing chintzy there. So Mike was in around forty Gs already when Louis was still fighting for chicken feed. Rickard always gets the credit as the top-drawer gambler with the big vision, but from where I sit Mike had it all over him. Don't forget Tex operated in the boom days. Mike had a depression going against him. Everything mean and small you can think of you can put down about Mike, and the odds are ten to one you'll be right. But if you want to keep the picture in focus you've got to get in somewhere how Mike thought big and shelled out big, always looking for the big angles where a Jimmy Johnston was playing for the little ones."

That summer, while the Garden operators looked on in helpless confusion, 62,000 people in Yankee Stadium saw Joe Louis cut down the hapless superstar Primo Carnera in six rounds. The firm of Jacobs & Louis Inc. was on its way to the greatest financial coup in the history of the business.

Statistics are usually the province of the fellows in the green eyeshades. Magazine writers are supposed to run from this like malaria mosquitoes. But you can't ignore a couple of statistics that went off with the roar of sixteen-inch guns, almost blasting the Garden high command from the desks of its flagship on Eighth Avenue. Just two weeks before Mike's first big outdoor show had filled the ballpark, the Garden-promoted championship bout between Max Baer and Jimmy Braddock drew only half as many fans to the Long Island Bowl and did less than two-thirds the business of Mike's nontitle fight.

But Mike had just begun. While Jimmy Braddock and the Garden sat on their championship, Mike promptly signed the ex-champion, Baer, to meet the Brown Bomber in another huge outdoor fight that September. Louis was now the biggest attraction since Dempsey, and sportwriters estimated that the fight would draw over half a million dollars. But they underestimated Mike, who with this match set the pattern for all the great outdoor promotions of the next decade.

If Mike sold every seat in the house his gross should have been $750,000. But Mike confounded the experts that September by coming up with the first million-dollar gate since the crash. Adding that extra quarter of a million is about in a class with dealing seventy cards out of a regular fifty-two-card deck. And like all sleight of hand, it's simple when you see how it's done.

Mike kept an eye on his ticket sales the way an old man does on an attractive young wife. If he saw a greater demand for thirty-dollar seats than twenties, he'd revise his seat plan to stretch the thirty-dollar section at the expense of the twenty-dollar seats. A little foresight in having printed differently priced tickets for the same seat gave Mike flexibility. Similarly, if the line was a block long at the three-dollar window while the customers seemed to shy away from the five, he'd drop the window on the threes so bleacherites would have no choice but to go for the next price range.

Another cute innovation of Mike's was a new section euphemistically called "raised ringside." These seats, set up behind the already ever-enlarged ringside, turned out to be bleacher seats at ringside prices. With apparent benevolence, Mike would give away hundreds of these seats as "complimentaries." On a "raised ringside" ticket the benefactee would have to pay only the tax plus a "service charge" of five to ten dollars. Since Mike's generosity did not include sharing this income with his fighters, he could net nearly as much on his comps as with his regular ticket sale.

This is probably the only time a man has ever played a seventy-thousand-seat arena as if it were an accordion.

On Broadway they say, "Old scalpers never die." Old scalper Mike Jacobs doubled in brass as a promoter who gave himself the choice tickets with which to speculate. First he'd turn over the first three or four rows of official ringside to the Jacobs Ticket Agency, which, it was announced many times, had no connection whatsoever with the Twentieth Century Sporting Club. Quick thinking on the part of brother Jake, apparently, nabbed those prize seats before the other agencies could get around to them. Next came one of the most ingenious devices for making money since Gutenberg invented the printing press. For important fights there were always three or four rows for the working press between the ring and the first row of the regular ringside. While a majority of these went to boxing writers, a large number were gifts to city officials and influential friends or were sold for the high dollar to Hollywood, Broadway stars, wealthy New Yorkers, and others who enjoyed paying an extra C-note or two for the privilege of sitting among the working press.

There would usually be a call from one of the boxing commissioners for seats for the top officialdom. Mike would invariably say the demand for press tickets was much greater than expected. To accommodate the commissioner he would have to set up a few extra rows, a condition to which the commissioner would agree.

This casual addition of a "few extra rows" would give Mike several hundred additional seats in front of "ringside" for his own play. It was an open secret in the fight game that these seats were usually sold in blocks to such well-heeled sports fans as a certain well-known racketeer with the same name as a prominent Hollywood comedian. He would go for whole rows of these seats, parting with five or ten thousand dollars as casually as you drop a coin in the phone slot. The big man would then distribute his seats among the politicians and various others who might be useful. Any boxing reporter can tell you of the strange and wonderful gathering liberally sprinkled through the working press. With this little gimmick, Mike would probably pick up an extra fifty thousand or more, a nice bit of gravy, none of which ever showed on his vest or in his books.

Since this was a slice off the top before the fighters' cut, I asked the manager of a former Jacobs main-eventer if he and his colleagues had been aware of the practice and whether they resented Mike's doing them out of gross income they should have been sharing with him. The answer was, "Nah, everybody knew what Mike was doin'. But he was makin' more money for us than anybody else could, so we figured let 'im have his little larcenies."

Jacobs & Louis Inc. went on expanding through 1935–1936 until an unexpected setback at the hands of Der Führer's most prominent exponent of Strength Through Joy, Max Schmeling. Oddly enough, Schmeling was managed by that droll little enemy of the English language who spoke only the purest basic American ("I shoulda stood in bed"), Joe "Yussel" Jacobs. An unconfirmed rumor has it that when the two fighters were called to the center of the ring for final instruction, the referee wound up with, "And may the best Jacobs win."

Schmeling's incredible victory—Louis's only defeat in a brilliant thirteen-year run before his retirement and sorry comeback—appeared to be a body blow to Uncle Mike's ambitions. Herr Max went back to the Third Reich where the party leaders made him their poster boy of the Master Race, the perfect example of Aryan supremacy over the decadent, mongrelized democracies. The following summer he was to return to meet Braddock for the championship under Garden auspices. It looked like a sure victory for Joseph Goebbels's favorite athlete as well as a clean-cut decision for Jimmy Johnston and the Garden over Uncle Mike and his defeated heavyweight.

At this point Uncle Mike began to demonstrate the shiftiest footwork since Benny Leonard's, only matched by that of Braddock's pilot, Joe Gould, a managerial Fred Astaire, who could spin so rapidly that no one ever was able to tell in which direction he was really looking. Together with the Schmeling directorate and the Garden management they began to play a game of "Braddock, Braddock, Who Gets to Fight Braddock?" that was to involve more techniques of high-level intrigue than even occurred to the Borgias. Before old Jim Braddock finally put his championship on the line, not only rival boxing promotions were involved but rival state boxing commissions, rival political organizations, and eventually President Roosevelt and Adolf Hitler themselves.

Again, not just good timing but the very fortunes of the time were to carry Mike forward. For if the year had not been 1937, when Nazi bestiality was beginning to shock the entire civilized world, even Mike might have hesitated before so brazen a move as attempting to "steal" Champion Jimmy Braddock from the Garden and the title match with Schmeling that had the official sanction of the New York Boxing Commission.

Fortunately for the firms of Jacobs & Louis Inc. and Gould & Braddock Inc., the Anti-Nazi Boycott League, headed by such civic leaders as Samuel Untermeyer and Jeremiah T. Mahoney, took a dim view of Herr Schmeling, arguing, not without reason, that he was an outstanding representative of Goebbels's propaganda mill and that a victory for Max would be a source not only of American dollars for Germany but of invaluable ammunition for its psychological warfare machine. If the heavyweight championship went to Germany, the Anti-Nazis feared, the astute Mr. Goebbels would see to it that it remained there.

At this point Mr. Gould, a charter member of the No-Stone-Unturned Club, ripped a page out of Gallup's book by polling boxing writers on the respective box office strength of a Braddock-Louis and a Braddock-Schmeling fight. According to his pollsters, anti-Nazi feeling was running so high that a Schmeling fight would be effectively boycotted and could draw two or three hundred thousand at most while Louis-Braddock looked like a sure three-quarters of a million.

From that moment on Mr. Gould became an even more confirmed Anti-Nazi than he might have been before, while Uncle Mike, sublimely oblivious of Gould and Braddock's contract with the Garden, began pulling out all the stops in an effort to talk the champion into breaking with the Garden and meeting his Brown Bomber instead.

Throughout this crucial period Uncle Mike was the epitome of generosity and benevolence. Gould's and Braddock's every wish, as we used to say, was Mike's command. He even sent them his personal tailor to make them as many suits as they wished at his expense. When Owney Madden, one of Braddock's sponsors, strolled back into town after having been officially banished, and the city's reformed police force threatened to lay hands on the eminent visitor from Hot Springs, somehow Uncle Mike saw to it that Mr. Madden wasn't embarrassed during his stay. Meanwhile he and Joe Gould began feeling each other out in a memorable series of tête-à-têtes combining the most accomplished arts of seduction, poker, chess, and Big Three conferences.

When rumors of Gould's defection floated back to Schmeling, he was outraged. He made daily calls on Gould, begging him not to pull out of the fight. Not only had he promised his Führer that he would grab off the world's chamiponship for Der Vaterland but he stood to make himself a hatful of Uncle Sam's certificates, something he always showed the highest respect for, no matter what his Berchtesgaden friends may have thought of what else we had to offer.

Finally, in a fit of frustration, Schmeling sailed home to the Reich. Meanwhile, with Braddock's crown in the pot, the poker game went on. The Garden raised, and Uncle Mike raised again. For Gould it was every fight manager's wish-dream come true. The has-been he had rescued from the relief roles and shrewdly resurrected just a few years earlier was now the prize over which the mighty Garden and Mike Jacobs the mighty upstart were struggling for promotional supremacy. Whichever syndicate could stage a Braddock fight first had the heavyweight title, and whoever controlled the title controlled this multi-million-dollar industry. It was as simple as that. The fact that Schmeling had been declared the rightful challenger and that Braddock and the German had contracts with the Garden hardly gave Uncle Mike a moment's pause. His attitude toward contracts had always been somewhat unorthodox. No man had greater respect for them when they were to his advantage, or was quicker to shrug them aside if they got in his way. Said General John Reed Kilpatrick, who seemed to admire Uncle Mike in a quizzical way, "Mike's philosophy was always to do it first and worry about the legalities when he came to them."

With a "damn-the-injunctions, full-speed-ahead" attitude, in the face of the boxing commission edicts, previous contracts, and threatened lawsuits, Uncle Mike kept his sights fixed on the heavyweight championship that had been for so many years an established Garden property. Using his Garden contract as a wedge, Gould was determined to pry Mike loose from more money than any pugilist had ever received, but the steepest demands Gould could make (and he was an inspired demander) would not stop Mike from coming on.

During these hectic crossfire negotiations, Joe Gould was at the home of his aged mother when her phone rang and she said to Joe in her halting accent, "What's this? Somebody is making a joke maybe? Germany is calling us?"

Joe picked up the phone. It was Max Schmeling. After tender inquiries into the state of Joe's health and that of his family (while indescribable pogroms were raging thoughout Germany), Schmeling said, "Joe, I am speaking from the office of one of the most important people in Germany—in the world," he corrected. "Reich Minister Goebbels wants to talk to you personally."

"Mr. Gould," Goebbels began in broken but understandable English, "we are ready to make you a very interesting offer to bring your champion to Germany to fight Max."

Said Gould, "Just a minute, Mr. Goebbels, has Max told you the kind of a deal we want?"

"He has given me a general idea," Goebbels answered. "But let me hear from you exactly what you want. The match will be very popular in Germany, and I am confident we can meet your terms."

"All right," Gould said. "I've got three conditions. If you can agree to them I will bring Braddock to Germany."

"Excellent," Goebbels said. "I feel sure I can arrange everything to your satisfaction. Now your three conditions, please."

"In the first place," said Gould, "I want five hundred thousand in real money—I mean American dollars—deposited in my name in a New Jersey bank before we get on the boat."

"I can promise you that will be done," Goebbels said without hesitation. "Go on, Mr. Gould."

"Secondly, I want to bring over an American referee, and one of the two judges must be an Englishman. We won't mind if the other's a German," Gould continued.

"One minute, please," Goebbels said, and apparently after conferring with Schmeling he told Gould, "Yes, we will agree to that also. And now, please, the third point."

"The third point," Gould said matter-of-factly, "is that you get Hitler to stop kicking the Jews around. Unless he opens the concentration camps, gives them back full citizenship and property rights, you know what you and Max can do with your fight."

But before Gould could finish, the receiver had been slammed down at the other end.

"Nu?" Gould's mother asked. "What is all this big conversation with Berlin?"

"Aw nothing," Gould said, "I just told Goebbels and Hitler what they could do with themselves."

Mrs. Gould looked at her son with an affectionate skepticism. "Oh Joe, you're always such a kidder," she said.

Soon after Goebbels's failure to grab the title fight away from Mike Jacobs, who was working around the clock to grab it away from the Garden, Gould announced that the champion would not go through with the Schmeling fight but would meet Joe Louis in Chicago for Uncle Mike instead. The boxing commission called Gould on the carpet, where he stoutly maintained that it was his responsiblity to protect the economic interests of Mr. Braddock and that he would be derelict in these duties if he were to permit him to go through with the Schmeling fight in the face of the threatened anti-Nazi boycott.

Gould's sense of duty was to be profoundly influenced by Uncle Mike. Not even a demand for a guaranteed $400,000 seemed too much to ask by Gould for his renovated titleholder. Tomcats yowling on a back fence had nothing on Jacobs and Gould as they went round and round in the final stages of their deal. But Mike had to have Braddock and that title at any price, and he finally acceded to Gould's unprecedented demand for 10 percent of the net receipts of all Jacobs's heavyweight promotions for the next ten years.

Gould had him over a barrel, but as soon as Mike got back on his feet he quickly talked Joe Louis into kicking in 10 percent of his purses for the next ten years and taxed each of his partners 5 percent. Gould's haymaker was neatly sidestepped by Mike, allowing his partners to absorb the blow.

With unerring judgment, Uncle Mike chose Chicago as the site of the title bout, for the Windy City was not only the scene of Louis's early triumphs but a convenient distance beyond the jurisdiction of the New York Boxing Commission that was trying to block the bout. Two steps ahead as usual, Mike had also foreseen that in welcoming a chance to put one over on New York, Chicago and Illinois officials would give him every possible protection. Lawyers for the Garden were trying to stop the Louis-Braddock fight by injunction, but Mike lined up behind an impressive forward wall of legal heavyweights who formed a flying wedge against the Garden diehards. The injunctions were gradually shaken off, and the game was won when a New Jersey judge whose name really was Guy W. Fake decided that Gould and Braddock's service contract with the Garden would not prevent the champion from placing his title at the disposal of the new firm.

While Louis and Braddock were getting ready for the fight that Uncle Mike had already won, regardless of the outcome, Max Schmeling returned to go through the motions of his quixotic "phantom fight" with Braddock's ghost. In an effort to strengthen his and the Garden's legal case, he went into training, weighed in the day of the "fight," and made a token appearance at the empty arena that evening.

On the night of the real fight, Gould says he insisted that $400,000 in thousand-dollar bills be delivered into his hands at the hotel before he would consent to bring Braddock to Comiskey Park. "Whatsa matter, Joe, don't you trust me?" Uncle Mike exploded.

"Sure I trust you, Mike," said Gould. "But I'll trust you even more when I've got the four hundred big ones in my pocket."

Despite the machinations that had surrounded it, the Louis-Braddock fight reestablished the prestige and dignity of the heavyweight title. Louis fought at the top of his power and skill;

Braddock went down as old champions are expected to, with proud and unflagging courage.

Mike had the Garden on the ropes now. Like his star, Louis, he was ready to move in for the kill. "Now I want to show 'em who's boss," he confided to sportswriter Wilbur Wood. "I wanna do something twice as big as any promoter ever thought of."

"Twice as big," Wood thought a moment. "Why don't you stage two championship fights the same night. No one's ever pulled that off before, Mike."

For a moment Mike chewed restlessly on his bridgework. "I'll double that. I'll give 'em four championship fights," he said.

That September his Carnival of Champions lived up to its name when two great titleholders, Barney Ross and Lou Ambers, retained their crowns while Harry Jeffra and Fred Apostoli reached the top of their divisions in brilliant battles. But the real winner, of course, was Uncle Mike. Although his grandiose promotion was in the red, he now had a corner on the boxing market. Monopoly Mike, as he began to be called, had exclusive contracts with five champions, and since no contenders could meet these champions without first signing over to Mike complete control of their future services—a device the Garden operatives somehow had overlooked—he could write his own ticket, for a price Mike was never shy about marking up.

The Garden was ready to cry Uncle. "Uncle" Mike was officially invited in. Mike's rival, Jimmy Johnston, a congenital up-and-downer, was on the outside looking in. He swore he would wipe Twentieth Century Sporting Club off the fistic map. His first move in that direction was to form the Thirtieth Century Sporting Club. He was going to top Mike in everything, including ten millenniums. Unfortunately for Jimmy, his millenniums didn't last out the year.

Just a little short of fifty years from the time Mike first hustled up to the box office in knee pants as a digger at the old Garden, he was the unchallenged czar of the fight business, with the Madison Square Garden for his winter palace and Yankee

Stadium for his Midsummer Nights' dreams of further million-dollar gates.

V.

When Mike Jacobs was dominating the fight world as single-handedly as Hitler did in his sphere of influence, I happened to spend a weekend at his first country estate in Rumson, New Jersey.

My personal friends Billy Soose, the newly crowned middleweight champion, and his manager, Paul Moss, were going down to talk over possible opponents for Garden matches that fall and asked me along. Remembering my Emily Post on uninvited guests, I hesitated. "Listen," my objections were brushed aside, "half the people there will be brought by somebody else. As long as we've got the title and Mike needs us, he wouldn't care if we brought our two-headed cousin."

Thus assured, if not flattered, I was headed for the Fontainebleau of the undisputed monarch of the cauliflower kingdom.

I found a sprawling twenty-five-room New Jersey mansion in a section known locally as millionaire's row, overlooking close-cropped rolling lawns and beautifully kept gardens. The house and veranda were already crowded with weekend guests, boxers, managers, members of Mike's staff, sportswriters, and several individuals who always seemed to be in the money without any readily identifiable occupation.

Except for tagalong freeloaders like me, every one of the guests was there for tactical reasons. Mike's business fever never slacked at nightfall or weekends. He knew exactly what he wanted from each invited guest.

Lunch was an elaborate and drawn-out barbecue of prize steaks and homegrown corn and tomatoes in which Mike took justifiable pride. A delicious sauce was announced as Mike's own recipe. At Mike's insistence, everyone ate twice as much as he really wanted. Like moneymaking, eating seemed to be a ritual feverishly indulged in though divorced from need. For an introverted but hardly introspective personality, apparently these activities helped fill a social vacuum.

Defensive, suspicious, obsessed, and ceaselessly driven—not from miserliness or power-madness, as one able sports columnist believed, but by a tight, hidden knot of insecurities—Mike impressed me as a victim in a contemporary Inferno doomed to run all his life at full speed in a giant squirrel's cage.

At least he seemed to be the only one at the picnic who wasn't having any fun. All weekend he moved restlessly among his guests like a campaign manager at a political convention. The late Hype Igoe, a beloved sportswriter of the old days, stretched out comfortably on a hammock after a rich meal and began to soliloquize: "Ah, what a day—a wonderful meal, the sky as clear as glass, the trees full of singing birds, the air perfumed with all these flowers, the soft hum of the bees in the garden, what an unforgettable sense of peace."

Near the hammock, Mike had been pacing as if this broad terrace were a confining cell. "Aaaah, yuh nuts," he growled at Igoe, "there ain't no action."

All during the barbecue the talk around Mike was fight business. Then he spent the rest of the afternoon in conference with managers and boxers, one or two at a time, in his circular garden house decorated with photographs and cartoons of famous fights and fighters. That evening the talk around Mike was more fight business. Never could this one lick that one but how much would they draw? An interested manager would suggest a match, and Mike would veto it with a contemptuous "Nah" and a clacking of the false teeth of which he had dozens of sets, none of which he had ever had the patience to have properly fitted.

After dinner Mike hurried his guests into his cars, raced to a small New Jersey fight club, caught the main event, and whisked them back again. Nearly everyone sacked in without delay. I picked up a book on the nightstand. It was one of Nat Fleischer's colorful biographies of ex-champions. Then I heard someone prowling around the hall and opened the door to find Uncle Mike in a bathrobe. I followed him downstairs into the kitchen for cold chicken and back to his study. He started his record player, and while the room filled with Sam Taub's blow-by-blow description of one of Mike's Garden fights, he paced the floor. When the long transcription came to an end, Mike played another one. Instead of reading himself to sleep, he listened himself to sleep with round-by-round playbacks of his own promotions. I could imagine him finally dropping off by counting customers as they passed through the turnstiles.

Although he was known to dose himself with sleeping pills, I heard him moving around several times during the night. When I mentioned this later to Bobby Dawson, for years Mike's personal attendant, Bobby said, "Whenever he couldn't sleep he'd wake me up, two, three o'clock in the morning. Sometimes he'd even want to go for a ride. You'd've thought sleep was tryin' to cheat him the way he hated it."

Next morning at 6:30 Mike was fully dressed and miraculously refreshed and reinvigorated. At eight o'clock, with a portable radio at arm's length and the volume turned up to a deafening blast, Mike was talking to several other early risers about a possible opponent for welterweight champion Red Cochrane. Out of the depth of my innocence I found myself, in a timid voice, suggesting Ray Robinson, universally recognized in those days as "the uncrowned welterweight champion." Uncle Mike looked down the table at me in teeth-clacking disgust. "Aaaah, we got too many colored boys on top now. Public's gettin' tired of 'em."

This opinion, it occurred to us, was not tainted with racist sentiment. In fact it was not to be confused with any sentiment, living or dead. It was completely regardless of race, color, or creed, as one of Mike's leftenants Mushky Jackson might say. It was cold-blooded showmanship, in the same golden rut with the Hollywood producer who decides that "The public's tired of platinum blondes" or "child stars."

Next day at the Jacobs manse was not unlike the first, except that we dined inside at one of the two dining room tables that had been bought as a compromise solution to the running argument between Mike and Josie as to which table had the most class.

Theirs is a union that apparently thrives on argument, for after thirty years Mike and Josie could not seem to agree even on what flowers to plant in their garden. As a result they each had their own flower garden, identified by their names painted on wooden signs.

Unexpectedly Mike has a genuine but inarticulate appreciation for flowers. He made sure we noticed the size of the peonies and sunflowers that had been planted for him, and gloated a little over their superiority to Josie's. "I got the biggest fuckin' flowers around here," he said. A number of rare plants and flowers in his garden were given to him by wealthy neighbors in exchange for fight tickets.

Mike's only other diversion that weekend was reviewing his horses as they were jumped over barriers for him. He watched this a few minutes, barking out crisp orders for particular hurdles he wanted the animals to clear, then suddenly lost interest and led a prominent manager back to his garden house to do some business.

I watched in a kind of horrified awe as Mike fastened himself on guest after guest like some insatiable bee, drawing from each whatever he had to offer. A new opponent was written in for Louis. A fight was switched from New York to Detroit because of Uncle Mike's shrewd hunch that it would have greater appeal for Midwesterners. A match in London couldn't go on until it had Mike's approval. A boxer who had beaten the champion of his division several times in nontitle bouts was vetoed because he lacked color and box office appeal. A manager who had been holding out stubbornly for 30 percent agreed to take 25 percent for his fighter after Mike had softened him up with a thousand-dollar "personal advance." That extra 5 percent would have taken around five thousand off the top of Mike's promotion. Since the manager would have had to split this with his fighter, he did just as well by taking Mike's advice to "put this in yuh pocket an' forget it."

None of these practices were original with Mike. They were as much a part of the fight business as the collodion used to close the wounds of the hirelings who provided the Garden entertainments. What Mike did was what any successful monopolist must do, perfect the techniques of total control.

That afternoon Mike rushed us to a nearby army camp to watch Buddy Baer, who was getting ready for Louis on Mike's Bum-of-the-Month road show. When we got back, a restless, aggressive house guest, expected twenty-four hours earlier, finally put in an appearance. It was Billy Conn, the feisty light heavyweight champion.

"What yuh havin' for dinner?" Conn wanted to know right away.

"Chicken fricassee," Josie Jacobs said.

"Aaah, fricassee my ass," said Conn. "I'm leavin' for a steak."

"Who needs yuh, yuh bum?" Josie yelled after him when the highly combustible Mr. Conn had departed, not to appear again that weekend.

"Aaah, lay off him, he's a good kid," Mike snapped. He had just begun the buildup on Conn as Louis's next major opponent.

The young cock o' the walk among Pittsburgh toughs and the crafty old man from the waterfront with the strip-hammer mind had something in common, one couldn't help feeling. It just went to prove once more what softheaded mush all racial generalizations are. The youthful boxer and the aging promoter were moneymen with the same insecure arrogance and graceless drive.

Perhaps it's because he's been so systematically cadged that some visitors have considered Uncle Mike an ungracious host while others are impressed with his openhanded if uncouth hospitality. When Colonel (later General) Kilpatrick called one Sunday afternoon, he noticed that Mike was serving his fight crowd, along with beer and ordinary domestic wine, some bottles of prewar Chateau d'Yquem. A connoisseur of wines, the Colonel knew how precious that scarce and famous sauterne was, and it horrified him to see it being guzzled by roughnecks as if it were draft beer. "For heaven's sake, Mike," the Colonel exclaimed, "if you're lucky enough to have Chateau d'Yquem, don't waste it on them. Save it for someone who appreciates it."

Uncle Mike's guests usually enjoyed the run of the house with the best of food, whiskey, and cigars. But always a quick-tempered, quick-changing man, Mike's inability to work out the bugs in a promising match or some other momentary frustration could bring about a startling transformation from generosity to unabashed inhospitality.

Joe Bannon, the Hearst executive, perhaps the nearest thing to an old friend Mike had, was down with some associates one weekend when Mike suddenly flew off the handle about the obscene spongers eating him out of house and home. Bannon was so shocked he locked himself in his room while he packed to leave. Uncle Mike was genuinely hurt by this reaction. After all, he and Bannon had hawked newspapers together fifty years before. Bannon had helped him along with fight tickets at the turn of the century. For one of the few times in his life, Mike was actually contrite and anxious to make amends. "Joe, I didn' mean you, fer Chri'sake. You c'n drink all the fuckin' Scotch you want. I meant those two grabbin' friends o' yours."

Mike was genuinely mystified when Bannon still insisted upon leaving and on canceling out their friendship.

On another occasion an erudite sportswriter dropped a sarcastic remark about the skimpy, catch-as-catch-can collection of old detective stories, moth-eaten novels, and boxing books that didn't begin to fill the bookcases in Mike's library. "Mike, once in a while you get somebody down here who knows how to read," the newspaperman said. "This is the crummiest collection of books I've ever seen." Mike turned to one of his lieutenants and snapped, "Go out n' get enough books to fill all them spaces. The best they got in the store."

When I left Rumson that Sunday night, I was convinced that not even in Hollywood, where shoptalk is as insistent as any place I know, had I ever run into such unrelieved single-mindedness. For three full days, with only a few hours off to rest those super-charged batteries, this man had talked about fighters, talked to fighters, watched fighters train, watched fighters fight, dealt with their managers, or, in desperation, when everyone else had gone to bed on him, listened to transcriptions of old fights he had promoted.

Mike's critics attributed his success to his having been born completely devoid of scruples that would slow down the ordinary man. But in fairness to Mike, Jacobs Beach has never lacked for a full complement of gentlemen who are not exactly weighed down with ethics and yet who remain on Hungry Street. The boxing business undoubtedly offered Uncle Mike an ideal field for his kind of operation, but anyone who combined his intuitiveness with such marathon energy and dawn-to-midnight concentration probably would have been a tycoon in any business.

No one could watch Mike at his job of putting over a big fight and make the mistake of ascribing his success entirely to ruthlessness and chicanery. Even when Mike was a millionnaire grossing three to five million a year, he ran his powerful corporation with the minute-to-minute personal touch of a hot-dog vendor. He had squeezed out his original partners, Runyon, Frayne, and Farnsworth, reducing the latter to a humbled minion who had to come to him for small loans. He had everything sewn up so tight that a rival promoter couldn't hire himself a hall in New York, not even one of the armories. Yet he not only continued his incredible practice of reaching his office by 8 a.m. and supervising all the office work down to the smallest detail, but even went in for the legwork of a common usher.

At million-dollar fights Mike could be seen serving as his own sentry between the ringside and the next expensive section. "If ya don't watch everything yerself, they'll rob ya blind," he used to say. If he spotted any confusion he'd beeline to the argument and personally escort the customers to their seats. Once, when general admissions were lagging, Mike grabbed a megaphone in reversion to his excursion-boat days and started barking, "This way, fella. Lotsa good seats left." At another championship fight Mike was found outside the stadium directing traffic. At one of the Louis title bouts, a particularly conscientious usher grabbed Mike as he brushed by him at the entrance to the ringside section. "Hey, Bud, where you think you're goin?"

"I'm Mike Jacobs," said Mike Jacobs.

"How do I know, lemme see your ticket," the usher insisted.

Mike was starting to lose his renowned temper. Then suddenly in the middle of an eloquent profanity, the nearest thing to a warm smile in Mike's possession spread over his face. "What the hell am I talkin' about? You're protectin' me—keep up the good work, kid, don' let nobody in, no matter how they con ya," and he pumped the confused usher's hand enthusiastically.

Mike's ability to police his fights was another distinctive talent. Ragged policing can be the margin between a financial winner and a loser. Mike has said that he solved his police problem "by invitin' the Mayor as my personal guest in the workin' press. To pertect the Mayor the Police Department sent inspectors, captains, and lieutenants. Lieutenants gotta have sergeants and corporals to boss around. I never had no trouble gettin' my fights policed." It was also a question of knowing how to get his working-press tickets into the right hands, he might have added. In the same way, when Mike wanted to squeeze into his arena several thousand more spectators than the laws of public assemblage allowed, he could be confident that the key officials were on his side.

Like many great captains of industry, Mike seemed to have an intuitive sense of public relations. It is hardly fair to attribute this—as do some of his enemies—to his systematic staking of certain boxing writers, a practice inherited from Rickard's day. Emile Gauvreau, when he was the fiery editor of the old *New York Graphic*, was asked by his publishers to find out from Rickard why he never advertised his fights in their paper. Gauvreau told me that Tex's answer was, "Why should I pay for an obvious ad when I get better advertising this way?" Rickard proceeded to show the editor a list of boxing writers on his weekly payroll. None of the major boxing writers today would compromise themselves in this way, and Mike is usually canny enough to know which men would be tempted and which ones insulted by such an offer. One time he erred, though, was when he sent John Kieran a hundred-dollar gift certificate for Christmas with a note asking the eminent columnist of the *New York Times* to accept the gift in the spirit offered. Kieran returned the certificate in the next mail with his own note telling Mike to take back the certificate in the same spirit. "I always got along fine with Mike after that," Kieran told us, with that twinkle in his eye. "I have a hunch the people he can't control are the only ones he really respects."

Whether this open-mindedness could be stretched to include his severest critic, Dan Parker, is somewhat doubtful. Mike's staff, whose fear of him actually sent several members to the hospital with nervous breakdowns, learned to anticipate his moods by the tone of Parker's columns in the *New York Mirror*. On the mornings when Parker lowered the boom on Mike, his employees braced themselves against his tantrums. "If Parker would only stop beating the Boss over the head," a member of his staff said once, "I think I could cut my breakdowns to one a year."

One of Parker's needles that jabbed deepest under Mike's skin, strangely enough, was over the paltry sum of five hundred dollars. Although Mike's promotions ran to many millions every year, he insisted upon operating his St. Nicholas Arena "farm club" under his Garden license, though the cost of a separate license was a mere tax-deductible five hundred, much less than he spent on various personal indulgences every week. Parker kept badgering the boxing commission to make Uncle Mike pony up the extra fee until at last even that amenable organization was nudged into action. Since Mike needed that extra five hundred about as much as he needed a comb and brush, his stubborn efforts to hold out on the State of New York seem to us to fall into the province of the psychoanalyst rather than the moralist. Second cousin to the wealthy ne'er-do-wells who hold up dance halls for the thrill, Mike seems forever driven to see just how much he can get away with, even when he's already gotten away with enough to retire on.

Not even a blast from Dan Parker could rouse Mike to anger more quickly than the sight of Joe Gould after a Louis title fight coming up to collect his 10 percent. The contract he had signed with Gould and Braddock in his determination to lure them from the Garden was a repugnant document to him now. If you have ever seen a giant tarpon trying to throw the hook you have a graphic picture of Mike fighting to extricate himself from Gould's hold. He would ignore Gould's calls, refuse to see him, try to bulldoze him into settling for a fraction of the amount accumulating under the contract, and even tried legally to set the agreement aside on the grounds that it had been signed under duress. But Gould, one of the sharpest ever honed, had taken care to postdate his contract *after* the Braddock-Louis fight, and when Gould sued Mike for holding out on him, Mike reluctantly settled out of court.

At one point Mike owed Gould eleven thousand dollars and stubbornly refused to pay. When Gould finally cornered him, Mike said, "All right, tell ya what I'll do with ya, I'll settle for ten thousand."

"The one grand didn't mean a thing, it was just Mike's way of showing 'im who could outsmart who," observed an Eighth Avenue philosopher. "Mike's always had the courage of his unprinciples."

But it would be a mistake to conclude from this that Mike is totally devoid of business ethics. He could be impeccably reliable when dealing with the strata he still looked up to—the Stanton Griffises and Bernard Gimbels. Ed Barrow of the Yankee Stadium, for instance, will tell you that in his rental dealing, Mike's word was so dependable that they could actually dispense with a contract. The face Mike presented to those whose respect he coveted, apparently, was in striking contrast to the one he showed the people he considered beneath him.

One attack that never failed to set up storm warnings in the offices of the Twentieth Century Sporting Club was the charge that Mike played footsie with the mob, whose fighters had an inside track to Garden bouts and Garden victories. Dan Parker pointed openly to the sale of titles with the apparent blessings of Uncle Mike and a spineless boxing commission, and fingered a number of suspicious matches between boxers generally conceded to carry the colors of the mob. In the *Post* Jimmy Cannon described the familiarity with which muscleman Frankie Carbo would stroll in and out of Mike's office.

As with so many other phases of Mike's career, there's plenty of evidence both to hang and acquit him. Mike has, at times, shown his contempt for the adventurers who safari through darkest Manhattan. When a mob-controlled champion was going to meet a challenger I knew, talk around town had the mob buying off the referee and one of the judges. The challenger's manager wrote an anonymous letter to himself ostensibly warning him of the impending steal. The manager then showed this letter to Uncle Mike. Mike went straight to Commissioner Phelan and, with oratory that was eloquently loud if monosyllabic, demanded that the untainted young challenger be given full protection against the sordid influence of "them motherfuckin' thieves." The commissioners, and in turn the referee and judges, were so intimidated that they leaned over backward to take the title away from the mob on a hairbreadth decision, breaking the underworld's hold on a crown that had been its personal property for years.

On the other hand, Carbo's performers were frequently booked on Garden cards, and Mike's relations with the mob were usually cordial. He found it easier to do business with legitimate managers, however, and for that reason he looked their way whenever he could. A pragmatist with no set code of ethics, presiding over what might be called the septic tank of American sports, Mike would neither encourage nor squeeze out the racketeers.

As a showman, though, he knew how fixed fights could sour the fans, and his influence was largely on the side of legitimate contests. If Uncle Mike had been tempted to tamper with the results of his own matches, he certainly would have the night Lou Nova, the Nature Boy with the Cosmic Punch, met Joe Jacobs's Tony Galento, of the publicized beer belly and the pier six style. This fight was so painfully on the level that Mike lost his best propect for a ballpark fight with Louis that summer. Ordinarily the new challenger coming on should dispose of Louis's last victim in less time than the champion had taken. If Louis had run up a score of four rounds on Galento, for instance, Nova might have been expected to mark his card for a birdie three.

But Nova was knocked out by the already discredited Galento. It took Mike and his crack PRO, Harry Markson, two years to re-sell the public on the far-fetched idea that Nova had enough of a chance with Louis to attract a gate of $600,000. To round out the Galento fiasco, the match turned out to be one of Mike's few box office mistakes. In the vast Philadelphia stadium they drew an anemic $68,000, and Harry Markson, Rose Cohen, and the rest of the loyal Jacobins came back to the hotel in a funereal mood. But instead of brooding in his room that evening as might have been expected, Mike reversed his field by seeking out the sportswriters and displaying more cheerfulness than they had ever seen in him before. He laughed and joked with the reporters all evening and even cut loose with an improvised tap dance. "Why, he was al-most human," one newspaperman recalled.

Harry Markson, Jacobs's appointed director of boxing at the Garden, was fascinated by this almost inexplicable trait of Mike's. A literate, quiet-mannered, college graduate who looks like a ra-dio writer or an English instructor that somehow wandered into Jacobs's offices by mistake, he told me, "One of the most amazing things about Mike was the way he acted in adversity. When things were going great, when he had a sellout, he'd be in a terrible tem-per. But every time he suffered a big setback, like that Nova-Galento night, he'd fool everybody by being so pleasant you'd hardly recognize him."

"Like the day of the first Louis-Buddy Baer fight. We only had the Washington ballpark for this one night, and if we were rained out we'd be sunk. That afternoon it started to shower and by evening it was a regular storm. Everybody but Mike is going crazy. He's the only one who doesn't even mention the weather. Instead he starts telling us funny stories about the old days when he was running excursion boats to Coney Island. The rain cut our gate at least by half. But coming out after the fight, Mike still doesn't say a word about it. To make it worse, it was still drizzling and there wasn't a cab in sight. There we were standing in the rain with nothing to think about but our hard luck. 'Tough night, boss, looks like you got the elements against you,' someone said. Mike just shrugged. 'Aaaah, what's the difference, I been battlin' the fuckin' elements all m' life.'"

Why a man who has made the pursuit of a buck a personal crusade for half a century should laugh off his losses and fly into his worst rages on his biggest paynights is one for the head doctors. Meanwhile Markson had a ready explanation. Like all champions, Mike knew intuitively when to dig in and when to lay back. He'd come up through a tough enough school to learn how to roll with the punches in order to live and fight another day. And from his excursion-boat days he knew the weatherman was one fellow who couldn't be influenced with a couple of ringside tickets.

In the last days of a Louis-Schmeling or Louis-Conn promotion, Mike's office was a madhouse—thousands phoning for tickets, wanting to speak to Mike personally, begging for a chance at a pair of ringsides, or willing to let Mike name his own price for a couple in the working press. There were last minute requests from the big men for whom seats had to be found up close. This called for fancy juggling and hair-trigger decisions on the phone. It was uncanny, said Markson, how Uncle Mike could carry the entire ringside seating plan in his head. In these last minute switches he'd say, "Put White in Row 4 Section C and give Brown those two seats in Row 1 Section A next to Senator Green." According to Markson, "He could remember where ten thousand people were sitting. When it came to tickets he had a mind like an IBM machine."

As the fight grew closer and the pressure on Mike intensified, he began to do a frighteningly convincing imitation of a high-tension wire. On D (for Dough)-1, the manager of a former Garden headliner came in to hit Mike for his usual complimentary tickets. The manager had been on particularly friendly terms with Mike when his fighter was a drawing card. He was so sure he could still count on Mike that he had already asked a friend to see the fight with him. Mike noticed him out of the corner of his eye and pulled one of his old tricks. He flew into such a profane rage at one of his secretaries that she burst into hysterics. He picked up the phone and shouted an obscene insult at someone trying to con him into free seats. He wheeled on one of his oldest executives and screamed, "Tell your fuckin' brother-in-law he c'n buy his own fuckin' seat." Then he turned on the waiting manager. "Well, whatta *you* want?" "Nothing—nothing at all," stammered the now thoroughly intimidated supplicant, and slunk out.

During the war Mike's unpopularity, as well as his fortune, increased when he insisted on pushing ringside prices to twenty and thirty dollars because he knew the money was around even if the boxers who rated that kind of admission price were doing their fighting with M-1s. This annoyed some of the boxing writers who held to the quaint notion that monopoly involves a sense of social responsibility. But it was the proposed Louis-Conn Army Relief show that had sports fans ready to turn Mike in as everything from a black marketeer to a fifth columnist, or a Fifth Communist, to quote Mike's Vice-President in Charge of Malaprops, Mushky Jackson.

Louis and Conn were ready to fight for the title with all receipts going to Army Emergency Relief when suddenly Secretary Stimson canceled the match because "this promotion would not be in the best interests of the War Department." Inevitably Mike became the scapegoat. Up to his old tricks, a majority of fight fans thought.

According to John Kieran, vice chairman under Grantland Rice of War Boxing, Inc., what really happened was this: A general representing the War Department came up with the idea of staging an Army Relief bout between its two famous GIs, Corporal Louis and Private Conn. With War Department approval, Rice and Kieran asked Mike Jacobs to promote the fight without compensation.

It was at a press conference set up to launch the publicity campaign for the fight, ironically, that Grantland Rice first heard of the alleged arrangement by which Louis and Conn were to repay Mike's advances of $135,000 out of Army gross receipts. Rice resigned, and Kieran inherited this hot potato.

According to Joe Louis, a War Department spokesman had told him he could receive an additional sum to pay off his back taxes if he put his title on the line. Kieran, who somehow managed to keep his head in the crossfire of charges and countercharges, tried to remind everyone of the goal—one million dollars for Army Relief, a sum that could not be raised at a single stroke in any other way. After all, Louis was being asked to sacrifice the one asset with which he thought he could surely clear up his debt to the government after the war. And since the money from Mike had been advanced against a rematch with Conn, it wasn't exactly a Truman Committee scandal that Joe should want to write it off so he could come out of the army in the clear.

When Louis held to his original understanding of the terms, a major general threatened to send him overseas into the front lines.

Louis looked at him impassively. "General, I'm in the army. I'm ready to go anywhere anybody else in this army goes."

Without warning, Kieran was summoned to the Pentagon and told the fight was off. In the course of a routine press conference that morning, he learned, a Washington correspondent, looking for something to spice his story, had asked, "Mr. Secretary, what about the hundred thousand Mike Jacobs is getting out of this Louis-Conn fight?"

This was a bombshell to Stimson, who knew nothing of the arrangements made by his own department representatives. Without investigation, he made the decision to cancel the fight. Kieran tried to give Stimson a firsthand report that had Jacobs completely in the clear. But the secretary of war refused to reconsider. Perhaps Mike had played wolf so often that even when he honestly wanted to help the flock, the shepherds—from force of habit—shuddered at his presence.

When told the fight was off, Mike sent Secretary Stimson this message: "I offer my services free in an advisory capacity to any officials designated by you to stage a championship bout between Sgt. Louis and Corporal Conn who have both advised me that they will engage in such a bout without any compensation." Mike went on to say that he was willing to advance the money necessary to promote the show, that all revenue from radio and film rights would go to Army Relief, and that he already held $250,000 for the army in advance sales.

Although it seemed to be an army snafu, Stimson replied that his decision was final. The real loser was Army Relief—by some million and a half dollars.

Of course certain Eighth Avenue cynics will tell you that even a 100 percent benefit fight could be of personal benefit to Uncle Mike because he still could work his old tricks with those ringside and working-press seats.

Jacobs & Louis, in Dunn & Bradstreet terms, was a multi-million-dollar concern that was out of business the first time any challenger succeeded in putting Joe down for ten. Thus the champion—and indirectly Mike—made a contribution not to be passed over lightly when the title was twice put on the line in 1942 with all receipts going to Navy and Army Relief. It was Walter Winchell who asked Mike if he would promote a benefit show for the navy. Mike asked, "How much money d'they want?" Twenty-five thousand, he was told. "Hell," Mike sneered, "that kind of money ain't worth my time. I'll get 'em seventy-five thousand." He did, by presenting the first heavyweight championship bout ever fought for charity.

Did Uncle Mike have any particular friends among the thousands of boxers he presented? Barney Ross, Jim Braddock, Billy Conn, and Joe Louis, I was told. I couldn't help observing that each of these men marked a significant step upward in Mike's fabulous ascent. Ross was the first champion to line up with Mike against the Garden. Braddock brought him the heavyweight title. Conn was the lever to his biggest gate. And, of course, Louis was the jackpot.

No, Mike had an interest in these boys beyond their earning power, Mushky Jackson insisted. Especially affecting was his feeling for Joe Louis, I was told. "Why in some ways they were almost like father and son."

In what way did Mike reveal this tender, little-known side of his character?

Mike's apologist paused, frowning in deep thought. "Well, no one can say that Mike ever held out a nickel from Joe. He paid him every cent Joe's contract called for."

In Mike's business, apparently, you must love a fighter like a son to allow yourself to be swept to such extremes of generosity.

As soon as the war ended, Uncle Mike went to work on the Louis-Conn rematch he had been nursing all these years. His first edict was that neither man should engage in the usual tune-up bouts, even though both were obviously rusty after four years of inactivity. But of course it was this very lack of condition that Mike was most anxious to hide.

Next he manipulated the appearance of a claque of old champions, managers, and assorted experts at both training camps. Their ostensibly objective reports described the sluggishness of the champion and the splendid condition and undiminished skill of the challenger who had come so close to whipping Louis in their first fight. Mike paid off his Charlie McCarthys with fight tickets and an extra buck or two if they could get him to hold still long enough.

Discerning sportswriters nailed this for the empty come-on it was, but Uncle Mike had mastered the high-pressure art of repeating the fiction till it passes for fact. Under his bombardment, the odds began to shrink and fight fans began to seethe with the old fever that grips them when they think they smell blood and the promise of a new champion. Even Jackie Conn, the challenger's brother, wasn't immune. "You know, Billy's so worked up that I'm honestly worried about his injuring Joe permanently," he confided to me in Toots Shor's on the eve of the fight.

The first Louis-Conn had been scaled from a twenty-five-dollar top, and it was believed that Mike would raise the price of ringside seats to forty or fifty dollars. One afternoon a sports columnist, Stanley Frank, asked Mike what price he had finally decided on. Mike, always keenly aware of the value of trial balloons, said he hadn't made up his mind yet, and added, apparently as a laughing afterthought, "Hell, I might even charge a hundred dollars, who knows."

Frank used the hundred-dollar figure in his column, and the following day, to the amazement of Mike's staff, requests for tickets, backed up by checks as large as a thousand and two thousand dollars, began pouring in. That, of course, fixed the price at an all-time high. Sportswriters abused Mike for bilking the public, but Mike just shrugged off the epithets and kept on working the old ticket squeeze he had perfected.

Those hundred-dollar tickets, ten thousand of them, brought in one million dollars alone, a record of its kind. Mike's personal contribution to inflation hardly made him an object of affection among boxing fans, but the second Louis-Conn was the greatest attraction since Dempsey-Tunney, and every true follower of the game had to be on hand.

The fight itself turned out to be an odiferous anti-climax, for here was a slower and clearly less effective champion while the intervening years had left the challenger with nothing but a wooden and overcautious style that made a mockery of Mike's overexuberant price scale. Mike's fatherly regard for Billy Conn cooled rapidly.

A heart attack at the age of sixty-seven benched Mike temporarily, but it was impossible for him to stay away from his office. "What ya want me to do, Doc, stay down in the country and listen to my fuckin' heart?" he had protested. He dropped by the office when Harry Markson and Mike's counsel and first cousin, the Honorable Sol Strauss, were pegging the price for the first Louis-Walcott fight at twenty-five dollars. "Thirty," Mike growled. But Walcott was hardly considered a worthy opponent for Louis, Mike's aides pointed out. "Twenty-five dollars would be safer." Mike shook his head. "Thirty," he grunted.

He drove back to Rumson and immediately called his office on the phone. "How much ya chargin' for the fight?" "Thirty," he was told. Mike sighed with relief. "Good. I worried all the way out. I thought maybe I let ya talk me into twenty-five."

With Mike's thirty-dollar top, the Louis-Walcott gate set a Garden record. Louis was fading fast, and Mike knew the fans would pay to see him closing out his career, no matter whom he fought. As it turned out—though not even Mike could be credited with that much forethought—the aged Walcott who wasn't expected to last a round knocked Louis down twice and came within a sentimental hair of scoring the greatest upset in the history of the title. It was like a farewell present from the boxing business to the faltering Uncle Mike, the perfect buildup for his final million-dollar gate.

Depite doctors' warnings that he must slow down, Mike was back working at his usual pace—on the forthcoming middleweight match between Marcel Cerdan and Georgie Abrams, when he dropped in to see Doc Crozier, the chiropractor with whom he was on unusually friendly terms. "He'd sneak in a side door into a small private office as if he was trying to get away from people. He said he could relax with me. He'd talk about the old days, investments, a million different things, but he'd get grouchy and shut up if you switched to boxing. Or if any of the fight crowd happened to come in."

On this particular day Mike was feeling particularly expansive. He had just cleaned up a small fortune in a New Jersey real estate deal. Tickets for Cerdan-Abrams were moving nicely. The day after the fight, he was leaving for Florida. "There's plenty of money to be made these days," Mike was saying. "Tell you what I'll do with you, Eddie. I'll give you some stocks to buy. Do what I tell you and you'll make a bundle."

Crozier noticed, as Mike was talking, that he had begun to stammer. The words seemed to catch in his throat. "Plenny money," he repeated, then he half rose and started to remove his shirt. "Think I need a little rub, Eddie. Feel kinda worn out."

Then he collapsed over the chair. As he fell, Crozier said, a huge wad of money disgorged from his pocket and fell on the floor near his head. When Crozier counted it later, it added up to a thousand dollars in small bills.

Mike lay in a coma for several days. Jimmy Walker and Jimmy Johnston had just passed on, and superstitious Jacobs Beach was convinced that Mike would complete the fatal trinity. Or maybe it was just wishful thinking. When one disgruntled manager heard that Mike was fighting for his life, he said, "I haven't been inside a church in years, but today I'm goin' in an' really pray." "I never knew you liked the guy so much," said a Garden hanger-on. "Like him!" the manager exploded. "I'm goin' in an' pray like hell he don't recover."

That seemed to be the sentiment of an overwhelming majority in the fight world. But Mike was crossing them up as usual. He didn't care what the doctors said. Or that the columnists had already started to write his obituary. He wasn't ready to check out yet. As usual, he had the last word. To everybody's amazement, including his physicians, he began to rally. Though partially paralyzed, he was back on his feet sooner than could have been expected.

Along Jacobs Beach the fight mob that had lived in his shadow for years laughed off his amazing recovery: "Mike's just too stubborn mean to die."

The House of Jacobs might have been left without heir or heiress if it hadn't been for an unexpected turn of events a few years earlier. At their winter home in Florida one afternoon, Josie was visited by a manager's wife who was trying to adopt a baby. Impatient with the red tape, she was about to give up the idea when Josie said, in her rough, impulsive, good-natured way, "You wan' a baby, I'll get ya a baby," and she put through a mysterious call. When the baby arrived, it was, the two women agreed, about the poorest excuse for a baby they had ever seen, homely, scrawny, and suffering from acne. Josie's friend said it wouldn't do, and Josie waved it away impatiently. "Take it back. Take it back."

But the image of this scrawny, unwanted infant seemed to haunt her. After a few beers she picked up the phone and asked, "You still got that homely little excuse for a baby?" Each time she'd hear that no one seemed to want this sickly little foundling, she'd be more disconcerted. One afternoon, when she and her friend were sufficiently beered up to feel particularly sentimental, she called about the infant once more. Suddenly she said, "So nobody wants the homely little thing? Bring it here. I'll take it m'self."

The fairy tale of the ugly duckling has nothing on the Jacobses. Joan grew up to be a bright and attractive young lady on whom Mike seemed to lavish all the affection he'd been saving up in the seventy-year war of attrition he'd been waging against his fellow man.

The last time I visited the big country house at Rumson, Mike was sitting in an easy chair, apathetically enfeebled, barely able to raise his left hand in greeting. Everyone had told me what a lonely man Mike was these days. The essential friendlessness of his life was weighing on him at last. Now that the boxing game was struggling along without him, almost no one came to see him. He had been a single-O guy all his life, but a busy one. Now there was nothing for him to do but sit there and stew and listen to the countdown of his own heart.

Little Joan came over with two doll dresses Josie and her Aunt had made for a children's party the following day. The warm paternal smile that came over his face looked almost grotesque on this hard old man. "Look, Daddy, which dress do you like best?" Joan wanted to know. The one with the best dress would win the prize at the party, she explained.

"You think you'll win?" I asked.

"Sure, I'll win easy," Joan said, in a way that made me wonder if she hadn't already acquired some of her foster father's drive. Mike grinned at her proudly.

Watching her go skipping off with her dolls, I suddenly felt overwhelmed by the thought that all the scrapping, the hustling, the conniving, the blood and sweat and larceny and ruthlessness that goes with control of America's most brutal business winds up in a multimillion-dollar fortune to be inherited by a little girl who arrived from nowhere one afternoon and, thanks perhaps to that extra beer, was allowed to stay. As fairy godfather and godmother, Mike and Josie are right out of Damon Runyon at his best. Only Runyon, with the help of the brothers Grimm, could have dreamed this one up.

A little while later I was in the kitchen with Josie, who was reaching way back for adoring stories of her father, a traveling actor who, she said, had fought with Napoleon III.

Suddenly Mike lurched through the door in a black temper. His strength had returned surprisingly. "Don' blab everything you know!" he shouted. "You'll help 'im knock my brains out."

"But I was only talkin' about my old man. . . ." Josie protested.

"Aaah, shut up!" Mike growled and, miraculously, he slapped her with the arm that had seemed useless an hour before.

When he stormed out, Josie wiped the corners of her eyes with her sleeve. "It ain't his fault. He just don' know what to do with himself now that he ain't workin."

I tried to understand. I thought of Mike as a kid on the waterfront battling for survival. There the golden rule was twisted out of shape to read: "Do it to him before he does it to you." In his great mansion on millionaire's row, with his black servants, ex-fighters as drivers and handymen, and his fleet of Cadillacs, he was still battling for survival in the only way he had ever learned, by striking out at everything he couldn't control.

Josie walked us to the door. She was still apologizing for the business in the kitchen. "Mike's gotta have action," she said. "Without action, he's nothin'. But whatever you write, you gotta put this in. He was the best goddamn promoter there ever was, or ever will be. After him, they threw away the combination."

Yes, and maybe that's a good thing, I couldn't help thinking as I turned back for a last look at this vast estate that had become a desolate mausoleum for a lonely and friendless old man who had made such a spectacular success in life and had nothing to show for it but money.

[1950]

Index

A NOTE ON THE AUTHOR

Budd Schulberg was born in New York City, the son of Hollywood film pioneer B. P. Schulberg, and was educated at Los Angeles High School, Deerfield Academy, and Dartmouth College. After a brief stint as a screenwriter in Hollywood, he served in the United States Navy during World War II and was in charge of photographic evidence for the Nuremberg Trial. Mr. Schulberg was *Sports Illustrated*'s first boxing editor; he has also covered title fights for *Playboy*, *Esquire*, *Newsday*, the *New York Post*, and currently the Glasgow *Sunday Herald*. He is the only nonfighter to receive the Living Legend of Boxing Award from the World Boxing Association. His writings on the fight game have also won him the Notre Dame Bengal Bouts Award and the A. J. Liebling Award from the Boxing Writers Association as well as induction into the Boxing Hall of Fame. He lives in Quiogue, Long Island, New York.